D0154192

GRAPPLING WITH DEMON RUM

GRAPPLING WITH DEMON RUM

The Cultural Struggle over Liquor in Early Oklahoma

James E. Klein

UNIVERSITY OF OKLAHOMA PRESS : NORMAN

Library of Congress Cataloging-in-Publication Data
Klein, James Edward, 1964–
Grappling with demon rum : the cultural struggle over liquor in early Oklahoma / James Edward Klein.
p. cm.
Includes bibliographical references and index.
ISBN 978-0-8061-3938-8 (hardcover : alk. paper) 1. Prohibition — Oklahoma — History. 2. Oklahoma — History. I. Title.
HV5090.O5K54 2008
363.4′109766 — dc22

2008002829

The paper in this book meets the guidelines for permanence and durability of the Committee on Production Guidelines for Book Longevity of the Council on Library Resources, Inc. ∞

Copyright © 2008 by the University of Oklahoma Press, Norman, Publishing Division of the University. Manufactured in the U.S.A.

All rights reserved. No part of this publication may be reproduced, stored in a retrieval system, or transmitted, in any form or by any means, electronic, mechanical, photocopying, recording, or otherwise — except as permitted under Section 107 or 108 of the United States Copyright Act — without the prior permission of the University of Oklahoma Press.

1 2 3 4 5 6 7 8 9 10

Contents

Illustrations

All photos are courtesy of the Research Division of the Oklahoma Historical Society.

Acknowledgments

For their gracious help and patience, I am indebted to the librarians and staff at the Oklahoma Historical Society Archives and Newspaper Archives, the Archives Division of the Oklahoma Department of Libraries, the Western History Collection at the University of Oklahoma, and the Special Collections Department at McFarlin Library, University of Tulsa. I also received indispensable assistance from the Special Collections and University Archives Department, the Government Documents Department, the Microform and Media Department, and the Interlibrary Services Department at the Edmon Low Library at Oklahoma State University.

Several scholars have assisted in the completion of this work. Ronald Petrin, L. G. Moses, Michael Logan, and Charles Edgley provided insight and helpful criticism in the early stages. Theodore Agnew, Laura Belmonte, and David D'Andria served as sounding boards, helping me frame and clarify the topic. Lisa Guinn, Thomas Jorsch, Steven Kite, Todd Leahy, Shelly Lemmons, and Mark Van de Logt offered encouragement and different perspectives on the liquor question. Claudia Gravier Frigo edited the manuscript in its later incarnation, providing helpful suggestions.

Matthew K. Bokovoy of the University of Oklahoma Press was instrumental in moving this project forward toward publication. As an editor and a friend, his efforts have been invaluable. I also acknowledge the innumerable contributions to this work by Teresa Lee Klein, my wife and life partner. She patiently listened while I discussed the details of my research, offering insightful observations and encouragement at critical junctures throughout the creative process. To all of these individuals, I am deeply grateful.

GRAPPLING WITH
DEMON RUM

Introduction

The week of November 17, 1907, the date on which Oklahoma became the forty-sixth state, witnessed widespread revelry throughout the region. It was a unique statehood celebration because Oklahoma entered the union as a dry state. Both proponents and opponents of the liquor ban were boisterous, though for different reasons and in different manners. Prohibition supporters rejoiced when the ban took effect on November 17 at the culmination of years of campaigning in Washington, D.C., and across Oklahoma and Indian territories. They had brought the first dry state into the union. Opponents of prohibition celebrated also, but not on the 17th. During the last days of territorial status, Oklahoma saloons slashed prices to draw customers and liquidate their stock. Business boomed as thirsty Oklahomans crowded into saloons and other liquor outlets to purchase this soon-to-be-illegal commodity and to celebrate statehood. These establishments fell quiet on the 17th, and the euphoria shifted to those who had campaigned to ban the saloon; however, the saloons would not remain quiet for long.

Oklahomans were not the first to wrestle with the liquor issue. The consumption of alcohol as a beverage was common in colonial America, and opposition to that consumption was slight. The first concerted anti-liquor campaign in the United States began during the religious revivals of the early nineteenth century. Evangelical ministers and middle-class reformers worried over liquor usage among the growing wage-earning population. Of the numerous antebellum temperance groups, one of the more effective was the Washington Temperance Society (popularly known as the Washingtonians). It differed from most other temperance groups in that it comprised mainly working-class men who pledged to abstain from liquor and acted as a support group for fellow teetotalers.

The voluntary temperance campaigns of the 1830s and 1840s gave way to coercive prohibition efforts in later decades. Maine and twelve other states legally banned liquor in the 1850s, but these laws proved ineffective and generally fell into disuse by the Civil War. Support for prohibition, rather than voluntary abstinence, continued to grow in the late nineteenth and early twentieth centuries. The Woman's Christian Temperance Union (WCTU) was formed in 1874 to pressure officeholders for legal restrictions on liquor. Kansas and Iowa adopted prohibition in the 1880s, but enforcement again proved elusive. The Anti-Saloon League of America formed in 1893 to better organize political campaigns against liquor. Both the WCTU and the league were instrumental in the Oklahoma campaign.

In the first decade of the twentieth century, prohibition forces began a string of successes at the state and local levels. In 1900, Maine, Kansas, North Dakota, New Hampshire, and Vermont prohibited liquor, though the federal government's control of interstate commerce allowed distillers and brewers to ship liquor into these dry states for personal use. Georgia and Alabama banned liquor in 1907; a year later Mississippi and North Carolina adopted prohibition; and Tennessee went dry in 1909. Thus the campaign to make Oklahoma a dry state can be seen as part of a larger aridity crusade, which was particularly effective in the American South at this time. The Anti-Saloon League orchestrated much of this crusade and formed state affiliates throughout the nation, including one in Oklahoma, to mobilize voters in support of liquor restrictions and dry candidates.

The league did not dwell on these victories. In 1913 Congress, pressured by the league, passed the Webb-Kenyon Act, ending the exemption that liquor shipments into or through dry states had enjoyed as interstate commerce. The league and its supporters followed this breakthrough legislation with several successful state anti-liquor campaigns. In 1914, Washington, Oregon, Colorado, Arizona, and Virginia banned liquor; the next year, Idaho, Iowa, Arkansas, and South Carolina followed suit. In 1916, Montana, South Dakota, Nebraska, and Michigan went dry; Utah, Indiana, and New Hampshire adopted new prohibition laws in 1917. The league's successful Oklahoma campaign, then, was one of the first in a series of victories for dry supporters that culminated in the adoption of national prohibition in 1919. The nation was officially dry from 1920 until 1933, when the Twenty-first Amendment, repealing the Eighteenth Amendment, was ratified.

The campaign for and enforcement of prohibition in Oklahoma in some ways mirrored efforts in other states and foreshadowed some of the problematic aspects of national prohibition. Even though Oklahoma became a dry state in 1907, illegal liquor remained available for the next three decades — before and during the national liquor ban. This book examines the social and cultural impulses that led Oklahomans to outlaw liquor and the consequences of that decision. The liquor issue clarified divisions — roughly along social class lines — between "respectable" and "nonrespectable" elements of Oklahoma society. Middle-class merchants and professionals, including evangelical ministers, formed the vanguard of the prohibition movement in the state. The middle-class, respectable Anti-Saloon League and the WCTU organized and gave political voice to this movement, whereas the state's large working-class population, largely unorganized as far as prohibition was concerned, generally opposed the liquor ban. Wage earners continued to patronize saloons after the state had declared them illegal, and they contributed to the considerable vote against prohibition in 1907 and 1910 referendums.

Because early Oklahoma contained significant numbers of American Indians and blacks and a small but concentrated immigrant population amid a white native majority, the region's cultural diversity shaped the contest between drys and wets. Competing definitions of propriety and the area's reputation for frontier lawlessness encouraged prominent middle-class residents to adopt a rigid standard of respectability and to apply this standard to the entire population through the force of law.

Liquor prohibition had enjoyed a long heritage in the region that became Oklahoma. The Cherokee Indian government passed the first prohibition law in the United States in 1819. The federal government, in the Indian Intercourse Act of 1834, forbade the sale of liquor to American Indians at the same time that it forcefully relocated American Indians from the Southeast and from the Old Northwest to lands west of Arkansas. The Chickasaw Indians formed their first temperance society in 1842. Despite these efforts, liquor sales continued in the region, in part because of the growing non-Indian population. According to published reports, some American Indians also engaged in the liquor traffic, ignoring both federal and tribal bans.

A characteristic common to both tribal and federal prohibition was lax enforcement. American Indian law applied only to tribal members and was enforced unevenly. For its part, the federal government provided few marshals and judges to enforce the ban on liquor sales in the extensive Indian Territory between Kansas and Texas, and the light presence of the law in the territory attracted outlaws and desperados. As the region's non-Indian population continued to grow in the late nineteenth century, so too did the illegal liquor industry. The opening of coal and, later, zinc mines and the construction of railroads drew a significant working-class population into the region, which formed the customer base of the liquor industry. As statehood drew near, proponents of a liquor ban drew on the established belief that American Indians were particularly susceptible to alcohol and were prone to violence when intoxicated. This rationale held sway in Oklahoma, even though by the turn of the century, the region's white population had far eclipsed the number of American Indian residents.

The region's black population also grew markedly in the closing decades of the nineteenth century. The earliest blacks in Indian

Territory were slaves of the Five Tribes. After emancipation, many of these freedmen continued to reside in the area as sharecroppers and farm laborers. Shortly after the federal government formed Oklahoma Territory in 1889, rumors began to spread that this new region would serve as a refuge for former slaves from the American Southeast, and black emigration to the region accelerated. This trend alarmed white Oklahomans who, after statehood provided them sufficient autonomy, took measures to restrict blacks' rights and to demonstrate that the Sooner State did not welcome black émigrés. The presence of blacks provided at least some of the rationale for prohibition, but Oklahoma did shy away from the overt race-baiting employed in some of the former Confederate states as a justification for the liquor ban.

At the margins of respectable society in many communities before statehood, the area liquor industry found itself further alienated from the respectable core as it became the target of middle-class reformers — many of them active in evangelical churches — who asserted that the saloon held no redeeming social value. They saw this institution as fomenting crime, obstructing social progress, and distracting men from their familial responsibilities. That these reformers succeeded in making prohibition a part of the state constitution in 1907 is a testament not only to their organizing efforts but also to their social standing in local communities and throughout the state. Prohibition supporters' prominence in their communities served them well when striving to convince voters to ban liquor. Through their propaganda and by emphasizing their own social standing, the reformers cast the retail liquor industry, its supporters, and its patrons outside the bounds of social respectability.

The illegal liquor trade persisted in the Sooner State because laborers continued to patronize liquor establishments despite admonitions from their middle-class neighbors. By the twentieth century, the saloon in Oklahoma, as elsewhere, had become a basic feature of working-class culture. The continued demand for liquor encouraged bootleggers to exploit legal loopholes in the state's liquor codes, forcing state officials and dry proponents to repeatedly tighten those codes, each time with limited results. By 1930

Oklahoma's illegal liquor industry remained prosperous. Thus, the conflict surrounding prohibition in Oklahoma was a conflict between middle-class and working-class definitions of social propriety. The socially and politically dominant middle class succeeded in defining the saloon as improper and nonrespectable but failed to extinguish it.

Charged with enforcing prohibition and backed by the respectable (generally white, middle-class) elements of Oklahoma's population, state and local officials attacked institutions and individuals responsible for public drinking in the new state. In some instances, residents themselves went after bootleggers and illegal saloons when they believed local officials had failed to carry out their enforcement duties. Public drinking, whether at a legal saloon or an illegal liquor joint, had become a central part of working-class culture in the United States. Historian Jon M. Kingsdale, citing sociological studies of the saloon from the turn of the century, describes it as "a neighborhood center, an all-male establishment and a transmitter of working-class and immigrant cultures."[1]

Though these studies focus on the urban saloon, many of the conditions that led to its designation as the "poor man's club" existed in Oklahoma also; workers lived in cramped dingy dwellings and sought human interaction and recreation in liquor joints. They could not afford or were barred from membership in middle-class social clubs, such as the Eagles and the Elks. Thus, the saloon formed a prominent part of working-class culture in Oklahoma as elsewhere. Because prohibition posed a direct threat to that culture, most wage earners quietly opposed the liquor ban; they did not challenge the moral authority of the dry campaign and continued to defy prohibition by patronizing illegal joints as they had saloons previously.

Reports from enforcement officers indicate that counties with large wage-earning populations contained the most flagrant violation of the liquor ban. In the Glenn Pool and Cushing oil fields of Tulsa, Osage, and Creek counties, in the later Healdton oil fields of Carter County, and still later in the Seminole oil fields of Seminole and Pottawatomie counties, liquor flowed freely. The mining districts of Coal and Ottawa counties likewise sported persistent liquor violations. The state's urban centers—Oklahoma City, Muskogee, and Tulsa—also experienced widespread violation of the liquor ban. Like the oil fields and the mining districts, these cities contained large wage-earning populations that patronized bootleggers. Some middle-class Oklahomans patronized saloons as well, but enforcement was most problematic in regions containing large numbers of working-class men because middle-class men were more likely to drink at home. The laboring classes' affinity for public drinking did not sit well with respectable Oklahomans; the better element of society sought to eliminate this scourge to improve the lives of everyone, and the results were mixed.

This cultural contest over respectability lies at the heart of the liquor question in Oklahoma. Whereas some previous studies have asserted that prohibition pitted rural populations and sensibilities against those of a rising urban United States, socioeconomic class played a much larger role in determining Oklahomans' stance on the liquor issue. Some rural communities in the Sooner State did strongly endorse prohibition, but others—such as the predominantly rural Creek, Coal, Osage, and Carter counties—offered some of the most stubborn resistance to state and local enforcement officers. Residents of these locales financially supported bootleggers as customers; voters regularly returned to office men who failed to enforce the liquor ban; and juries repeatedly acquitted bootleggers despite substantial evidence of their guilt.

Similarly, support for prohibition was not a fundamentally rural issue. Supporters of prohibition resided not only in small towns and farming communities but also in the state's largest cities. Oklahoma City and Tulsa contained populations that continued to violate the liquor ban, but many of the officers of the Oklahoma Anti-Saloon League, which was the leading dry organization in the state, also resided in Oklahoma City, and rough and tumble Tulsa sported one of the state's more active chapters of the WCTU. Rather than a rural-urban split on prohibition, the issue divided Oklahomans according to economic class, and increasingly, social standing: merchants and professionals, respected in their communities and in the state, sought to curb the public drinking habits of the laboring classes.

Other previous studies of prohibition have emphasized ethnicity and religion in explaining the disagreement over the liquor question. Paul Kleppner, Richard Jensen, and others have argued that evangelicals within the Methodist, Baptist, Congregationalist, Presbyterian, and Christian (Church of Christ) denominations formed a pietistic political culture that sought cultural reforms, such as the prohibition of liquor. Opposing the pietists were the ritualists or liturgicals, drawn from the Roman Catholic and Episcopal denominations, and some portions of the Lutheran faith. Liturgicals emphasized religious tradition and ritual over the emotion of pietists or evangelicals and generally discouraged political reforms designed to change individual behavior. One issue that split pietists and ritualists most clearly was the regulation of liquor; pietists supporting prohibition and ritualists opposing it.[2]

Prohibition was a religious and cultural issue in Oklahoma, but many nonreligious groups also opposed the ban. Roman Catholic, Episcopal, and Lutheran populations remained so slight in the region that they, alone, cannot account for the political opposition to prohibition when the question came before voters in 1907 and again in 1910. The 1906 religious census conducted in the territories indicates that the Southern Baptist Convention drew the most adherents (49,978), followed by the Methodist Episcopal Church, South (40,473), the Roman Catholic Church (36,548), the Disciples of Christ Church (24,232), and the Methodist Episcopal Church (23,309). The small Lutheran population, which totaled less than 3,000, belonged to an evangelical synod. The Episcopal population was smaller still. The liturgical faiths, taken together, drew fewer than 45,000 adherents.[3] Compare this to the 112,258 who voted against prohibition in September 1907. Further, the religious census included women and children, neither of whom could vote in Oklahoma in 1907. (Oklahoma adopted women's suffrage in 1918.)

The 1916 religious census of Oklahoma indicates considerable growth among pietistic denominations, notably the Southern Baptist Church, the Churches of Christ, and the Presbyterian Church in the U.S.A.[4] Membership in each of these denominations grew by more than 70 percent between 1906 and 1916. The Roman Catholic and Episcopal churches grew also during this period but much less than these denominations. In the latter year, 47,427 Roman Catholics and 3,566 Episcopalians resided in Oklahoma. Compare these numbers to the 105,041 who voted against prohibition in 1910. Even assuming that these congregations voted in large numbers against the liquor ban, it becomes clear that a nonliturgical population also opposed the liquor ban in Oklahoma.

The state's growing evangelical majority increasingly shaped moral debates, including consideration of the liquor question, and brought these issues beyond the realm of religion and into politics. This progression was seamless and uncontroversial in most Oklahoma regions because the ministers and other religious leaders, such as those who occupied top positions in the Oklahoma Anti-Saloon League, were influential not only in their respective churches but also in their communities. The absence of liturgicals — Roman Catholics, Episcopalians, and Jews — in the league and similar dry organizations alienated these minority religious groups from mainstream respectable Oklahoma as well.

Similarly, the assertion that immigrants voted against prohibition does not explain the level of wet sentiment in the Sooner State. During the first decades of the twentieth century, Oklahoma's foreign population never reached 10 percent of the total. In 1910, the year of the second Oklahoma referendum on liquor, the state contained a combined foreign population of 134,128 — 44,167 residents of mixed foreign and native parentage, 49,877 residents of entirely foreign parentage, and 40,084 foreign-born residents. Considering that these figures include non-voters (women and children), the wet vote of 1910 (105,041) was much larger than Oklahoma's immigrant-based population. The 1910 figures were not an anomaly: The 1900 census lists the foreign population of the territories at 68,652, which was 8.69 percent of the total; the 1910 foreign population accounted for 8.09 percent of the total; and the 1920 foreign population comprised 7.01 percent of Oklahoma's total population.[5]

According to the ethnocultural argument, a large majority of Oklahomans should have voted to ban liquor because relatively few liturgicals and immigrants lived in the region in the early twentieth century. Further, these populations overlapped somewhat as a number of the immigrant coal miners of southeast Oklahoma, the German-American farmers of north central Oklahoma, and the small but growing foreign population of Oklahoma City and Tulsa were Roman Catholics. In the referendums conducted in 1907 to consider the liquor ban and in 1910 to continue or end it, more than 45 percent of voters opposed prohibition. These were clear victories for the dry campaign, but not as overwhelming as expected given the minor presence in Oklahoma of the traditionally wet populations.[6] This illustrates that a substantial non-immigrant, non-liturgical population also voted against prohibition in the Sooner State.

The immigrant population was sufficiently slight that it had little effect on social norms and notions of respectability in the region. Several of the smaller foreign groups—those of Italian, English, and Austrian descent—were concentrated in the coal fields surrounding McAlester in southeastern Oklahoma. Although these immigrants and their children might have influenced the culture and attitudes of small, relatively self-contained communities, their impact on the overall social milieu of the state was small. Oklahoma Germans gained attention during the prohibition debate for their vocal opposition to the measure, but their limited numbers suggest that the German population represented only a small portion of wet Oklahoma. They became more conspicuous during the First World War when the surrounding population demonized German culture and urged the Americanization of its German neighbors; their German heritage somehow discredited their wet arguments as unpatriotic in the minds of native Oklahomans.

The liturgical and immigrant populations were also too small to explain the continued prosperity of the state's bootlegging industry following statehood. Many Oklahomans continued to purchase contraband liquor, raising the demand for it and making the industry sufficiently profitable that numerous liquor men defied prohibition. This created an enforcement conundrum for state and local officials who labored to discern the mood of the voting public concerning the availability of liquor. Repeated but inconsistent crackdowns and refinements of the ban temporarily slowed but did not stop the flow of liquor. In 1922, fifteen years after Oklahoma officially went dry, Governor James B. A. Robertson publicly stated that prohibition was a failure and that corn whiskey was available in every county of the state. Given the volume and prosperity of the illegal liquor industry, the ethnocultural argument is insufficient in explaining opposition to prohibition in early Oklahoma. A significant nonimmigrant, nonliturgical population opposed prohibition at the election polls and at the illegal saloons. Much of this additional wet sentiment came from Oklahoma's large wage-earning population, which included not only many immigrants and liturgicals, but also natives and nonreligious groups.[7]

The development of coal mining and railroads drew large numbers of wage earners to the territories in the last decades of the nineteenth century. Cotton and wheat farming brought itinerant farm laborers to the region. The discovery of oil near Tulsa during the first decades of the twentieth century attracted wage earners with the promise—sometimes unmet—of high-paying jobs. Reports by enforcement officers and correspondence by local residents indicate that those areas that contained high concentrations of laborers, such as the mining camps surrounding McAlester, the zinc- and lead-mining camps near Miami, and the boomtowns of the Glenn Pool and Cushing oil fields, also contained bootlegging operations that most stubbornly defied the liquor ban.

Among the region's dry population, the Anti-Saloon League deserves primary credit for organizing and directing the campaign to bring Oklahoma into the union as a dry state. Though the WCTU organized in the region soon after the formation of Oklahoma and Indian territories and served as the leading temperance group at the turn of the century, the league gradually overshadowed it after 1900 to become the area's leading anti-liquor association. Clergymen, doctors, lawyers, and merchants from around the region directed the Oklahoma league's activities. These men, prominent and respected in their communities, shared the middle-class view that the saloon was without redeeming social qualities. League agents worked diligently both in Washington, D.C., and in the territories to convince others of the merits of prohibition. Their assertion that saloons spawned crime — assault, theft, prostitution, graft, and murder — and hindered the growth of respectable, stable business resonated with merchants and professionals in the region; their social prominence gave the dry camp an air of respectability and implied that their opponents did not possess the same virtuous qualities.

The league also involved itself in enforcement issues. These issues originated during the territorial period, when the long-standing federal ban on liquor sales to American Indians produced violations. After statehood, enforcement fell to local and state officers, and the league willingly stepped in to goad reluctant officials into applying the ban. This was no small task because the exact provisions of the liquor ban remained unclear during the early years of statehood, and liquor dealers took advantage of this uncertainty to continue their trade. The state gradually closed the early loopholes in the liquor codes, yet liquor remained available in most locales; the state had achieved prohibition on paper but not in the streets or along the roads of many Oklahoma communities.

Wet proponents not only suffered from a lack of organization when pitted against the Anti-Saloon League, but also from a lack of social standing that league supporters enjoyed. The various wet organizations that formed during the debate over prohibition were of short duration and received only limited support from Oklahoma laborers. These shortcomings largely account for their lack of success against the league's organizational and propaganda onslaught.

Despite the adoption of prohibition and subsequent attempts to tighten the ban, the illegal liquor trade remained vibrant in Oklahoma through the first three decades of the twentieth century, as wage earners in particular continued to frequent saloons. The liquor ban, however, did place this aspect of working-class culture outside the bounds of polite, respectable society in Oklahoma. In fact, those friendly toward the liquor culture in the years following prohibition found themselves out of step with the social attitude dominant in the state. A person's liquor stance served as a litmus test for respectability. Respectable people — righteous, established, and prominent in their communities — publicly abstained from drinking and sought to restrict others' access to alcohol; those who did not share this view were stained as less virtuous, less than righteous.

Vestiges of this mentality remain in Oklahoma a century after the state banned liquor; the prohibition experience has left a deep imprint on social propriety in the state: a prominent outspoken population expresses disdain for the liquor culture whereas a less visible, less vocal population continues to consume alcohol as a beverage but does not attempt to justify its actions in the public forum.

CHAPTER ONE

Liquor and Liquor Policy in Territorial Oklahoma

The roots of Oklahoma's anti-liquor campaign stretch back to the early nineteenth century. As early as 1819, the Cherokee Nation, residing in Georgia and North Carolina, enacted the first liquor prohibition law anywhere within the boundaries of the United States.[1] In 1833 the Cherokees established the Cherokee National Temperance Society, and in 1849, after being forcefully relocated to the region west of Arkansas by the United States, they outlawed the sale and use of liquor by tribal members in their region of Indian Country. In 1842 the Chickasaws, another of the Five Tribes relocated to the region that became Oklahoma, formed their nation's first temperance society.[2] Opposition to the liquor trade, however, was not uniform among these American Indians: liquor consumption continued. The seizure of seventeen hundred gallons of whiskey at an international Indian council at Tahlequah in 1843 indicates the persistent desire of some to flout the ban and engage in the lucrative liquor trade.[3]

Liquor enforcement in the Indian Country (subsequently Indian Territory) remained problematic throughout the nineteenth century. Each of the Five Tribes passed legislation regulating the behavior of members and established judicial systems to enforce those laws. Although these legal systems were substantial, they suffered from the same laxity and corruption that marked federal and state codes of the period.[4] The tribes formed groups called light-horsemen to enforce their laws, but they had no legal authority over non-Indian residents of Indian Territory. Tribal governments could ask the federal government to expel non-Indians from their lands, but because a few federal officers were expected to cover the entire region, enforcement was uneven and slow. The development of mines and railroads in the late nineteenth century attracted more white residents, which further complicated these problems.

The growing white population also expressed concern at the effect liquor consumption had on American Indians. As one resident subsequently noted, "All crimes in the calendar were committed under its [liquor's] influence. Peaceable citizens were terrified in their homes and on highways by drunken Indians."[5] Banning liquor from American Indians to protect local white residents remained a prominent argument for Oklahoma prohibition into the twentieth century, even though the 1900 federal census indicates that American Indians constituted less than 10 percent of the region's population. In the 1905 Enabling Act, which permitted creation of the state of Oklahoma from Indian and Oklahoma territories, the U.S. Congress prohibited liquor in the former Indian Territory for the first twenty-one years of statehood.

To better control the region's American Indian and growing white populations, the U.S. government established three federal judicial districts and in 1898 authorized these courts to try all criminal cases and those civil cases involving at least one non-Indian. These courts remained the basis of federal law in Indian Territory until statehood came in November 1907.[6]

The federal government also commissioned enforcement officers for Indian Territory, but understaffing remained chronic. Marshals and their deputies were responsible for immense areas; most of which could be reached by horse only. The region contained few judges, and the dockets soon became backlogged. By 1906, the federal courts of Indian Territory reported that they had resolved 3,612 cases in the past year leaving 5,512 cases unsettled.[7] Oklahoma Territory, which was organized in 1889 from the western portion of the original lands assigned to the Five Tribes, saw a similar judicial backlog. Judges spent much of their time traversing the expansive region and the legal process slowed even further.[8] Consequently, enforcement officers rarely pursued liquor offenders unless they had also committed violent crimes.

The region's inadequate law enforcement systems attracted criminals from other regions to Indian and Oklahoma Territories, which also contributed to the liquor problem. The Doolin-Dalton gang used the area as a base from which to rob trains and banks. Jesse and Frank James periodically resided in Indian Territory as did Belle Starr. Less famous criminals also flocked to the territories, particularly to the wooded hills and thickets of the southeast. Other rough men followed the railroads into the territory and settled in the various towns created at the rail stations; some engaged in the lucrative but illegal liquor trade. The federal government's limited enforcement presence allowed illegal saloons to operate with impunity throughout the area.

In 1889 Congress created Oklahoma Territory in response to lobbyists' demands for white settlement lands in the area, and the territorial government legalized liquor in this region. The saloon became a staple feature of many communities. This was particularly evident in Pottawatomie County, bordered by the Seminole lands in the east and the Chickasaw lands to the south. It contained Corner, Keokuk Falls, and other towns so dependent on the saloon industry that they disappeared shortly after statehood and statewide prohibition took effect. These saloon towns gained violent reputations; fist-fights and shootings were common, and American Indians formed a part of the saloon clientele even though the sale of liquor to American Indians in either territory was illegal.[9] The Cherokee Strip, jutting into the Osage and Creek lands, also contained a considerable liquor presence. By 1903 Ponca City contained fourteen saloons, three breweries, and a whiskey distillery. Saloons were also commonplace in the Pawnee County towns of Blackburn, Cleveland, Jennings, Keystone, Osage, Pawnee, Ralston, and

Federal marshals destroy liquor at an 1889 Guthrie saloon as patrons and a distraught saloon keeper look on. Saloons remained open in Guthrie until statehood in 1907, even though federal officials stepped in if an establishment violated federal law such as the ban on sales to American Indians.

Sinnett. American Indians were regular liquor customers here also, even though the saloon owners also served a large number of local white men.[10]

The region's burgeoning liquor industry did not go unnoticed by critics. Frances Willard, the dynamic national president of the Woman's Christian Temperance Union (WCTU), visited Indian Territory and organized a local chapter at Muskogee in 1888. Within two years, the WCTU had organized in Oklahoma Territory as well.[11] The union was active in the territories throughout the 1890s; women formed local organizations in Vinita, Claremore, and Prior Creek in Indian Territory and in Oklahoma City, El Reno, Kingfisher, and other Oklahoma Territory communities.[12] They urged local and territorial officials to restrict liquor sales.

Though still vibrant after 1900, the WCTU found itself overshadowed by the religiously based Anti-Saloon League of America.[13]

Congregationalist minister Howard H. Russell founded the inter-denominational league in 1895 and targeted public drinking estab-lishments: saloons. Protestant ministers, notably Methodists, Presby-terians, Baptists, and Congregationalists held prominent offices in the national league and in its state affiliates; attorneys, doctors, and businessmen also filled leadership positions. Rather than support-ing a third political party devoted to prohibition, Russell urged his followers to work within the two major parties to create leverage for liquor restrictions. This approach proved effective, and national, state, and local officials came to appreciate the league's growing political might.

On January 20, 1899, Rev. Russell convened a meeting at the First Baptist Church of Oklahoma City to organize the Oklahoma Anti-Saloon League. Tipton Cox of Hennessey served as the first president, Reverend J. W. Sherwood of Kingfisher as vice president, Reverend Thomas H. Harper of Oklahoma City as secretary, F. E. McKinley of Guthrie as treasurer, and Reverend H. E. Swan of Okla-homa City as superintendent. Swan, a Congregationalist minister, became the most prominent league agent in the region until state-hood.[14] These men organized residents of Oklahoma communities to pressure their local officials for stricter enforcement of saloon closing hours (typically midnight and on Sundays). Dry proponents in the rough and tumble town of Perry formed one of the earliest leagues to curb saloon excesses and gambling in the saloon district called Hell's Half Acre.[15]

Although the league, like the saloon, became a staple of many Oklahoma communities, the more established National Prohibition Party entered the region later and thus never matched the league's presence in Oklahoma. Dry advocates formed the party in Chicago in 1869 as a single-issue proponent and insisted that supporters swear off the Democratic and Republican parties. The party orga-nized its first territorial convention in Guthrie in June 1902. As in the league, Protestant ministers held prominent positions in this organization. Reverend E. S. Stockwell of Perry became the party's state chairman, and Reverend L. T. Van Cleave of Oklahoma City its territorial delegate to Congress. As at the national level, banning the sale of liquor in Oklahoma was the party's central goal, but its third-party strategy hindered its growth in the Sooner State. Even at the national level, the party never seriously challenged either of the two major parties. It enjoyed significant support in rural north-western Woods County in the late territorial period, but little else-where throughout the territories, and it rarely drew a mention in the press following the adoption of statewide prohibition.[16]

Unlike their parent organizations, the party and the league in Oklahoma worked together and even shared some members. The 1908 Oklahoma Prohibition Party convention named as a national delegate Reverend J. M. Monroe, a member of the Oklahoma Anti-Saloon League headquarters committee, Reverend J. J. Thompson, formerly state superintendent of the league, and Reverend I. C. Rankin, a league trustee. That same year, the two organizations jointly supported a state-operated liquor dispensary system (for scientific, industrial, and medicinal purposes only) as the surest means of achieving effective prohibition enforcement.[17] However, the party's influence waned in subsequent years as that of the league grew.

After the turn of the century, the league and the WCTU gained an unwelcome ally when Carry Nation brought her personal anti-liquor crusade to Oklahoma. She had attained national prominence attacking Kansas saloons with a hatchet. She and her husband, David Nation, had homesteaded in Dewey County, Oklahoma, in the 1890s. He had served as minister of a local church, while Carry toured area communities, organizing charity groups and preaching the gospel. She railed against the use of liquor and tobacco and gained a reputation among the area's saloon keepers for stirring up trouble. In a preview of her Kansas exploits, she traveled to Ed-mond, Oklahoma, in 1899 and proceeded to smash whiskey bottles, beer kegs, and various furnishings in each of that town's saloons.[18]

That same year, Nation returned to Kansas and began her famed crusade against illegal saloons (Kansas had outlawed liquor in 1881) in Wichita, Topeka, Kansas City, Enterprise, and Holt.[19] She returned to Oklahoma Territory in 1901 but received a chilly response from the anti-liquor forces there. The Guthrie chapter of the union advised her not to come to their city and refused to endorse her work. Nation visited the territorial capital anyway, and discovering that no church would grant her permission to speak during their weekly services, she preached against the evils of alcohol on street corners. She blasted saloon proprietors as a threat to society but destroyed no property. Chagrinned at her reception by fellow drys, she left the region shortly after.[20]

Nation returned to Guthrie in 1905, intent on establishing a prohibition federation in the territory. Through this organization, she proposed to dismantle the liquor industry, achieve constitutional prohibition for the proposed state of Oklahoma, push legislation to outlaw cursing, and elect a prohibitionist to the White House.[21] Large crowds gathered to hear the famous saloon smasher in Edmond, El Reno, Holdenville, and Wewoka. The editor of the *Shawnee News* granted her complete editorial control of his newspaper for one day. She brought nationally renowned anti-liquor speakers to Guthrie, launched her federation, and began printing her own journal, *The Hatchet*. In this publication and her speeches, she urged Oklahomans to remove elected officials who failed to enforce existing liquor laws.[22] Traveling into Indian Territory, she tried to attend the grand opening of Tulsa's Robinson Hotel to protest liquor sales there, but she was locked out of the ceremony. Her relationship with other dry leaders in the territories worsened as she became more militant and radical. In the summer of 1906, she was charged with sending obscene materials through the mails: in an issue of *The Hatchet* she had provided a lesson to boys on controlling their sexual urges that included a graphic description of the male body. As the state constitutional convention opened in Guthrie in 1906, she left Oklahoma Territory and settled in Arkansas.[23]

Nation's presence in the territories had a significant impact on the anti-liquor campaign. Although she attracted people to the cause initially, dry Oklahomans disdained her radical approach. Established temperance organizations and churches distanced themselves from her, fearing she would discredit their own efforts. Her presence and radical ways allowed the union, league, and the Indian Territory Federation of Churches (allied with the Anti-Saloon

League) to portray themselves as moderate voices in the liquor debate. The image of Nation as the wild-eyed reformer with a hatchet established her as the radical fringe of the temperance crusade in Oklahoma.

The league and the union sought distance between themselves and Nation. Reminiscent of her previous conflicts with dry organizations in Kansas, which viewed her activism as unladylike, Oklahoma drys resented her presence in the territories;[24] but her antics did aid the dry cause in the Sooner State. When convention delegates met in Guthrie to draft a state constitution and debate prohibition, they were inundated with petitions from the league and the union; this extensive lobbying effort seemed moderate and reasonable when compared to Nation's tactics.

Long before talk of statehood escalated, the Oklahoma territorial government took steps to regulate liquor sales. The legislature authorized boards of county commissioners to grant liquor licenses. These boards required each applicant to submit a petition signed by thirty tax-paying residents of the township or voting precinct in which the saloon was to be located. Further, applicants had to make their intentions public to allow residents to voice opposition; two weeks before the board's vote, they were to post their request in the county's two largest newspapers or in five public places. Those seeking a license were to be of respectable standing in the local community, and the board was to consider any objections. These stipulations allowed dry organizations, such as the league and the union, considerable influence over the number of licensed saloons in a community.[25] Additionally, the social character requirement (i.e., that applications by nonrespectable residents would be rejected) granted area clergymen, and by extension the league to which many belonged, some influence in this process. From their respected positions in the community, ministers could establish or tear down an individual's standing, and the league also exercised its moral authority to pressure community leaders who opposed its efforts.

For example, in 1900, the Anti-Saloon League of Hennessey circulated a petition against a saloon license. When Reverend

George N. Keniston refused to sign it, the league publicly attacked him. He responded that the consumption of alcohol was a personal liberty issue and should not be dictated by the majority, but the league held fast in its rebuke. Oklahoma Anti-Saloon League superintendent Rev. Swan sent letters to citizens throughout Oklahoma Territory questioning the moral fortitude of anyone who signed a petition in favor of a saloon license.[26] Through such actions, the league not only attacked the saloon in specific locales, but also kept the issue in the minds of the voting public and hammered home its portrayal of the liquor question as one that pitted organized religion, which the league portrayed as the paragon of respectability, against the liquor industry, which was viewed as the leading threat to respectable society.

Pressured by the league and other respectable organizations, the territorial government placed other restrictions on the liquor industry. Victuallers could not sell liquor to minors or habitual drunkards, after midnight or before five o'clock in the morning, or on Sundays and election days. Further, saloons could not have chairs or seats, pool tables, or gambling paraphernalia.[27] Some county and municipal officers strictly enforced these laws, whereas others did not: enforcement often reflected the mood of the local voting public. According to the territorial attorney general's commissioned report on crime statistics for the period June 1, 1901 to June 1, 1902, county attorneys handed down indictments for selling liquor on Sunday, for selling liquor to minors, and for selling liquor without a license. However the lack of indictments for liquor violations in Oklahoma County, which included Oklahoma City and its approximately eighty saloons, strongly suggests an uneven approach to liquor enforcement in the territory. Reports that some saloon keepers regularly violated territorial liquor laws became a leading rationale for the elimination of the regulated saloon.[28]

The league also fought the saloon industry in the courts. In July 1900, Rev. Swan filed a remonstrance with the Oklahoma County board of commissioners to block the issuance of a liquor license to an Oklahoma City man. The board issued the license, declaring that the time period within which to file the challenge had expired. Swan appealed this decision to Oklahoma Territory's Supreme Court, which ruled that county boards were required to consider all remonstrances and that the Oklahoma County board should not have ruled on the liquor license until it considered all complaints.[29] This decision established a precedent for subsequent territorial rulings and granted drys greater leverage in blocking liquor licenses.

The league used pressure politics to influence liquor enforcement. In Oklahoma City, the league threatened charges of corruption against the city police chief and others if they did not enforce saloon closing laws to its liking.[30] City residents, in conjunction with league operatives, formed a law-and-order league early in 1900 to assist elected officials in enforcing closing hours and Sunday closing laws. Drys smeared Oklahoma City mayor Henry Overholser as an anarchist when he criticized the influence of these private agencies.[31] An El Reno saloon brawl between the local marshal and a city police officer that took place after midnight sparked the development of a law-and-order league in that community.[32] The cities of Mangum and Chickasha also formed law-and-order leagues, which employed detectives to monitor and publicize the names of those who patronized saloons and houses of prostitution.[33]

By November 1900, the Anti-Saloon League boasted 15,000 members in Oklahoma Territory.[34] Its base of support may have been much larger, however, because many ministers endorsed the league's work without formally joining.[35] As with the national league, local merchants and professionals (i.e., doctors, lawyers, and ministers) dominated the Oklahoma league. Because clergymen held positions of prominence in state and local leagues, these bodies served as conduits by which local pastors attained considerable political influence in the region. They also provided the middle-class league officers with the means to redefine public drinking as a non-respectable activity.

The Oklahoma league also fought the saloon in the territorial government. Operatives drafted several bills restricting or banning liquor sales. None of these bills passed, but the Oklahoma House did allow Reverend D. W. Keller of the Logan County league to address that body concerning a prohibition bill.[36] The Oklahoma league's political activism produced only limited results initially, though its officers gained valuable political experience that they later used during the campaign for dry statehood.

Until statehood, drys worked to limit the sale of liquor locally. The *Daily Oklahoman*, a leading critic of prohibition, estimated that forty towns in Oklahoma Territory had banned liquor sales by 1906.[37] The Sayre *Headlight* placed the number of dry towns at one hundred. Washita County was completely dry except for one saloon in the small town of Bessie; Comanche County was dry except for Lawton; a Lincoln County court ruling dried up all of the towns in that county except Chandler and Stroud; all of Beaver County was dry; and Weatherford, which had supported fourteen saloons in 1900, had closed all liquor establishments by the end of 1906.[38] Additionally, league operatives blocked the annual renewal of liquor licenses, which reduced the legal sources of liquor in wet communities. League officers persuaded the Anadarko city council to increase liquor licenses from three to five hundred dollars.[39] The league's success in local politics made statewide prohibition feasible because drys ignored the enforcement problems in Indian Territory.

As the nineteenth century closed, enforcement of the federal liquor ban in the eastern territory remained lax as a result of the small number of U.S. marshals stationed there. The governments of the Five Tribes also adopted liquor prohibition, but these laws did not apply to non-Indians in the region who sold liquor without worry of local prosecution. Additionally, the federal penalties for liquor violations did little to hinder liquor purchases. The fine for intoxication was one dollar, which was approximately a day's wages, whereas the penalty for "introducing" liquor into the territory was a fine of twenty-five dollars and a jail term of thirty days. Federal marshals and town sheriffs generally tolerated the presence of liquor establishments unless they aroused the ire of the local community as centers of violent crime.

In 1906, concerned about the liquor situation in the territories, President Theodore Roosevelt commissioned William E. "Pussyfoot" Johnson as "Special Officer for the Suppression of the Liquor Traffic in Indian Territory" with a twenty-five hundred annual stipend plus reimbursement for expenses.[40] A member of the Anti-Saloon League of America and a former operative of the Prohibition Party, Johnson carried out his mission with gusto. He acquired the nickname "Pussyfoot" for his ability to enter communities unnoticed before the liquor men could hide their wares. Once divulging his identity, Johnson arrested proprietors and employees and destroyed the establishments. He smashed the furnishings of saloons, joints, and gambling halls (also illegal) throughout the territory. He dumped confiscated liquor into the streets or nearby streams. (One such raid led to the spectacle of thirsty patrons from a victimized saloon scooping the spilled liquor from the streets with their hands.[41]) Johnson quickly gained regional notoriety.

Soon after his arrival in Indian Territory, Johnson and local officials raided illegal saloons in the booming oil town of Tulsa and arrested eight men. He next raided the joints in the railroad towns of Eufaula and South McAlester, dumping two thousand gallons of whiskey at the latter site.[42] At the McKee post office, he dumped one hundred gallons of spiked cider that had been sent there through the mail service.[43] He descended on Collinsville, Mounds, Red Fork, Tullahasee, and Sapulpa and destroyed gambling and saloon fixtures. During a second visit to Tulsa, he and his officers confiscated and dumped 25,000 bottles of liquor into the Arkansas River.[44]

Over the next year, Johnson and his deputies launched similar raids in Ada, Ardmore, Chickasha, Durant, Okmulgee, and smaller communities throughout the territories. They invaded joints in Tulsa, Muskogee, and McAlester on numerous occasions, determined to stamp out the liquor industry. Their return visits speak to their determination, but also highlight the liquor men's resiliency in facing such staunch opponents. Furthermore, Johnson and his deputies were not content to fight the liquor traffic only in the streets. During his fourteen months in the territories, he supervised over six thousand cases in court, most involving liquor. He achieved a 95 percent conviction rate in those cases he brought to trial.[45] Johnson and his associates sought to make prohibition a reality in Indian Territory; their abrupt tactics certainly shook up the region, but the liquor industry remained prosperous.

Though Indian Territory remained the focus of Johnson's attention, he also conducted liquor raids in neighboring Oklahoma Territory. Because the federal liquor ban applied not only to all of Indian Territory, but also to individual American Indians elsewhere in the United States, Johnson broadened the scope of his operations. Oklahoma Territory contained sizeable Arapaho, Cheyenne, Comanche, Kiowa, and Apache populations, and numerous smaller tribes. Despite the federal ban, these American Indian groups also had liquor available to them. In March 1907, responding to reports of illegal liquor sales, Johnson arrested thirty-six Oklahoma City saloon keepers for introducing whiskey to an American Indian patron.[46] Johnson warned the remaining liquor men that he might return if liquor sales to American Indians persisted, and then he returned to Indian Territory.

Johnson enlisted the aid of federal officers, such as Bud Ledbetter, already stationed in Muskogee.[47] Before Johnson's arrival, Ledbetter intercepted several shipments of liquor, which local citizens had ordered from Kansas City and St. Louis distributors, at the Missouri, Kansas and Texas Railroad yard. In December 1905, he arrested several prominent Muskogee businessmen when they picked up their holiday spirits at the depot. Despite these and other efforts, liquor remained available in Muskogee. Johnson stepped up raids at train yards. In December 1906, he destroyed 1,920 bottles of alleged temperance drinks at the Ardmore express office and smashed twenty-three separate consignments of liquor shipped to the Durant railroad yard from Texas distilleries and breweries.[48]

Johnson also received assistance from federal officers Grant Cowen, Bass Reeves, Sam Cone, Frank West, Sam Roberts, and enlisted the thirty-three American Indian police officers scattered around the territory. These men faced considerable danger. During the course of Johnson's stay in Indian Territory, liquor men killed several of his enforcement officers in skirmishes and reportedly placed a three-thousand-dollar bounty on Johnson's head. Two outlaws known throughout the region, Eugene and Ben Titsworth, were tried in court for offering this reward, but juries failed to convict either man despite testimony from others that the Titsworths had offered the bounty.[49] Johnson persisted in his campaign, but this lack of local support blunted his efforts and denoted considerable area resentment toward his heavy-handed methods.

Johnson's fervent approach to his job encouraged some local officials to take a harder stand against the liquor men. Early in 1907, a grand jury investigated liquor selling and gambling in Chickasha, near the western edge of the Chickasaw nation, and prohibition supporters briefly became hopeful that the territories might be dried up permanently.[50] These local enforcement campaigns soon lost momentum, and liquor joints reopened in Muskogee, Tulsa, and McAlester soon after Johnson's raids. Further, alcohol remained available to many people in small towns and villages, such as Kiefer, Drumright, Checotah, and Coalgate.

To enforce the federal ban effectively, authorities sought an exact definition of liquor, that is, the amount of alcohol a beverage must contain for officials to declare it intoxicating and thus illegal. Many people did not consider beer or wine intoxicants because most people did not become noticeably drunk unless they consumed generous amounts of these liquids. Indian Territory stores, saloons, hotels, and restaurants regularly sold near-beers, such as Choctaw, Uno, Ino, Tintop, Hiawatha, Pablo, Long Horn, Short Horn, under the assumption that they were not intoxicating; they contained roughly 3 percent alcohol by content. In August 1906 in Muskogee, federal judge William R. Lawrence ruled that beverages containing 2 percent alcohol or more were liquor and thus illegal in Indian Territory; special agent Johnson wasted no time and added the joints that served Uno and Choctaw to his itinerary of raids. Most local authorities lacked the facilities to conduct immediate chemical analyses of suspicious beverages and thus improvised their methods. For example, when a South McAlester proprietor told the marshal that the cider he served did not inebriate his customers, the officer, to prove the opposite, served it to five onlookers who then staggered about. The marshal promptly arrested the business owner.[51]

Although the federal officers raided several establishments that served Uno and Choctaw and seized numerous shipments, they enjoyed little success in stamping out this trade all together. As of May 1907, more than eight months after Lawrence had defined Uno as intoxicating, the city of Muskogee continued to order the nine joints within city limits that served Uno and Mistletoe (another low-alcohol drink) to pay a twenty-five-dollar monthly license for permission to operate.[52] In September of that year, Lawrence refused joint owner Joe Lightle the injunction he sought to block Johnson from raiding these establishments. Emboldened by this decision, Johnson went after the near-beer joints in Muskogee, Tulsa, and in smaller towns, such as Coweta, Broken Arrow, Red Fork, Porter, and Clarksville.[53] His efforts interrupted the availability of these drinks, but the near-beer joints continued to operate.

Johnson did not limit his activities to the retail liquor industry or the territories. In September 1907, he arrested Sam DePriest in the Cherokee Hills near Melvin for keeping liquor distillation equipment at his home. The newspaper account indicated that several stills operated in the hills, which produced liquor that was sold in Ft. Gibson.[54] Johnson further ordered the brewers of northeast Texas to stop selling beer in Indian Territory or risk federal prosecution.[55] His efforts clearly exceeded those of previous federal officers. Nevertheless, liquor remained available in the area during the late territorial period for anyone who wanted it.

In some quarters, Johnson's extreme methods produced angry rebukes. A resident of the mining community of Coalgate publicly protested that the liquor laws were enforced by "carpetbaggers" who possessed a "nonsensical disregard of common sense and decency. The homes of private citizens were entered and in some instances the lonely quart which was intended only as a remedy for the sick wife or aged parents, was ruthlessly confiscated."[56] At times, Johnson's critics reacted violently to his activities. In addition to death threats, Johnson was physically assaulted during raids at

Eufala and Chelsea.⁵⁷ Certainly a portion of the population, most notably those associated with the Anti-Saloon League, applauded Johnson's campaign against the liquor joints, but others just as vehemently opposed him.

Johnson also encountered difficulties in the courts, which often viewed his methods unfavorably. In February 1907, the U.S. Circuit Court of Appeals overturned the conviction of L. L. Ellis for introducing liquor to American Indians. Federal authorities had arrested Ellis when they found liquor in his house, but the court ruled that this did not constitute introduction of liquor. It ruled, rather, that the perpetrator must be caught with liquor on his or her person or in a mode of transportation. This ruling led officials to dismiss many of the pending liquor cases.⁵⁸ The issue continued to haunt the newly formed Oklahoma legal system when statehood took effect.

To add to the problem, some local officials actively contested the federal authorities. In October 1907, Johnson and his deputies conducted raids on Muskogee's near-beer joints despite testimonies from the proprietors that their beverages were nonalcoholic. Word of the impending raid spread, and several joints served free near-beer to the crowded onlookers until Johnson and his men arrived. The Muskogee police accepted the joint operators' assertion that their drinks were nonalcoholic and arrested the federal officers for disturbing the peace and committing malicious destruction of property. Johnson was ordered to post a five-hundred-dollar bond.⁵⁹ Three days later, the Muskogee mayor discharged the federal officers because all of the near-beer had been dumped into the streets, preventing a chemical analysis of the beverage to determine its alcohol content.

Five days after the arrest in Muskogee, Tulsa police arrested three of Johnson's deputies for conducting a raid on near-beer joints in that city. Federal judge Lawrence put the matter to rest the following week when he ruled that Johnson and his men were under the jurisdiction of the federal courts only, and all local charges against them were dropped.⁶⁰ The combative stance of elected officials in

Indian Territory's two largest communities received at least passive support from a local electorate that regularly reelected these men to office.

Lawrence's reassertion of federal authority regarding the liquor issue had a somewhat muted effect because the previous September, voters in the two territories had made prohibition a part of the new state constitution, which was to take effect when Oklahoma joined the United States. At that point, the federal government would surrender responsibility for liquor enforcement to the new state government or so most people in the region believed. As for Johnson, a week after the fiasco in Tulsa and a month before Oklahoma statehood, he returned to Washington, D.C., for future assignment. He never returned to the territories in an official capacity. Instead, he gained authority over all of the American Indian reservations in the United States, shifted his headquarters from Muskogee to Salt Lake City, Utah, and focused on liquor sales to American Indians in California, New Mexico, and Idaho.[61]

The federal officers who had assisted Johnson continued their assault on Indian Territory's illegal liquor industry as statehood neared. They arrested liquor joint owners and destroyed liquor in Glenn Pool, Bartlesville, Kiefer, Marlow, and Wewoka in late October. On November 1, 1907, federal officers received word from Washington that, in lieu of the impending statehood date, they were to discontinue these raids. The liquor men learned of this order and announced that they would resume uninhibited liquor sales.[62] The jointists' commitment to their industry, then, matched that of Indian Territory's dry forces. The situation in neighboring Oklahoma Territory was quite similar.

Despite efforts by the Anti-Saloon League and like-minded groups, the liquor industry persisted throughout the existence of Oklahoma Territory. Within a year of the 1889 land run, the Anheuser-Busch company established a series of breweries around Oklahoma. Guthrie, the territorial capital, sported one of these breweries, and others operated by the Ferd Heim Brewing Company and the Schlitz Brewing Company.[63] In 1894, a Texas company announced plans to open a brewery in Hennessey, home of the territorial Anti-Saloon League's first president, Tipton Cox. W. H. Baker operated a federally licensed distillery in Ponca City across the street from the justice of the peace office. This establishment caused numerous court recesses and delays because judges, attorneys, plaintiffs, defendants, jurors, and witnesses stepped across the street to treat one another.[64] In 1902, N. Moss and Company opened the Oklahoma Brewery in Oklahoma City, which was scheduled to produce 25,000 to 30,000 barrels of beer annually and announced plans for a malt plant in the region to service breweries in the southwestern United States. The following year the Moss Brewing Company began construction of a $200,000 brewery in Oklahoma City, which was advertised as one of the largest in the southwest.[65] The Pabst Corporation of Milwaukee established wholesale beer operations in Guthrie and in Stillwater.

Oklahoma Territory produced wine as well. A 1901 territorial report asserted that wine was manufactured in many counties. The rocky, uneven ground was ideal for growing grapes, and farmers refined their bounty into wine to reduce spoilage and financial loss. The marginal mention of this industry in subsequent newspaper accounts and communications between enforcement officers suggest that, although present in a number of counties, wine production comprised a relatively small part of the region's liquor industry, as was the case elsewhere in the nation.[66]

The retail liquor industry also thrived throughout Oklahoma Territory. Lawton, which officially opened to white settlement by lottery between June 9 and August 6, 1901, contained sixty saloons by August 22 of that year.[67] Shawnee, a town of 12,000 at the time of statehood and constitutional prohibition, contained thirty licensed saloons, which reportedly dispensed seven hundred gallons of beer and twenty-five gallons of whiskey each day.[68] Saloons also were a standard feature of many smaller communities in Oklahoma Territory: Ponca City, with a population of 2,528, supported twelve licensed saloons in 1900;[69] Granite and Sayre contained thirteen saloons in 1901 and 1903, respectively, though each contained fewer than 2,500 people;[70] El Reno supported twenty-one saloons in 1901, though its population was 3,383;[71] Weatherford, with a

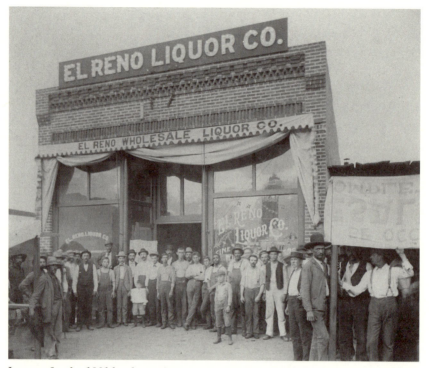

In town for the 1901 land opening, a group of men and boys gather outside the El Reno Liquor Company building. Liquor establishments such as this often were among the earliest businesses to open in new communities.

population less than 2,500, contained eighteen saloons and seventeen gambling houses in 1903.[72] Saloons were a basic feature of many Oklahoma communities and formed a dominant part of the business district in some towns.

Numerous saloons sprouted in Oklahoma City, which quickly became the territory's largest urban center soon after its incorporation. Its retail liquor business remained prominent throughout the territorial period and became particularly raucous during special events. One early resident recalled that downtown saloons were so jammed with customers during the 1900 Independence Day celebration that several sawed additional door space in their front walls to accommodate greater customer traffic.[73] Mayor Overholser's anti-prohibition meeting of that year drew five hundred like-minded city inhabitants, confirming the city's wet stance and fostering, according to critics, vice and crime.[74] Oklahoma City reportedly contained eighty-five saloons by 1904.[75] Among the more notorious were Robert D. Kerr's Sasaric Saloon on Robinson Street just south of Main, Madam Daisy Clayton's Red Onion just off of Broadway Street, and Two Johns, all located in what was labeled "Hop Boulevard."[76] Despite the efforts of the Anti-Saloon League and other dry advocates, liquor remained available in many parts of Oklahoma Territory; 550 territorial saloons remained open until Oklahoma became a state.[77] Many of the saloons would continue to operate, illegally, after prohibition and statehood passed. And even though Oklahoma dry proponents failed to kill the saloon, they did separate it from respectable society.

The coarse nature of the liquor industry inadvertently propelled the prohibition campaign forward. The entrenched, lucrative liquor trade violently opposed any bent on destroying it. In the tiny community of Orlando in 1901, a three-week war ensued between supporters of the saloon and the local league over the issuance of liquor licenses. As tensions rose, two men beat and stabbed a locally prominent league supporter. The public turned against the saloon men, and the league successfully blocked the issuance of a saloon license in Orlando.[78] In Guthrie, saloon men attacked Reverend Swan of the Oklahoma league, beating him so severely that he required two weeks rest at home to recuperate. In the summer of 1907, with the vote on prohibition nearing, saloon men assaulted the league's Reverend Thompson on the steps of the Beaver County courthouse because he vocally opposed the issuance of saloon licenses.[79] These types of violent outbursts by Oklahoma liquor men pushed a number of voters to the dry cause, and the league played these incidents to maximum political effect to pass their agenda.

CHAPTER TWO

Oklahoma Goes Dry

Oklahomans' vote to make prohibition a part of the state constitution was less a reflection of overwhelming popular support for a liquor ban than a result of the extensive lobbying and political organizing by the Woman's Christian Temperance Union (WTCU) and the Anti-Saloon League of America. By the time of statehood, the league and its supporters had managed to ban liquor in several counties and towns, but they still faced an entrenched liquor industry in Oklahoma Territory. Indian Territory also contained a thriving liquor business despite the long-standing federal liquor ban in the region. Federal officials encountered considerable opposition to strict enforcement in many communities. Despite these stubborn areas of wet sentiment, the league continued to work methodically toward dry statehood. The adoption of statewide prohibition in 1907 was the culmination of a campaign by area ministers and others, mobilized by the league, to limit access to liquor in the territories, and it was through the efforts of these men and women that Oklahoma became the only dry state to enter the union.

The campaign for and enforcement of prohibition in Oklahoma also was part of several larger trends in the late-nineteenth-

and early-twentieth-century United States. One of these was the nationwide shift from voluntary temperance to coercive prohibition. Previous temperance organizations, such as the Washingtonian movement, had promoted abstinence among working men before the Civil War. Although the Washingtonians enjoyed considerable success in reducing drunkenness among wage earners, avid temperance supporters remained dissatisfied with voluntary abstinence and gravitated toward legisled liquor bans. Prohibition was also wrapped in the broader issues of gender identification and working-class culture because a liquor ban would most significantly affect the saloon-going population — working-class men.

As for political leanings, Indian Territory, which comprised roughly the eastern half of the present-day state of Oklahoma, allied itself with the Democratic Party of the Old South, from which many residents had come. Oklahoma Territory, which constituted approximately the western half of Oklahoma, was much more Republican, reflecting the politics of neighboring Kansas. Because Democrats, like Muskogee's Charles Haskell and Tishomingo's William H. Murray, were instrumental in merging the two territories into a single state, their party and the southeastern region of the new state gained a tenuous dominance over the early Oklahoma government. Thus the Democratic Party would become an uncomfortable ally of dry organizations in the Sooner State.

In 1904, Reverend Purley A. Baker, general superintendent of the Anti-Saloon League of America, came to Oklahoma Territory and reorganized the Oklahoma Anti-Saloon League with the goal of banning the saloon throughout the proposed state. By this time, the national league's leadership had grown increasingly concerned about the direction of the Oklahoma organization and sought greater influence over it. Baker brought with him Reverend J. J. Thomson, recently of the Ohio league, to serve as the new superintendent of the Oklahoma Territory organization. Thomson replaced Reverend H. E. Swan, a Congregationalist minister from Oklahoma City.

Baker also met with prominent Indian Territory clergymen in Muskogee and founded the Church Federation for Prohibition

Statehood. This group named Captain A. S. McKennon as its president. McKennon, as a member of the Dawes Commission, had been charged with the task of allotting lands to the individual members of the Five Tribes. He also had been a vocal critic of the liquor industry. For the all-important position of secretary (equivalent to superintendent in state leagues), the federation tabbed Reverend Evander M. Sweet of Muskogee's Methodist Episcopal Church, South. Men, such as Dr. A. Grant Evans (president of Henry Kendall College in Muskogee), Reverend J. S. Murrow (a long-standing missionary in the region), and many other ministers from around Indian Territory were also active in the church federation. Like the Oklahoma Territory league, the federation organized dry sentiment among respectable members of middle-class society. It held its own convention in 1905, but it worked in conjunction with the Oklahoma Territory league and the Anti-Saloon League of America throughout the territorial period. In 1907, the two territorial organizations merged to form the Oklahoma league.[1]

Baker's visit to the territories in 1904 exemplifies the effort by the Anti-Saloon League of America to tighten its hold on regional affiliates. In replacing Rev. Swan with Rev. Thomson, Baker exchanged an established Oklahoma City steward of the anti-liquor cause with a newcomer to the area. Although Swan was personally acquainted with other dry advocates in the region, Thomson knew Baker and the national officers much better than the officers and trustees of the Oklahoma league and likely depended on the national league for guidance more than his predecessor had. (Oklahoma was not the only instance in which the national league attempted to increase its influence over regional leagues; Anti-Saloon League of America founder Howard H. Russell reorganized the Wisconsin league in 1898 under a new superintendent whom Russell found more agreeable.)[2]

The selection of McKennon, Thomson, and others to lead the prohibition campaigns in Oklahoma and Indian territories also reflected the region's political circumstances in the opening years of the twentieth century. Having identified grassroots support for a liquor ban, the league labored to organize and mobilize these people. And Thomson and McKennon further used their clout in Washington, D.C., to effect change through the Congress. In addition to his work on the Dawes commission, McKennon had gained a personal audience with President Theodore Roosevelt to discuss the liquor question in the territories. Soon after assuming their new offices, Thomson and the others lobbied Congress as it considered an enabling act, which would permit the creation of one or more states from the territories. The lobbyists further urged Congress to continue the long-standing liquor ban in Indian Territory (subsequently the eastern portion of the new state) as a condition of statehood.

Additionally, dry proponents in Indian Territory sent other supporters back East to discuss with influential groups the merits of a liquor ban in regard to the area's shrinking American Indian population. Dr. Evans, a trustee in the Oklahoma league, made several such trips calling for a prohibition clause. Reverend Murrow, a forty-year missionary to the American Indians in the region, sent members of Congress memorials from thousands of American Indians praying for prohibition. The Indian Territory Federation's Rev. Sweet attended the Lake Mohonk Indian Conference and gained its vocal support for prohibition in Oklahoma, and in 1905, Dr. Evans attended and spoke at the twenty-third annual Lake Mohonk Conference.[3] These well-connected men capitalized on personal acquaintances in the federal government and national organizations to promote a liquor ban in Oklahoma.

In 1905, dry proponents throughout the territories formed a central committee to organize the campaign for prohibition throughout the proposed state. The committee included Rev. Swan; Mrs. M. S. Fellow of the Alva, Oklahoma WCTU; Leslie Baker of the Oklahoma City Order of Good Templars; S. W. McCann of the Oklahoma City civic federation; and Reverend Marion Porter of the Lawton Methodist Episcopal Church (and future secretary of the Oklahoma league). They lobbied the Oklahoma Territorial government in Guthrie and continued to pressure Congress to pass prohibition.[4] Rev. Thomson held weekly meetings around the region in support of prohibition, and dry advocates sent petitions signed by 20,000 supporters to Congress urging prohibition for the area.[5]

The Anti-Saloon League of America worked in conjunction with its regional affiliates toward prohibition statehood. Its legislative superintendent in Washington, D.C., Reverend Edwin C. Dinwiddie, became the de facto leader of the Oklahoma anti-liquor campaign at the capitol. He stressed to congressmen the importance of prohibiting liquor in the region and emphasized the popular support prohibition enjoyed in the region, presenting the petitions from the territories as evidence. Dinwiddie was a well-heeled Washington lobbyist. On behalf of the national league and in conjunction with such veteran lobbyists as Wilbur F. Crafts and the WCTU's Margaret Dye Ellis, he convinced Congress to ban the sale of liquor on military bases, in the capitol building, and at federally operated homes for veterans in 1902.[6]

Dinwiddie and his colleagues lobbied Congress for prohibition in Oklahoma while it crafted the 1905 Enabling Act, by which Congress relinquished its authority over the territories and allowed for the creation of a state. Dinwiddie even authored an amendment to the bill that prohibited the "manufacture, sale, barter, giving away, or otherwise furnishing . . . of intoxicating liquors" in the regions designated as the Indian Territory and the Osage Reservation for twenty-one years following statehood, and this change became a part of the final language of the Enabling Act.[7] Back in the territories, the local press acknowledged the league's influence on the wording of the measure: "There is no doubt but that the organized efforts of the Anti-Saloon people was (sic) responsible for the Gallinger amendment (calling for prohibition in the proposed state for twenty-one years) being inserted into the statehood bill. . . ."[8] The league had maneuvered well and ensured prohibition for the eastern half of the new state through the next two decades.

Dinwiddie's amendment was integral to the development of statewide prohibition in Oklahoma. Two years later, liquor ban supporters at the Oklahoma constitutional convention, such as Charles N. Haskell, argued that delegates should prohibit liquor throughout the state because Congress previously had banned it from the eastern portion of the new state for twenty-one years, and he held the belief that Oklahoma's laws should be uniform throughout the state and so pressed for statewide prohibition.[9]

The prohibition clause of the Enabling Act, then, was the result of active lobbying by critics of the liquor traffic as much as popular support for continuing traditional American Indian liquor policy. The perceived threat that intoxicated American Indians posed to white society had served as pretext for the federal liquor ban, but that justification seems increasingly hollow when examining the region at the turn of the century. The census of 1900 made clear that the American Indian population in Oklahoma, as elsewhere in the nation, was declining rapidly. Thus even though a large number of whites continued to accept the premise that American Indians became violently uncontrollable when intoxicated, the basis of this threat was declining with the American Indian population. Prohibition became a part of the Enabling Act as a result of the extensive politicking by dry organizations in the territory and in Washington. The league played a vital role in the creation of Oklahoma prohibition more than two years before statehood.

After the passage of the Enabling Act, league operatives in the territories accelerated their efforts toward prohibition. At the 1905 Sequoyah convention held in Muskogee to consider separate statehood for Indian Territory, delegates representing the various tribes named Captain McKennon as chairman of the prohibition committee. In addition to his other prominent posts, he became vice president of the Oklahoma league in 1907. He worked closely with Haskell and Murray at the meeting in Muskogee. Both men were rising political stars in the region. Haskell was elected as the state's first governor in 1907, and Murray became the first speaker of the Oklahoma House of Representatives. McKennon became chairman of the Sequoyah convention's prohibition committee and made a ban on liquor central to that convention's final report, which went beyond the provisions of the Enabling Act and called for perpetual prohibition in the proposed state of Sequoyah. Though Congress rejected the idea of a separate state comprising the eastern territory, this convention's unanimous support for prohibition bolstered dry arguments at the state constitutional convention that opened in late 1906.

Some American Indian leaders joined in urging the federal government to ban liquor in the new state. The Creek Nation's Chief Pleasant Porter addressed Congress late in 1905, stating, "We are asked to give up our right to govern ourselves. But we do not submit to the breaking of the other promises, to a change that would fill our country with saloons, that would poison the bodies of our people and demoralize their souls with the white man's liquor."[10] Porter accepted the loss of American Indian autonomy on the condition that the federal government continue to protect the American Indians from liquor sales.

Other American Indians did not share his acceptance of single statehood or his concern over liquor. Responding to the decision to merge the two territories into one state, which was contrary to the wishes of many American Indians, Little Frog, who was full-blood Creek Indian, stated, "He (Democratics) say Publican broke all Injun treaties, wouldn't let him have the statehood what he wanted, but give him Oklahoma, and then refuse to give 'em Oklahoma whiskey."[11] In the eyes of this speaker, the liquor ban, rather than benefiting the American Indians, merely represented another way in which the government sought to control and limit their activities.

White residents of the two territories began to pressure Congress for single statehood soon after passage of the Enabling Act. Several in this group sought prohibition for the new state and were concerned that Congress might act to hinder their cause. Revs. Thomson and Sweet, superintendents of the Oklahoma and Indian Territory leagues, respectively, and Reverend Thomas H. Harper, future treasurer of the Oklahoma league, traveled to Washington to make their case. Through Thomson's close friendships with two members of the House committee on territories, they secured a hearing before committee members at which they effectively discouraged any congressional declarations against a liquor ban.[12] The Anti-Saloon League, through its work in the territories and in Washington, D.C., laid the groundwork for statewide prohibition long before statehood boosters scheduled a constitutional convention for November 20, 1906.

While league supporters in both territories worked toward state-wide prohibition, they also continued to address immediate conditions in the region. Enforcement efforts in dry Indian Territory increased dramatically in 1906 when William E. "Pussyfoot" Johnson arrived as a federal liquor enforcement officer. Johnson, whose efforts against the illegal liquor industry made his a household name throughout the territories, was a prominent member of the Anti-Saloon League of America and had previously served as editor of the official League newspaper, *American Issue*. Reverend Charles C. Brannon, one of Johnson's commissioned deputies and a Methodist minister in the northeast region of Oklahoma Territory, was active in the territorial and later the state league. The state Methodist Episcopal conference elected him as trustee to the Oklahoma league in 1912 and 1913. Brannon took his federal post seriously and rooted out liquor violators during the week before taking the pulpit on Sunday.[13]

League operatives in Oklahoma Territory were not content with seeing local and territorial liquor laws enforced. They sought the elimination of the saloon at the county and municipal level by inhibiting saloon operators from renewing their annual liquor licenses. They dried up more than one hundred communities—mostly small ones—by late 1906. Asserting that the saloon was corrupting young people, the league targeted those towns that contained state educational institutions: Norman, Stillwater, Tonkawa, Alva, Edmond, and Weatherford. In the southwestern town of Arapahoe, the league defeated efforts to open a brewery and blocked the renewal of saloon licenses for two saloons.[14] They also pressured the territorial governor, Frank Frantz, to remove several county attorneys from office who were lax in liquor enforcement.[15] By June 1907, league officers claimed that they had helped reduce the number of saloons in Oklahoma Territory by one hundred.[16]

Having secured congressional endorsement of prohibition in Oklahoma, Rev. Dinwiddie came West to direct the prohibition campaign in the territories. In the fall of 1906, voters elected delegates to a convention in Guthrie to draft a constitution for the proposed state of Oklahoma. Dinwiddie, in keeping with the league's nonpartisan approach, directed activists in the Indian Territory Church Federation for Prohibition and the Oklahoma Territory league to endorse the election of men sympathetic to the prohibition cause regardless of their party affiliation. They sent circulars to known dry advocates urging them to involve themselves in the selection of delegates.

By September 1906 the league had organized local leagues in each Oklahoma Territory county save Caddo, Dewey, and Washita counties. Each of these local groups selected a president to direct it and to coordinate activities with the state league. Each also elected a vice president in charge of information and agitation to circulate literature and ensure that local newspapers published league material; a vice president in charge of legislative matters to meet with and advise city and county officials; and a vice president in charge of finances to solicit funds for league work from churches and civic groups.[17]

The Oklahoma WCTU worked in conjunction with the league during this campaign. Union President Abbie Hillerman of Cushing formed local chapters in each county of the territory. These chapters urged men to elect local officers and convention delegates sympathetic to the dry cause.[18] The union increasingly coordinated with and deferred to the leadership of the league. Despite these extensive efforts, the league and its supporters were unable to place a majority of confirmed dry proponents in the convention as voting delegates. Prohibition supporters' organizing would not pay dividends until a year later during the prohibition referendum campaign.

To counteract the lobbying of the union and the league, opponents of prohibition in the territories worked through several organizations to influence the convention. As early as 1897, the German-American Association of Oklahoma Territory had denounced prohibition as an affront to personal liberty. Although devout in its opposition to the ban, the association represented a relatively small portion of Oklahoma voters. Its 1897 convention drew fifty delegates from nine counties in the north central and central regions of the future state, and the area's small German population remained concentrated in these counties after statehood.[19] In 1904, the Oklahoma Liquor Men's Association organized to combat the campaign for prohibition. The Citizens League gained the highest profile of the anti-prohibition groups as the convention neared. This small group of businessmen and professionals was critical of the saloon, but they asserted that a system of high licenses and local option, rather than a liquor ban, was the best means to control the nonrespectable liquor industry. They further argued that a complete ban of liquor would reduce tax revenues significantly, discourage business investment in Oklahoma, and greatly increase disrespect for all laws.[20]

When the constitutional convention opened in November 1906, the Oklahoma league sent Revs. Dinwiddie and Sweet and others to attend and established headquarters in Guthrie from which to organize their lobbying efforts. The league found some convention delegates receptive to their arguments. William J. Caudill of Hobart, representing southwestern Oklahoma at Guthrie, supported prohibition. He later cemented his ties to the prohibition camp as a trustee of the Oklahoma league. League operatives introduced several of the many petitions calling for statewide prohibition to the convention.

Dry supporters gained a measure of comfort in the selection of Murray and Haskell, two dry champions, as convention president and floor chairman, respectively. These two men wielded considerable power in the convention, particularly Haskell who supervised the drawing of county boundaries and the selection of county seats. In this work, he gained the personal allegiance of many local factions and drew on this loyalty to push for statewide prohibition. Revs. Dinwiddie and Sweet met with him concerning liquor policy in the new state and concluded that prohibition in the east (as required by the Enabling Act) and local option in the west was the best they could achieve. Haskell assured them he could convince the delegates to adopt a liquor ban throughout the new state, using his influence from his county committee work and by counseling uniformity in Oklahoma's liquor code. Haskell also consulted Dinwiddie and Sweet concerning the composition of the convention's committee on liquor traffic. The committee he subsequently formed contained all of the names Dinwiddie and Sweet had recommended.[21]

Sweet provided telling remarks in later recounting that Haskell brought the prohibition issue to the unchurched population of the territories and pulled the region's middle classes into the prohibition fold, "I knew what the Church people as a class would do about it (prohibition). I knew what the saloon-keepers and gamblers of Indian Territory, together with the rough-necks who danced when they piped, would do about it. But between these two opposite classes were the great middle class, many of whom had not made up their minds. And I knew that victory or defeat was to come from these."[22] Sweet's comments encapsulate the arguments of the Oklahoma Anti-Saloon League: the prohibition struggle pitted organized religion against the liquor industry for the hearts and minds of middle-class men. No appeal was made to the region's laboring classes. In fact, Sweet's only mention of laborers was the reference to the roughnecks (semi-transient workers in the oil fields) as the dupes of the liquor industry, and they were a lost cause in the eyes of Sweet and many other league supporters.

Once the committee on liquor traffic was set, the league, the union, and other dry proponents demonstrated organizational skills far superior to those of their opponents. The committee deliberated on the issue of liquor from December 1906 through January 1907, as dry advocates inundated the convention and the liquor committee with petitions calling for statewide prohibition. They recruited, circulated, and submitted one hundred and six petitions for prohibition from seventy-six different communities scattered across the two territories. Some petitions contained more than one thousand signatures. Many of these entreaties stated that the signers were praying for prohibition. Of special note is a petition signed by 1,350 women from around Oklahoma; petitions from school children at Wakita, Cameron, Poteau, and Falls Sunday school; a petition from sixty-five Kiowa Indians at Mt. Scott; a petition from the Preachers Association of Tulsa; a petition from 2,390 "young people" of Oklahoma; and a petition from students at Northwestern Normal School in Alva. All called or prayed for statewide prohibition. Of course, the league had directed much of this petitioning. The league's Revs. D. W. Keller and D. G. Murray met with convention President William Murray and convinced him to read several of these entreaties to the entire convention before referring them to the committee on liquor traffic. During the same two-month period, the convention heard only four petitions favoring local option.[23]

When compared to the one hundred and six petitions for prohibition, the four petitions for local option indicate overwhelming popular support for prohibition. Sentiment toward liquor policy, however, was not so one-sided in Oklahoma. The imbalance in petitions to the convention more accurately reflects the superior organization of the dry forces in Oklahoma. At the local and county levels and at the convention, dry advocates created a network to urge the convention, and the liquor committee in particular, to make prohibition a part of the proposed state constitution. As a result of the lobbying of the league and the union and the efforts of Haskell and William Murray, statewide prohibition became a tentative part of the Oklahoma Constitution, contingent on a referendum scheduled for September 1907. Oklahomans were to vote on a state constitution at the same election, but prohibition was to be a separate question. Voters could adopt the constitution while rejecting the prohibition clause.[24]

Opponents of prohibition worked against the liquor ban but with little effect. Ledru Guthrie of the Citizens League had lobbied the convention actively, hoping to keep prohibition out of the constitution. Ultimately, he managed only to convince delegates that voters should weigh in (via a referendum) on any prohibition clause adopted at the convention.[25] In the late spring of 1907, this became the focus of wet and dry organizations alike.

In the summer of 1907, the two territorial prohibition groups merged to form the Oklahoma Anti-Saloon League and set about campaigning for dry candidates in the August political primaries and for statewide prohibition at the September referendum. The

Oklahoma league named Rev. Dinwiddie as its superintendent. His previous work in the halls of Congress had gained him considerable notoriety among dry advocates and his energy quickly made him popular in Oklahoma. He toured the territories, speaking in churches on the merits of prohibition and collected contributions and subscriptions from those attending.[26] To augment league revenues, Dinwiddie urged Oklahoma ministers to speak before Sunday school and church meetings on the liquor question and to send him all money collected in support of the dry cause.[27] He was careful to allow local supporters considerable influence during the campaign to stifle charges by opponents that outsiders were imposing the liquor ban on Oklahomans.[28]

Under Rev. Dinwiddie's direction, the league launched a broad campaign for prohibition. It established press bureaus throughout the state and blanketed the region with ten million pages of literature during the weeks before the referendum. The league sent forty speakers to barnstorm every region of the state, including John G. Woolley (a former candidate for president of the United States) and R. N. Holsaple (superintendent of the South Dakota league). Horatio T. Laughbaum (attorney for the Oklahoma league), Reverend Sweet, and Captain A. S. McKennon also spoke in churches throughout the region, urging congregations to vote in favor of prohibition and for candidates committed to the liquor ban, such as Haskell.[29]

Several wet organizations attempted to counteract the efforts of the league and other Oklahoma dry proponents in the months leading up to the prohibition referendum. The Citizens League, the German-American Association, and other groups campaigned against the liquor ban in the newspapers. These groups spent freely on advertising, but many newspapers refused to run their ads.[30] None of them had developed the organization of the Oklahoma league, and the various groups did little to coordinate their efforts. Prohibition supporters painted the Citizens League as merely a front for the liquor interests in Oklahoma and neighboring states. The political impact of these unfounded charges likely was significant, particularly because the Citizens League produced no strong denial of the allegations at the time. It paid full advertising rates to place anti-prohibition literature in newspapers throughout the territories, which suggests considerable financial backing.[31] The *Muskogee Times-Democrat* reported that the liquor interests were spending $300,000 to defeat prohibition in Oklahoma and that paid lobbyists were active in Guthrie during the constitutional convention.[32] Given the slight mention of the wet lobbyists in the journals of the convention, these assertions appear dubious. At any rate, the efforts against prohibition paled in comparison to Rev. Dinwiddie's well-organized campaign. Despite his success and popularity in Oklahoma, his relationship with the national league deteriorated.

In May 1907, as he was organizing the new Oklahoma league and gearing up for the statewide referendum on prohibition the following September, the national league informed Rev. Dinwiddie that he was to leave Oklahoma for a new assignment in Washington. Dinwiddie protested, saying that he wished to remain in the territories through the end of the campaign, but to no avail. The league offered several explanations for the sudden move: Dinwiddie reportedly had campaigned for Senator Joseph Cannon of Illinois, an ardent opponent of the league and prohibition. Reports circulated that the national league also was unhappy with Dinwiddie's free-spending methods in Oklahoma. Dinwiddie denied any misappropriation of funds and resigned from the national league in protest. The Oklahoma league defended Dinwiddie against these charges. Fred S. Caldwell of the Oklahoma league conducted a financial accounting of the organization's receipts and expenditures, concluding that no misuse of funds had occurred. The Oklahoma league voted to keep Dinwiddie as its superintendent despite his estrangement from the national organization.[33]

The underlying cause of Rev. Dinwiddie's removal was tied to a personal dispute with Purley A. Baker. Dinwiddie's appointment to Oklahoma predated Baker's assumption of the superintendency in 1903, and this created some tension between the two. Dinwiddie asserted that Baker wished to replace him as superintendent of the Oklahoma league with one of his friends, and Baker found an opportunity to act against the popular lobbyist in 1907 when another league operative expressed concern over the appearance of impropriety in the Oklahoma campaign. Dinwiddie, though married, traveled without his wife while on assignment for the league. He brought with him Laura R. Church as a personal secretary. This situation alarmed the league's E. S. Chapman who spent time in the territories supporting the prohibition campaign. Though he admitted that he had no knowledge of infidelity, he informed Baker that others might view the arrangement of "two attractive young people" traveling together as scandalous. In response to this concern, the league temporarily reassigned Dinwiddie in May 1907 and permanently assigned Church to other duties. This sparked Dinwiddie's resignation from the national organization.[34]

Rev. Dinwiddie did spend a great deal of money during the 1907 campaign, though the vast majority of this was spent after the national organization ordered him to surrender leadership of the Oklahoma prohibition effort. In August, the league spent $3,347.73 on speakers and literature to bring the anti-liquor message to voters around the region. In September, expenditures climbed to $5,133.60, likely most of this before the September 17 referendum on prohibition. During the same period, the Oklahoma league totaled $7,766.25 in receipts, slightly less than the national league spent.[35]

In addition to their calls for prohibition, the Anti-Saloon League speakers paid particular attention to the Democratic nomination for governor because this office held considerable responsibility for enforcing state liquor laws. As a result in part of league efforts, the publicly dry Haskell defeated the popular Lee Cruce, a moderate on the liquor question, at the August Democratic Party primary. This was a significant victory for the dry advocates because most observers predicted that the Democratic Party would dominate Oklahoma's first government and likely would capture the governor's office.

Dry supporters, such as league operatives, then, did not leave the question of constitutional prohibition to chance. They mobilized support for the liquor ban. Drawing on their personal connections to the region's leading religious denominations, league speakers spread their anti-saloon message from church pulpits around the state. The role of the union at this time should also be noted. Local unions supported the efforts of the league and coordinated their own work with that of the ministers' organization. Because women were not formally a part of the political process in Oklahoma until 1918, the unions accepted the league's leadership in this and other political campaigns on prohibition.

The league and the ministers reaped the benefits of their efforts when a majority of those voting on the prohibition question checked the affirmative box on September 17, 1907, and the prohibition clause became a part of the state constitution. The referendum on prohibition tallied 130,361 votes for the liquor ban and 112,258 against. The prohibition vote was not uniform throughout the new state.[36] Of those voting on the question across the state, 53.7 percent voted dry, though the percentage varied from county to county. The standard deviation of these county returns from the state average of 54.3 percent is 8.4.[37] The vote in fifty-six of Oklahoma's seventy-five counties fell within the range of standard deviation. Of the remaining nineteen counties, eight reported notable opposition to prohibition, whereas eleven reported considerable support for the liquor ban. In Latimer County, in the southeastern portion of the new state, the vote ran more than two to one against prohibition. McIntosh County, in east central Oklahoma; Oklahoma County, dominated by Oklahoma City; and Coal County, in the state's southeastern quadrant, also reported results that were more than 60 percent wet. In five of the counties submitting significantly dry figures, more than 70 percent of voters favored prohibition.

These figures should be studied with some caution. Voter participation also varied widely throughout the state, from a high of 76.9 percent in Kingfisher County to a low of 42.2 percent in Cimarron County. Voter turnout was relatively high in most areas of the state: sixteen counties saw participation by more than 70 percent of the adult male population, and fifty-three counties reported voting figures in excess of 60 percent of that population. In only two counties did less than half of the adult male population vote on the prohibition question.

The wide variation in voting results from one county to another suggests that Oklahomans differed regionally on the liquor issue. Preelection concerns that Indian Territory residents would vote dry to "play a joke" on the western territory (because the Enabling Act banned liquor in the eastern territory for twenty-one years after statehood regardless of the referendum) were unfounded because western counties gave the strongest support for prohibition.[38] Early studies of national prohibition suggest that the liquor issue pitted dry rural areas against wet urban populations, and the 1907 vote in Oklahoma, at first glance, appears to reinforce this.[39] Oklahoma County, the most urban county in the new state, voted wet; the driest votes came from predominantly rural Jackson, Washita, and Beckham counties. The rural-urban dichotomy, however, does not explain the wet votes in Coal, Latimer, and McIntosh counties, all of which were predominantly rural; and the rural counties of Creek, Johnston, Logan, and Nowata returned more narrow majorities against prohibition. The wet sentiment expressed by voters in these counties suggests that factors independent of urbanity influenced Oklahomans' response to prohibition.

The prohibition clause that became part of the Oklahoma constitution was aimed at the liquor trade in the new state. It prohibited the "manufacture, sale, or barter, giving away, or otherwise furnishing, except as hereafter provided, of intoxicating liquor within this State" for twenty-one years after the date that Oklahoma joined the union.[40] Some Oklahomans considered the saloon a cancer on local communities, and this attitude gained wider adherence once the saloon was declared illegal. Liquor remained available in the Sooner State after 1907 because the statute could not touch out-of-state purchases that might be shipped into Oklahoma. Federal law placed such shipments under the purview of Congress alone. This traffic might have been addressed if the prohibition clause to the constitution, and the accompanying enforcement legislation adopted after statehood, had made possession of liquor an offense also. That it did not is a testament to the desire of Oklahoma's leading citizens to retain access to liquor for responsible drinkers, such as themselves, while they attempted to destroy the nonrespectable saloon.

The focus by prohibitionists on the retail liquor industry rather than the consumer was not unique to Oklahoma. The Maine prohibition law of 1851, the first such state law, banned the sale of liquor, but it said nothing of simple possession. It became the template for prohibition laws in thirteen other states in the late nineteenth century.[41] Kansas, bordering the future state of Oklahoma to the north, adopted prohibition in 1881; the Kansas attorney general ruled that the law implementing constitutional prohibition banned the sale of liquor but not its use.[42] The states that adopted prohibition after 1900, beginning with Georgia, Oklahoma, and Alabama, also made no attempt to ban the possession or consumption of liquor. Given the precedent set in other states and the prominence of middle-class reformers in the Oklahoma prohibition campaign, the targeting of the retail liquor industry rather than the liquor consumer is not surprising.

Officially "born" dry, a sober Oklahoma was another matter. Dry advocates who clapped each other on the back for a job well done in November 1907 came to find that liquor remained plentiful in the Sooner State despite prohibition and that the liquor ban was not politically secure; wet organizations urged lawmakers to revisit the liquor question and succeeded in placing prohibition before Oklahoma voters again in a 1910 referendum. The league and the union remained active in the new state to address these problems. The enforcement and evolution of Oklahoma's prohibition statutes is addressed in the next chapter.

CHAPTER THREE

Early Statehood

Dry Ascendancy and Wet Underground

Even though Oklahoma entered the union as a dry state with great fanfare, liquor remained plentiful in the region thereafter. Enforcement of the liquor ban fell to municipal and county authorities, with state officials stepping in on numerous occasions if they were dissatisfied with local efforts. Federal liquor enforcement agents remained in the eastern portion of Oklahoma after statehood, which reflected Congress's continued commitment to the American Indian populations there and caused jurisdictional confusion. Because effective enforcement cost more than local communities were willing to spend, local voters occasionally turned out of office those officers who enforced the liquor ban strenuously. In this environment, the illegal liquor industry thrived. As the state closed existing ambiguities in its prohibition statutes, liquor men found new loopholes and continued to ply their trade. When national prohibition took effect in January 1920, many Oklahoma officials gladly allowed federal authorities to take the lead in liquor enforcement.[1]

When Oklahomans adopted statewide prohibition, small businessmen, merchants, professionals, and others who obtained their liquor from outside the Sooner State initially felt little hindrance from the liquor ban, because it did not outlaw possession of liquor and the state had no jurisdiction over interstate commerce. Working-class men in Oklahoma also could order their liquor through the mail, though circumstances made this difficult. The transient nature of their work — particularly in the construction of buildings, rail lines, oil storage tanks, and oil and gas pipe lines and in seasonal agricultural work — and the considerable time demands of their occupations limited these workers' ability to order and receive liquor by mail. Also, laborers generally did not have the financial means necessary to purchase substantial quantities of liquor. They were much more likely to buy a single glass or bottle of liquor from a local retailer.[2]

Further, working-class men were drawn to the social setting of the saloon as an alternative to their small, rented dwellings. Middle-class men joined professional or social clubs, such as the Elks, the International Order of Odd Fellows, and the Moose Lodge. This option was not economically feasible for much of Oklahoma's working class. As elsewhere, the saloon served as the de facto working-class club.[3] Given the social importance of the saloon to wage earners, its resiliency against the efforts of dry advocates and enforcement officials is not surprising. Prohibition made the saloon illegal, but it did not kill it.

When Oklahoma became a dry state, communities throughout the region celebrated. The retail liquor industry went through its death throes in the days before the 17th. Some saloon operators embraced the impending liquor ban by staging prohibition sales. An Oklahoma City saloon sold quarts of bourbon for a dollar and pints of Old Crow for fifty to sixty cents. A drunken melee resulted by the time all liquor establishments closed at midnight.[4] Guthrie, the capital of Oklahoma Territory and of the new state of Oklahoma, experienced similar revelry in its saloon district as the Ferd Heim and the Pabst breweries dumped their excess beer into the city's sewers.[5] The New State Brewery Association did likewise in Oklahoma City. When its 75,000 gallons of beer proved too much for the city's sewer system, it piped the excess into the city's gutters, creating "a disgraceful scramble to keep the liquor from 'going to waste.' Buckets, barrels, vases, receptacles of all sorts, were utilized in carrying the beer away.'"[6] If a majority of Oklahomans supported prohibition as the 1907 referendum suggests, a large minority viewed the ban quite differently.

Unplanned celebrations also broke out in Oklahoma's smaller communities. In Cleveland, northwest of Tulsa, each of the eight local saloons conducted a rousing business on the sixteenth of November, selling between three and eleven hundred dollars' worth of liquor. Customers, including people not known as regular drinkers, bought as much as ten quarts each.[7] In Okarche, northwest of Oklahoma City, local saloons conducted a "good business in the jug and bottle trade," and the Eischen Brothers, owners of the town's largest saloon, announced they would sell all liquor at wholesale prices.[8] Oklahoma's saloon operators seemed resigned to the ensuing liquor ban.

Consequently, many saloons closed in November 1907. Okarche's Peter Eischen opened a pool hall, which served nonalcoholic drinks, in the building that had housed his saloon.[9] Guthrie's Henry Braun closed the breweries he managed for the Pabst Brewing Company and redirected his efforts toward several Pabst ice plants in Oklahoma.[10] August Ille, who had opened a saloon near Lawton in 1901, remodeled his establishment late in 1907 as Ille Brothers Hardware.[11] Prague's thirteen saloons closed after prohibition; Keokuk Falls and Violet Springs, notorious as sources of liquor for the residents of nearby Indian Territory, became little more than ghost towns shortly after statehood.[12]

Despite the ban, liquor remained plentiful in the new state, particularly in Oklahoma City. An Anti-Saloon League operative noted with chagrin that the city's liquor sources increased tenfold following prohibition.[13] Area liquor men appealed to the new state supreme court to preserve their trade in late 1907. They sought an injunction against prohibition enforcement until the courts determined its constitutionality. They also argued that liquor permits purchased before statehood were legal contracts that could not be canceled until they expired. When these efforts failed, the city's saloon operators dumped twenty-three hundred barrels of beer into the sewer, but Oklahoma City's liquor industry persisted. In 1908, United States marshals seized one thousand barrels of beer from the city's Moss Brewing Company. In that year, Attorney General Charles West described vice conditions in the city as worse than before prohibition.[14]

Liquor violations became problematic elsewhere in the state also. In the region around Shawnee, which had supported a vibrant saloon industry before statehood, liquor remained available even though some of the saloon towns dried up. As a local observer noted, "Statehood brought prohibition, but not for Pottawatomie County."[15] Enforcement by area officials remained sufficiently lax that Governor Charles N. Haskell sent Attorney General West to investigate the region personally.

In the eastern side of the state, Muskogee officials were so resigned to the presence of the illegal saloons that they ordered them to pay a fifty-dollar monthly license to the city. This practice continued into 1909. City officials based this practice on an 1898 law allowing the city to license taverns that sold nonintoxicating drinks.[16] Tulsa, after statehood and prohibition, licensed its numerous saloons at one hundred dollars per month, and Ardmore city commissioners considered a five hundred dollars annual tax on that city's near-beer joints.[17] The willingness of these cities to license establishments that violated the prohibition law is indicative of the daunting task that local officials faced. Because liquor remained available, local officials sought to regulate it rather than enforce the ban.

This activity was not confined to Oklahoma's larger towns. Predominantly rural Coal County quickly gained notoriety among prohibition enforcement personnel as a region in which illegal liquor was freely available. The *Coalgate Courier* reported that raids at Lehigh and Coalgate netted one thousand gallons and two hundred gallons of liquor, respectively, startling amounts given the small populations of these communities.[18] In Creek County, enforcement was so lax that state enforcement officer Fred S. Caldwell prosecuted the county attorney for dereliction of duty. He subsequently reported, "Conditions in Creek County have, during my entire administration (1908–1910), been extremely bad, especially at Sapulpa and Kiefer."[19] These were not isolated incidents. A resident of the small north central town of Glencoe asserted that the state's small towns were havens for bootleggers because these communities had fewer enforcement resources than their urban counterparts.[20] In 1908, Caldwell admitted that Oklahoma, in effect, contained wet and dry zones. The availability of liquor depended on local officials' enforcement efforts, which in turn depended on the mood of the voting public.[21]

State and local officials alike wrestled with effective enforcement of the liquor ban. On December 12, 1907, Governor Haskell delivered his seventh special message to the legislature. He expressed his firm commitment to constitutional prohibition and the pressing need for legislation to enforce it. Haskell's concerns were justified. The liquor laws of Oklahoma Territory expired with that government. The new state liquor ban seemingly superseded the federal liquor ban in Indian Territory also, but jurisdictional boundaries remained unclear. The authority of the federal marshals in the former Indian Territory was uncertain following statehood, and city and county officials were slow to organize their enforcement efforts. Many liquor retailers in this unsettled legal environment resumed sales following the declaration of statehood. Muskogee County attorney W. J. Crump vowed to drive the local jointists out of business, but he admitted near the end of 1907 that he lacked sufficient enforcement power. To aid his work, he called for legislation by which he could compel a person possessing liquor to testify as to the origins of that liquor.[22]

Crump and other county attorneys found little backing for such broad measures. A majority of voters had supported prohibition at the polls, but considerable opposition arose when officers attempted to enforce the liquor ban. In Wetumka, the sheriff and deputies plied drunks for information regarding illegal liquor sales. A newspaper account called into question their methods, stating, "when a man is found in an intoxicated condition some means are found to make him talk and tell where he got the cause of his trouble, and at once the guilty party is taken in hand. Some criticism has been made of the officers for their extreme activity in enforcing the prohibition law, but they are determined to give the people the real thing."[23] Conscientious enforcement officers soon discovered that they could not win this battle unless Oklahomans assented to dramatic increases in the police powers of public officials.

In the unsettled first months following statehood, officials and would-be criminals felt their way about the new legal code to determine its parameters. Early in 1908, Muskogee officials defined beverages containing more than 2 percent alcohol as intoxicating. In so doing, they ignored the ruling by federal judge William R. Lawrence, which was issued sixteen months previously that had set the legal limit at one-half of 1 percent alcohol by content. The Muskogee officers, apparently believing that this recent federal ruling did not apply in the new state, reverted to an older definition of "intoxicating."[24] County officials from around the state complained to Governor Haskell of their enforcement woes, which he mentioned in his December message to the legislature: "County attorneys of many counties advise me of their inability to control what they say is a constantly growing violation of the prohibition law. That the condition in many localities is growing worse daily. Give us the needed legislation and we will enforce it."[25] These officials and the liquor men, alike, waited for the state legislature to act on the issue of liquor.

The first state legislature tackled this thorny issue during its first session. Their task was complicated by many Oklahomans' tendency to use alcohol for medicinal purposed. In the nineteenth century, many people believed that alcohol could cure or at least alleviate the symptoms of numerous ailments, and even though early-twentieth-century medical research labored to dispel such notions of alcohol's curative properties, the general public continued to purchase alcohol and substances containing alcohol as medicines well into the new century. For a prohibition enforcement statute in early Oklahoma, to be effective then, it had to include provisions by which alcohol might be sold as a medicine. The legislature went about drafting such a law late in 1907.

Richard A. Billups, state senator representing Washita County and chairman of the Senate prohibition committee, introduced a bill in December that specified the penalties for violating the liquor ban and the exemptions from the ban, which included alcohol used for medical, scientific, and sacramental purposes. Reverend Edwin C. Dinwiddie wrote this legislation for Billups to present to the state senate. That body easily approved the measure and sent it to the state House of Representatives for consideration. At the insistence of speaker William H. Murray, the house added an article calling for a state-operated dispensary modeled after that of South Carolina.[26] This article provided a system by which Oklahomans might purchase alcohol or products containing alcohol as a medicine from state-sanctioned sources. Disagreement over the exact provisions of this dispensary held up the bill until the next year when a committee of senators and house members met with Governor Haskell and drafted the final version of the bill. Governor Haskell signed it into law March 24, 1908, and because the legislature attached an emergency clause to the law, it took effect immediately.

According to the final draft of the Billups Bill, as it became known, people seeking to purchase liquor (defined as any substance containing one-half of 1 percent alcohol by content) from designated dispensaries would need a sworn statement establishing the applicant's name, the purpose for which the liquor was to be used, and a prescription from a licensed physician. Medicinal liquor would be made available to the public at a state-run agency in each town of at least two thousand residents. In those counties containing no towns of that size, the state liquor superintendent would select one community as the site of a dispensary so that all residents of the state would have access to liquor for medicinal use. The governor would appoint the state superintendent and all local dispensary officers.[27]

The bill also provided the terms by which enforcement officers could collect evidence of violation and a range of punishments for those convicted of violating the new law. Judges of district or county courts could subpoena witnesses to testify against defendants and could issue search warrants allowing officers to enter the premises in question. Those who sold or provided liquor illegally could be found guilty of a misdemeanor, punishable by a fine of fifty to five hundred dollars and imprisonment for a term of thirty days to six months. Punishment differed for physicians who prescribed liquor for non-medicinal reasons and for local or state agents who sold liquor not provided by the state agency. The public consumption of alcohol combined with disturbance of the peace also became a misdemeanor punishable by a fine of ten to one hundred dollars or imprisonment for five to thirty days.[28]

However the Billups bill did little to reduce the confusion surrounding the enforcement of Oklahoma prohibition. Although it defined the crime and the consequences, the law remained unclear regarding the methods by which officers could enter a private building in search of evidence or suspects. Officers were required to demonstrate probable cause to receive a search warrant, but these provisions were left vague enough to allow judges latitude to interpret them according to the circumstances of each case. Search warrants were not to be issued for private residences unless these were used as a business or as a place of "public resort."[29]

The retail liquor industry was quick to criticize the search and seizure portion of the law as unconstitutional and did not wait long to test it in the courts. In May 1908, Mrs. Mary Brown of Shawnee sued the Pottawatomie County sheriff for entering her home illegally and seizing a barrel of whiskey that she said was intended for personal use only.[30] In August, judges in Coalgate and Oklahoma City declared the search and seizure provisions of the enforcement law unconstitutional because they did not provide hearings or trials for the dependents and merely allowed officers to confiscate the liquor.[31] By September 1908, enforcement personnel were anxious for the courts to clarify this part of the legal code. Given the Billups law's legal uncertainties, an Oklahoma City officer stated that his city was, "wide open and that nearly as much liquor is being consumed and (sic) in the days of free saloons."[32] The legislature had done little to settle the conflict between effective enforcement of the liquor ban and the safe guarding of personal liberties.

The dispensary provisions of the Billups bill created further confusion in Oklahoma's liquor codes. The act called for a liquor outlet in each town containing two thousand or more people. To deflect criticism that the bill discriminated against rural citizens, the legislature amended it to allow the creation of dispensaries in towns of one thousand if voters approved this change by referendum at the 1908 general election. A muddled campaign ensued between dry proponents (including the Anti-Saloon League) defending the dispensary as necessary for effective enforcement and other dry advocates (including initially some religious denominations that supported the league) who opposed the dispensary as a mockery of prohibition. Organizations critical of prohibition, such as the Sons of Washington, opposed the dispensary system as hypocritical.[33] Still others asserted that, in allowing dispensaries in towns of one thousand people, the proposed amendment violated the Enabling Act and the Oklahoma Constitution, each of which had stipulated that dispensaries could be located only in towns of two thousand people or more.

The 1908 referendum on the dispensary system produced unclear results befitting the wording of the question put to the electorate. It asked voters to approve the dispensary agency and the decision to locate such legal liquor sources in towns of one thousand residents or more. In November 1908, voters defeated the proposed amendment, 105,392 to 121,573. Governor Haskell took the vote as evidence that a majority of Oklahomans did not want the agency and closed all dispensaries throughout the state. The vote aside, Haskell was concerned about the public's infrequent use of the dispensaries and the cost of the agency to the state. In Oklahoma City with a population of more than fifty thousand, residents purchased a mere eight dollars of liquor from the dispensary between May and August of 1908. Lawton residents purchased six dollars' worth of liquor from the dispensary over the same period; those of Shawnee, less than ten dollars. Statewide, dispensaries took in $3,811.88 from whiskey sales and $1,000 from unspecified alcohol sales. The total cost of the dispensary system for the same period was $25,051.95.[34] These small amounts indicate that Oklahomans consumed little "legal" liquor, even though statements by enforcement officials and avid dry proponents suggest otherwise.

The existence of the dispensary system remained in doubt

through the spring of 1909. Supporters of the agency, in reaction to Governor Haskell's act of abolition, argued in court that the referendum was confusing and that many voters believed they were voting against the establishment of additional dispensaries rather than the existence of the agency. On appeal, the state supreme court ruled in *Robert Lozier* v. *Alexander Drug Company* that the Billups law and the dispensary agency remain in effect.[35] Before this ruling, a series of scandals cast doubt on the legitimacy of the dispensaries. In May 1908, less than two months after the agency system had begun operation, someone stole several wagon loads of liquor from the McAlester liquor agency,[36] and the state examiner later reported irregularities in the dispensaries' financial records. Haskell criticized the methods and accounting practices of the agency's first state superintendent, Robert Lozier, though he saw no evidence of criminal wrongdoing. He replaced Lozier with S. W. Stone in June 1909, and the number of dispensaries remained low thereafter, never exceeding twenty. The state legislature finally closed all of them in 1911.[37]

The confused reaction of local officials to Oklahoma's liquor codes was evident in Muskogee. A prominent newspaper reported that the Billups bill made violation of the liquor ban a felony, though the bill explicitly stated that violation constituted a misdemeanor.[38] Uncertainty at the future of the dispensaries and the Billups law contributed to the decision by several cities, including Muskogee, to license saloons despite the liquor ban. Muskogee saloon keepers, following the 1908 referendum, claimed that the vote on the dispensary system demonstrated a majority of Oklahomans disapproved of prohibition. Before the year was out, sixty-nine establishments were selling liquor in Muskogee.[39]

Political corruption compounded enforcement problems. In April 1908, Shawnee Democrats petitioned Governor Haskell to remove O. C. Strode as local liquor enforcement agent because he was drinking (to obvious intoxication) confiscated bootleg liquor.[40] Shawnee's situation was not unique. Seized liquor disappeared on numerous occasions from officers in large and small communities around the state. In 1911, a complaint to Governor Lee Cruce indicated that Judge R. A. Keller and Deputy Sheriff J. Y. F. Blake had removed confiscated liquor from the Love County courthouse in Marietta and had consumed it with others.[41] The problem was so persistent over the next decade that Senator Warren K. Snyder of Oklahoma City introduced a bill in 1919 that called for stiffened penalties against officials who gave away or sold confiscated liquor.[42]

In those areas where the officers on the streets enforced prohibition diligently, problems arose also because the courts quickly became backlogged with liquor cases and local governments labored under the financial burden of liquor enforcement. Late in 1908, the Muskogee court ruled that it would hold over until the next court term three hundred liquor cases. Defense lawyers saw this as, in effect, a dismissal of the charges because juries had voted to convict in only one of the six cases already tried and each of these cost the county fifty dollars.[43] County prosecutor Crump complained that he had achieved forty-three convictions in the fifty-four liquor cases he had tried during thirteen months on the job, but each of the defendants had appealed the decision a to higher court and continued to sell liquor while awaiting the appellate ruling.[44] The Oklahoma Criminal Court of Appeals became so inundated with liquor cases that it set aside a week in March of 1909 to hear only liquor cases. Later that year, newspapers reported that the appeals court had heard twenty-three cases involving bootlegging. It affirmed seven of the convictions from lower courts, but overturned sixteen convictions. Local and state court systems ground nearly to a halt in attempting to prosecute the numerous liquor offenders, and the backlog continued. In 1910, the Muskogee municipal police court heard four thousand cases, nearly two thousand of which were for public drunkenness. On average, then, thirty-six such cases were brought each week in that community.[45] This sea of liquor prosecutions inundated many local and state courts.

Furthermore, the costs of effective prohibition enforcement weighed heavily on the minds of Oklahomans. An informal poll of county attorneys in 1909 revealed that most believed prohibition enforcement cost their counties twice as much as they collected in fines for liquor offenses. Despite a common tendency by judges and juries to exonerate liquor offenders, prohibition dramatically affected the state's prison population. The Oklahoma penitentiary at McAlester reported an inmate population of 531 during 1909, and 137 of these prisoners were incarcerated on liquor offenses, which was easily the most common offense. The next most frequent type of conviction among the prisoners — larceny — accounted for the imprisonment of only eighty men.[46] Oklahomans who had opposed prohibition before statehood had predicted that it would make criminals of an otherwise law-abiding population, and the state's penitentiary report confirms this prediction, but it did little to sway those who supported the liquor ban.

In the face of rising expenses, the legislature began to scale back its financial commitment to prohibition enforcement, effectively shifting fiscal responsibility from the state to local governments. Local police officers, judges, and county attorneys who diligently performed their duties found themselves spending a disproportionate amount of time detecting, arresting, and prosecuting liquor offenders. The unwillingness of jurors in many areas to convict bootleggers meant that this expense often achieved nothing. Ignoring the limited financial resources of many Oklahoma communities, the state legislature severely limited funding for prohibition enforcement at the state level Legislators not only discontinued the dispensary system, but they also closed the prohibition enforcement office in 1911, thereafter allowing the governor to hire only one enforcement officer at the state's expense.

The legislature's aversion to extensive enforcement measures stemmed from two issues that stretched beyond the matter of liquor prohibition in Oklahoma: a desire to limit state expenses and a suspicion of gubernatorial power. Early Oklahoma's political culture emphasized reductions in taxes and government programs. This political culture was predominant in the old South, and Oklahoma's Democratic Party, who was in control of the state house, adopted it in Oklahoma. Oklahomans feared the concentration of political power in the hands of the governor; the state constitution made seventeen executive posts elective giving the governor considerable patronage influence. Legislators sought to restrict the number of appointments whenever possible in an effort to curtail executive prerogative.[47]

The tension between the executive and legislative branches of government was not constant, but it ebbed and flowed, depending on the person occupying the governor's mansion. From 1911 to 1914, Governor Cruce encountered great difficulty with the legislature though his own (Democratic) party controlled it.[48] James B. A. Robertson, governor from 1919 to 1922, also experienced difficulty with the legislature, and that body impeached and removed his successor, Jack Walton, from office in 1923. Individual personalities aside, all Oklahoma governors faced legislatures desirous of smaller government and suspicious of the governor's appointive power, and this severely limited the state's ability to enforce the statewide liquor ban effectively.

The shipment of liquor into Oklahoma from other states further complicated enforcement efforts. The Sooner State's prohibition explicitly banned the sale, giving away, or providing of liquor in the state. It did not address the issue of imported liquor, which was a form of interstate commerce and thus immune from state liquor regulations. Federal circuit court judges Ralph E. Campbell and John H. Cotteral ruled that the state infringed on interstate traffic when seizing out-of-state liquor while it remained in the possession of the shipper. The state of Oklahoma attempted to block these legal challenges through a writ of prohibition against such actions. The U.S. Supreme Court ruled in April 1911 that the state could not issue such a writ against the circuit courts and so the legal challenges continued.[49]

Oklahoma bootleggers pounced on this loophole and began ordering large quantities of liquor from other states that they then resold illegally. Some liquor men took orders from area residents, purchased the liquor in other states, and delivered it to their customers when it arrived in the local railroad yards.[50] Dry advocates and enforcement officers, alike, complained that these illegal sales might be stopped with relative ease if this flow of liquor could be dammed at the state's borders.

In March 1908, as the Billups law was announced, Oklahoma

attorney general West declared that interstate liquor could legally be taken from the railroad depot by the consignee to his or her residence. By this statement, liquor from outside the state maintained its exemption from Oklahoma liquor laws until the person who had ordered it brought it to his or her home, and they could only be prosecuted if they attempted to resell it.[51] The federal courts agreed with West. Caldwell, an ardent dry and a trustee of the Oklahoma league, challenged this ruling in the federal appellate courts, arguing that the interstate shipment ended when the shipper released the liquor to the consignee, but the courts ruled against his position. He sought recourse before the U.S. Supreme Court, but it refused to hear the case.[52] In January 1909, a Muskogee newspaper reported that the state supreme court had ruled that Oklahomans could ship as much liquor into the state as they wished, if it was for personal use only.[53] Such pronouncements in defense of personal liberties further hamstrung efforts to prevent the resale of out-of-state liquor. Effective enforcement of prohibition remained problematic until Oklahoma judges interpreted the powers of enforcement officers more broadly, which was at the expense of individual rights.

To further complicate matters, local officials interpreted their enforcement powers differently from one region of the state to another. Governor Haskell, pressured by the Oklahoma league, instructed state officials to look into instances of blatant non-enforcement of the liquor ban. Attorney General West investigated liquor violations in Pottawatomie County and eventually forced the resignation of several officials in the area.[54] As a state enforcement officer, Caldwell examined the lack of enforcement by local officials in Creek, Ellis, Kay, and Nowata counties. In Creek County, he filed charges against county attorney L. B. Jackson and Sheriff Henry Clay King in July 1909 for failing to enforce the liquor ban in their jurisdiction and sought to have them removed from office on this basis. King left office when Caldwell announced his inquiry, but Jackson awaited the outcome of the investigation. In August, Caldwell called a grand jury to hear the case against Jackson rather than the region's presiding judge, whom Caldwell knew to be critical of prohibition. Jackson was formally charged with failing to prosecute approximately 190 indictments for liquor violations in Creek County between September 15, 1908 and July 1, 1909. The majority of these violations had occurred in Sapulpa, the county seat located amidst the Glenn Pool oil field, and in Kiefer, one of the rough and tumble boomtowns in the oil patch. The grand jury found Jackson guilty of the accused misconduct, and Caldwell applied to the Oklahoma Supreme Court to have him removed as county attorney. Jackson challenged this application, arguing that Caldwell had swayed the grand jury in its deliberations; the removal process ground to a halt while a trial court considered the challenge. At the time of Caldwell's dismissal from his enforcement post in December 1910, the trial court had not issued a ruling on the challenge and Jackson remained in office. Former sheriff King was indicted for liquor violations including acceptance of bribe money, but that trial ended in a hung jury.[55] These incidents show how Caldwell (and others) encountered considerable opposition to his investigation, not only among Creek County liquor men but also among the general public.

Caldwell also assisted investigations in other counties around the state. In February 1910, he went to Newkirk to aid a grand jury investigation that brought approximately sixty indictments for the unlawful possession of liquor. In June 1910, he scheduled a hearing in Ellis County and recommended the removal of county attorney C. B. Leedy for failing to act against bootleggers. Leedy promptly applied to the Oklahoma Supreme Court for a writ of prohibition to stop the hearing and the investigation slowed. In November 1910, the court denied this application. Because Leedy was nearing the end of his term in office, Caldwell chose not to pursue his investigation, counting on Ellis County voters to unseat him the following spring. Caldwell next traveled to Nowata County to assist a grand jury investigation of liquor violations there. He demonstrated that liquor joints had been operating openly in South Coffeeville, Lenapah, and Delaware for more than a year, and he presented overwhelming evidence that the county attorney, sheriff, and judge knew of these activities and had failed to act. Despite this, four members of the grand jury voted to exonerate the county officials and Caldwell left the area, disgusted with the justice system.[56]

By the end of his appointed term in office, Caldwell had traversed much of the state and had seen considerable variation in the devotion to prohibition enforcement. His investigations did little to hinder the liquor industry in the regions examined. Creek County, dominated by the Glenn Pool and later the Cushing oil field, remained a problem area for state enforcement officials through the first two decades of the twentieth century. In 1912, a district judge removed county attorney Vic S. Docker and Sheriff John Berry for allowing saloons to operate in Sapulpa, and similar investigations subsequently were undertaken in Nowata and Muskogee counties.[57] Attorney General S. Prince Freeling attempted to remove the Creek County sheriff in 1915 and conducted investigations of liquor enforcement in Tulsa, Nowata, Ottawa, and Sequoyah counties shortly thereafter.[58] In 1917, Freeling convened a grand jury investigation into vice conditions in Muskogee; the city's leading newspapers split over the necessity for this inquiry.[59] It became increasingly apparent that these various state investigations suffered from a lack of support from the local populace, which continued to return to office men found to be derelict in the enforcement of liquor laws. The public also expressed its prohibition sentiment in court when juries regularly acquitted liquor defendants and officers who failed to enforce the ban. This sentiment is belied in a report that a judge's ruling, which required municipalities to try defendants with a jury, left the liquor ordinances in several eastern Oklahoma communities useless.[60] Sheriffs and county attorneys in several regions of the state did not actively pursue bootleggers because they knew that juries would not convict them.

Given the uneven enforcement of prohibition in Oklahoma, the decision to revisit the liquor ban at the election poles in 1910 is not surprising. Despite enjoying narrow bases of support, wet organizations, such as the Sons of Washington and the German-American Association, succeeded in placing the liquor question before Oklahoma voters in a second referendum: they proposed a local option law to supersede statewide prohibition. It would have granted counties and municipalities the legal authority to ban or license saloons on their own. As before, the Oklahoma league led the state's dry forces against this amendment in the ensuing election campaign.

Ignoring the great volume of liquor violations under prohibition, league officials urged supporters to vote to continue the ban by warning of increased law breaking if liquor became legal: "Vote to open the saloons again in Oklahoma and you vote to open the sluice gates for a carnival of crime."[61] Bishop William A. Quayle, before Oklahoma's Methodist Episcopal Church Conference, urged attendees to follow the league's guidance and "do business for God . . . country and state."[62] The state Baptist conference characterized the campaign as a contest between "Law, Order, and Righteousness . . . and Lawlessness and Sin. . . ."[63] Leading up to the referendum, the Oklahoma Women's Christian Temperance Union (WCTU) distributed prohibition materials, and Ernest H. Cherrington of the Anti-Saloon League of America lectured on the merits of prohibition throughout the state.[64] Though wet and dry proponents actively campaigned on the liquor issue in the weeks before the election, the league's superior organization again proved instrumental in the majority vote for prohibition. During this campaign, the league spent $4,684.71 on canvassing the state with speakers and literature; wet advocates reportedly spent much more.[65]

The league charged large brewing interests with spending a massive sum of money in Oklahoma to defeat prohibition. One newspaper reported that unnamed breweries had created a one-million-dollar slush fund to finance the local option campaign.[66] Although the million-dollar figure never was substantiated, it fueled the popular perception that opponents of prohibition received financial aid from large, out-of-state liquor interests who sought to influence the election for their own profits.

Also instrumental in the referendum vote were the social stations of the wet and dry parties. Although wet proponents attempted to characterize their cause as pro-business, dry advocates effectively countered that argument by portraying their opponents as outsiders who did not have the best interests of Oklahoma or Oklahomans at heart. Statements by league and church officers cast

Prohibition supporters gather at an Oklahoma anti-drink demonstration, circa 1910. The Woman's Christian Temperance Union and the Oklahoma Anti-Saloon League organized numerous demonstrations like this around the state to sway voters in anticipation of referenda on prohibition in 1907 and again in 1910.

this conflict as one pitting respectable, churchgoing people against the disreputable saloon crowd. The respected social positions of dry speakers, as local merchants and professionals, added credence to their arguments that their wet counterparts could not match.

Weighing these various factors, a majority of Oklahomans voted against local option. The dry portion of the statewide vote increased slightly from 53.7 percent in 1907 to 54.6 percent in 1910.[67] As with the 1907 referendum, the 1910 vote on prohibition varied from one county to another. Coal, Osage, McIntosh, Nowata, and Latimer counties voted wet, whereas Harmon, Alfalfa, Jackson, and Tillman counties reported overwhelmingly dry votes. Voter turnout, however, was down significantly from the 1907 vote, which makes significant comparisons between counties or between the 1907 and 1910 votes problematic. In the 1907 referendum, sixteen counties reported vote tallies on the prohibition question that represented more than 70 percent of the voting-age population. By contrast, in the 1910 referendum, only two counties achieved voter turnout figures above 70 percent. Of those counties reporting significant wet or dry votes in 1910, the wet counties of McIntosh, Nowata, and Latimer, and dry counties, Harmon and Jackson counties recorded vote totals representing less than half of the voting population. Statewide, only 51.7 percent of voting-age males voted on the prohibition question in 1910, which was down from 63.9 percent in 1907. The election figures for 1910, then, reflect the prohibition sentiment of a still narrower portion of the state population than the 1907 vote and provide no information on the liquor stance of nearly half of the population eligible to vote, to say nothing of those (i.e., women) disallowed from voting. The support that the WCTU continued to enjoy during this period indicates that many Sooner State women approved of prohibition, though union members tended to come from Oklahoma's white middle classes. The absence of significant numbers of working-class women suggests that wage-earning women either did not have time to join the union or did not support its goals.

Several factors might explain the low vote tallies for the 1910 referendum. The reduced figures could reflect a loss of interest in the liquor issue, but two other factors likely contributed as well. Because the 1907 election allowed adult men to vote not only on prohibition but also on the state constitution (in clearly distinct questions), the election held greater importance than subsequent elections that focused solely on prohibition, and this consideration likely produced a greater turnout in 1907 than in 1910. Another factor in the reduced 1910 vote was the grandfather clause, which was adopted statewide at the primary election in September 1910. This clause allowed the disenfranchisement of many black men, and at least some white voters, who had exhibited radical political leanings. This disenfranchisement took effect at the 1910 general election. Because the decision to prohibit black and radical Oklahomans from voting took place at local polling places, the exact impact of this law on voter turnout is unclear, though the law probably reduced it.[68]

Though the 1910 referendum on prohibition attracted less interest than the 1907 vote, it reaffirmed Oklahoma's political commitment to prohibition. Bills calling for the resubmission of the liquor issue to voters arose again several times after 1910, but it never received sufficient support to gain a place on the ballot. The liquor ban never again came before Oklahoma voters until after the repeal of national prohibition in 1933.

The confusion surrounding Oklahoma's early liquor codes eroded effective enforcement. The 1908 referendum on the dispensary system led some to believe that voters had rejected prohibition. Although the 1910 referendum seemed to settle that question, uncertainty over the jurisdictional boundaries of federal, state, and local officials remained, particularly in the lands of the former Indian Territory and Osage Reservation. Liquor also continued to flow into Oklahoma from other states, further exasperating exacting enforcement officials and avid proponents of the liquor ban.

Compounding these enforcement problems was a willingness by some locally elected officials to ignore conspicuous liquor violations in their locales. These men remained in office, sometimes in the face of criminal investigations, because they understood the mood of the voting public concerning prohibition. State enforcement officer Caldwell encountered numerous situations like this throughout the state. The persistence of a prosperous bootlegging trade also indicates a strong popular demand for liquor that ran counter to arguments by the league and its supporters. Although the league held considerable political influence in the early years of statehood, liquor remained available during Governors Haskell's administration; succeeding governors and their staffs would continue to tinker with Oklahoma's liquor enforcement provisions with mixed results.

CHAPTER FOUR

Paper Prohibition
Enforcement Problems Continue

As Governor Charles Haskell's administration gave way to that of Governor Lee Cruce in 1911, liquor continued to flow in Oklahoma despite prohibition. Up to this point, the efforts of state enforcement officer Fred S. Caldwell, Attorney General Charles West, and other officials had produced little meaningful prohibition enforcement in the state. Dry proponents blamed the situation on rampant corruption. This no doubt was a contributing factor, but prohibition supporters refused to admit that bootlegging persisted because the popular demand for liquor made it sufficiently profitable to outweigh the legal risks. From their perspective as respectable merchants and professionals, working-class men were dupes of the liquor industry who could not appreciate the benefits of prohibition and the respectability that it brought. Meanwhile, elected and appointed officers struggled to plug the leaks in the state's prohibition codes.

The situation in the eastern half of the state (i.e., the former Indian Territory) further compounded officials' task. The Enabling Act of 1905 not only banned liquor from the region for twenty-one years following statehood but also reaffirmed the federal government's role as guardian of area Indians. This led to many new questions: Was the state of Oklahoma bound by the federal liquor ban, or had state prohibition superseded it? More important, were federal or state officials responsible for its enforcement? In 1910, Attorney General West, mindful of the growing backlog of liquor cases in the Oklahoma court system and the mounting costs to the state, filed suit in federal court arguing that Congress retained responsibility for the prosecution of liquor cases in the former Indian Territory and Osage Reservation (Osage County after 1907). Federal judge John Campbell, equally concerned about the growing number of liquor cases on the docket in his and other federal courts in Oklahoma, ruled that the former Indian Territory and Osage Reservation were no longer under federal law and that state and local courts should handle liquor offenders.[1] Because neither federal nor state and local officials felt certain of their responsibilities, enforcement languished and violations increased.

In the summer of 1912, the U.S. Supreme Court ruled that American Indians remained wards of the federal government and that its long-standing ban on liquor sales to American Indians applied to everyone in eastern Oklahoma. Cases begun in municipal or county courts were thrown out, and those who had been convicted in those courts were released from prison.[2] In effect, the ruling put liquor men back on the streets and discouraged enforcement efforts.

The Supreme Court effectively defined shipment of liquor into these regions as the introduction of liquor to American Indians, which was a federal violation. A double standard developed as liquor shipments into former Oklahoma Territory remained legal and immune from state prosecution as a form of interstate commerce under federal law, whereas liquor shipments into the former Indian Territory and Osage Reservation lands violated federal law. State and local authorities in eastern Oklahoma surrendered primary responsibility for monitoring liquor shipments to the few federal marshals stationed there. As a result, liquor flowed freely in the region's largest cities, Tulsa and Muskogee, and also in rural areas, such as the oil fields of Creek, Osage, and later Carter counties, and in the mining districts of Coal, Latimer, and Ottawa counties.

Oklahoma dry proponents turned hopefully to federal officers to stem the tide of liquor coming into the eastern region not only from beyond the state but also from the former Oklahoma Territory lands. Liquor men had established regular transportation routes from the west region to the east during the territorial period, and they revived these amid the jurisdictional confusion following the Supreme Court ruling of June 1912. In the Tulsa area, bootleggers mixed clear glass jugs of alcohol with others containing nitroglycerin (used to blow open low-production oil wells) to deter enthusiastic enforcement officers. The high court's ruling seemingly placed responsibility for stopping such shipments with federal officials, but in November of that same year, the federal court in Muskogee ruled that liquor shipped from former Oklahoma Territory to former Indian Territory or Osage Reservation did not violate federal law unless prosecutors could prove that the liquor had originated from outside the current state of Oklahoma. As a consequence, three hundred indictments against Oklahoma bootleggers were thrown out.[3]

Liquor enforcement in eastern Oklahoma remained uncertain. In April 1913, a federal court in St. Louis ruled that those eastern Oklahoma liquor offenses committed on lands not owned by American Indians should be prosecuted in state rather than federal courts. Federal officials ordered continuances in 115 liquor cases they had begun in Tulsa, and authorities released liquor defendants on their own recognizance until their court date arrived. A subsequent newspaper report reiterated the federal government's responsibility for liquor enforcement in former Indian Territory, making no mention of the 115 defendants who had been released a few weeks previously.[4] In 1914, the U.S. Supreme Court again weighed in on the issue, ruling that possession of liquor in former Indian Territory was not prima facie evidence (sufficiently compelling to shift the burden of proof from the prosecution to the defense) of intent to sell liquor. In reaction to this judgment, federal officials in Muskogee released eighteen men from jail accused of introducing liquor.[5]

At times, state and local officials worked at cross purposes to the federal authorities. Chief federal enforcement officer Henry A. Larson and his deputies, brandishing rifles, had stopped and searched a caravan of liquor-laden vehicles on the bridge spanning the Arkansas River at the western edge of Tulsa. They seized seven wagon loads of beer and whiskey and arrested eleven men for introducing liquor. The city, reminiscent of William E. "Pussyfoot" Johnson's arrest by Tulsa officials in 1907, charged the officers with assault and jailed them over night until they could arrange bond.[6]

Prohibition also pitted state and local officials against one another. The state required all counties to ship confiscated liquor to Oklahoma City where state authorities arranged for its resale in other (wet) states. The county was to receive 26 percent of the proceeds from such sales to cover the salaries of enforcement officers. In 1911, Muskogee County officials stopped shipping liquor to Oklahoma City because the state had not given the county its share of the proceeds from previous sales. The state, in turn, sued Muskogee County to force the sheriff to surrender the confiscated liquor in his possession. The following year in defiance of state directives, Muskogee officials began dumping contraband liquor into the city's sewer system.[7] In this atmosphere, the astute bootlegger could conduct business with some assurance that his product would not be seized.

Indeed, some local authorities refused to enforce prohibition, either because they accepted bribes from bootleggers or because they understood that local voters would turn them out of office if they cracked down on the liquor industry. A Muskogee newspaper hinted at the latter motivation in a post-election report, "Now that the election is over and conditions are becoming normal, Judge Lipscomb has resumed the work of securing evidence against bootleggers and other illegal whiskey sellers."[8] In the 1910 election, when Oklahomans returned only eight of the seventy-seven incumbent county sheriffs to office, many outgoing sheriffs blamed their defeat on the prohibition statute: excessively strict enforcement turned the public against some, whereas lax enforcement doomed others.[9] With the 1914 elections looming, Texas County officials, stepped up enforcement efforts in Goodwell in response to public protests against their leniency. A local newspaper stated that these officials were attempting to "distinguish between what to do and what to let alone in the effort to retain their offices."[10] It became increasingly apparent that local officials needed to closely monitor the public's liquor sentiment if they wanted to retain their posts.

Authorities in Oklahoma's largest cities adopted a cyclical pattern of enforcement: lax enforcement, followed by a crackdown on liquor offenses in reaction to criticism by local dry advocates, and a return to inattentiveness after the reform movement spent its energy. Spurred by the opening of the nearby Glenn Pool oil field in 1905, Tulsa experienced phenomenal growth from 1,390 residents in 1900 to 72,075 in 1920. Though "Pussyfoot" Johnson and his federal deputies met stiff resistance in their Tulsa raids, the Oklahoma Anti-Saloon League optimistically reported that Tulsa had dried up in 1908.[11] This report proved premature because in 1910 Tulsa's liquor industry was thriving. Bootleggers evaded the authorities by hiding their product in coffins and in wagon loads of ear corn. In November 1915, local authorities arrested the city's leading bootleggers in a general cleanup. Despite these efforts, however, the illegal liquor industry remained vibrant in Tulsa. When the city police stepped up their enforcement efforts, the joints relocated to the outskirts of Tulsa or beyond. These roadhouses, such as the famed Bucket of Blood Saloon, fell under the enforcement umbrella of the understaffed Tulsa County sheriff's department and so prospered. Similarly, news reports noted in 1907 that Muskogee County had been wide open (allowing unhindered liquor sales) in the past and speculated that it would become wide open again after Pussyfoot Johnson left.[12]

Oklahoma City also contained extensive liquor violations despite the additional scrutiny the city drew as the seat of state government. City officials there also adopted a cyclical pattern of leniency and rigorous enforcement. Attorney General West, who assumed control of law enforcement in Oklahoma County, described conditions in the city as deteriorating after the adoption of statewide prohibition.[13] Oklahoma City was an eyesore for committed dry proponents, particularly as a result of the saloon district's proximity to the state capitol.

In late 1909, city attorney John M. Hays began a crackdown on Oklahoma City's saloons. He notified over one hundred individuals that they (and the saloon proprietors who rented space from them) were responsible for liquor sold on their property. Police chief Charles Post led a series of raids that closed many of the joints or blind pigs. The stubborn illegal liquor industry persisted, and in 1911, the city hired famed lawman William O. Tilghman as its new chief of police. He promptly arrested twenty-five bootleggers, which was called the most significant enforcement effort in years. Before the year was out, however, Tilghman told a newspaper reporter that he alone could not enforce the liquor ban in Oklahoma's capital city.[14] Another stepped-up campaign, led by Oklahoma County attorney John Embry and Mayor Ed Overholser, produced several arrests in 1915 and closed several of the most visible liquor joints. The liquor industry flourished in the city after 1920 under national prohibition, prompting the police chief at that time to echo Tilghman's previous characterization of the liquor ban as unenforceable.[15]

In some instances, this situation was the result of the corrupting political influence of bootleggers. William J. Creekmore, one of the most powerful liquor men in the state, developed a regional syndicate by 1915 that controlled liquor sales in much of Oklahoma. He had sold illegal liquor in Sapulpa before 1907, but under statewide prohibition he expanded to become the state's largest liquor dealer through a distribution agreement with a Kansas City wholesaler. From Joplin, Missouri, he shipped liquor (150 to 200 railroad car loads in 1913) to Enid and from there to Keystone where operatives loaded it onto wagons, hauled it to such towns as Sapulpa and Tulsa, and sold it at 25 percent above the wholesale price.[16] In Tulsa, Sapulpa, Oklahoma City, Muskogee, Miami, Claremore, Oilton, and other communities, he bought immunity from the police for his saloons and paid officials to raid his competitors and advance his own operations. The Creek County sheriff reportedly was working with Creekmore. In 1915, federal authorities convicted Creekmore of contempt of court and sentenced him to the federal penitentiary the following year.[17]

Significantly, his conviction came at the hands of federal officials rather than state or local authorities, among who Creekmore held considerable influence. In 1912, state commissioner of labor Charles L. Daugherty passed along to Creekmore changes in the Democratic campaign committee's speaking assignments for that election year and asked him for additional funds to continue his own stumping around the state.[18] Reportedly worth a million dollars by the time of his 1915 conviction, Creekmore had been arrested in 1912 by federal authorities and allegedly had paid a member of the U.S. House of Representatives twenty thousand dollars to have his sentence reduced to thirty days in jail. His ultimate conviction for jury tampering arose from his bribing a jury member to acquit him on liquor charges.[19]

Creekmore's conviction did not end Oklahoma's illicit liquor industry. Numerous smaller liquor dealers moved in to take his place. Arch Wright replaced him in the Muskogee liquor and gambling business and was described as worse than his predecessor in this capacity.[20] The rise and fall of Creekmore portended, on a proportionally smaller scale, the obstacles the nation would face under national prohibition in the 1920s.

In addition to this and less blatant examples of corruption, however, enforcement officers also pointed to another source of the lax enforcement in Oklahoma communities. Many people did not want the law enforced strictly. State enforcement officer Caldwell often encountered juries that refused to convict liquor offenders, as happened in Nowata and Creek counties. In the latter, Sheriff Henry Clay King, whose prosecution for dereliction of duty had ended in a hung jury, ran for sheriff again in 1910 and lost the primary by a mere fifty votes. Disgusted, Caldwell stated that this show of support for a man who had demonstrated an unwillingness to enforce the liquor ban "is decidedly typical and quite characteristic of the citizenship of Creek County."[21] In 1913, a news report described the population of Tulsa similarly, "The prevailing senti-

ment of the citizens is 'wet,' " adding, "Tulsa isn't the only city in the
state where the majority of the people hold this view."[22] Caldwell
and other enthusiastic supporters of prohibition became exasper-
ated with this open disregard for the law. In contrast to Caldwell, a
majority of people in some communities did not view the liquor
industry as criminal regardless of the law. They snickered at the
bootleggers' ability to evade authorities and did not want rigorous
enforcement.

Prohibition touched the lives of more than enforcement personnel and liquor runners. The ban also affected Oklahoma's retail pharmaceutical industry. Recognizing that many Oklahomans
considered alcohol a medicine, drug stores sold beer, which was
prescribed as a tonic, and patented medicines, such as Duffy's Malt
Whiskey and Haniford's Balsam of Myrrh (84 percent of which
was wood alcohol).[23] Many liquor men called their establishments
"drug stores" to give them an air of respectability. These sham drug
stores were particularly common in eastern Oklahoma, and legitimate druggists gradually became concerned at the damaging effect
these businesses had on the entire industry's image. The Oklahoma
Pharmaceutical Association, formed in 1890 as a watchdog over the
state's retail drug business, met shortly after statehood and called
for all drug stores to be directed by pharmacists registered with the
association or lose their licenses.[24] The liquor issue, then, uninten-
tionally spurred the development of a professional pharmaceutical
industry, seeking to differentiate itself from the liquor men.

Druggists also were involved in the regulation of medicinal liquor. Following the demise of the state dispensary system in 1911,
Governor Cruce designated the Alexander Drug Company of Oklahoma City as the state's wholesale distributor of alcohol to all licensed druggists in Oklahoma to monitor and control alcohol sold
through these outlets. Cruce, concerned about abuse in these sales,
commissioned a 1913 report by Alexander Drug of its alcohol sales
to licensed druggists throughout the state. His concern seems to
have been justified because numerous druggists and drug stores
around the state bought more than fifty gallons of alcohol during
the report's three-month period. The largest amounts were sold to

the Cheyenne Drug Company of Tulsa (190 gallons of alcohol), the Red Cross Drug Store of Sapulpa (185 gallons), druggists Bryant & Keith and Burke & Son both of Collinsville (137 gallons each), and Brown's Pharmacy of Tulsa (111 gallons). Many other drug stores throughout Oklahoma bought lesser, though still abnormally large, amounts.[25]

The governor then asked reputable druggists how much alcohol they bought each month to determine normal legitimate usage. Most responded that an average-sized drug store purchased roughly five or six gallons of alcohol each month to create liniments and tinctures and to sell to local hospitals.[26] These figures sharply contrasted the liquor purchased by druggists in Tulsa, Sapulpa, and elsewhere. Based on this information, Cruce limited the amount of alcohol Alexander Drug could sell to individual drug stores.

Governor Cruce also worried that he might hinder legitimate business. Consequently, he was generous in the limit he placed on monthly alcohol sales to pharmacists: no more than ten gallons. As a further concession, he allowed individual druggists to appeal for an increased allotment. He checked the reputation of petitioners with local residents and, in the first months of the new policy, he approved most requests for additional purchases, instructing Alexander Drug to sell up to twenty gallons of alcohol each month to these druggists. At the same time, he asked county attorneys to investigate local drug stores that purchased inordinate amounts and ordered Alexander Drug not to sell any alcohol to those drug stores that were known to resell it as a beverage.[27]

The governor's balance between liquor enforcement and support for business resulted in an apparatus similar to the abolished dispensary system. The state regulated the sale of alcohol for medicinal and industrial purposes, and, given the generous amounts Governor Cruce allowed many druggists to purchase, the state effectively sanctioned the sale by drug stores of some alcohol as a beverage. Cruce's efforts did curb the worst abuses by purported druggists, and he established the state's regulatory role over the evolving pharmaceutical industry.

Cruce's successor, Robert L. Williams, continued this regulatory policy throughout his term as governor (1915–1918). The Alexander Drug Company retained its state contract to sell alcohol to pharmacists, though the state added the Cardinal Drug Company of Muskogee as a liquor wholesaler for eastern Oklahoma. Illegal liquor sales from drug stores continued. In November 1918, Woodward's mayor H. R. Kent complained to Governor Williams that area druggists were selling patent medicines containing at least 50 percent alcohol. He inquired whether the state might restrict the sale of extracts, (i.e., bay rum, Jamaica ginger, and others) that contained alcohol. Mayor Ed Linthicum of Hugo, in the southeast, echoed these concerns.[28] Of course, many Oklahomans continued to sell liquor without the pharmaceutical pretense; much of this liquor originated from out of state.

Interstate liquor shipments continued to present a serious obstacle to dry proponents and officials in Oklahoma during this time. The U.S. Supreme Court had ruled in *Rhodes v. Iowa* (1898) that states could ban the importation of liquor for resale but could not block shipment of liquor for personal use.[29] When Oklahoma went dry, bootleggers commenced importation of immense quantities of beer and whiskey asserting that these were for their own consumption. Officials prosecuted those who resold this out-of-state liquor, though many dry advocates believed prohibition would be more effective if the flow of liquor could be dammed at the state's borders.

The Anti-Saloon League of America badgered Congress to place interstate liquor shipments under state jurisdiction. Caldwell proposed such legislation to lawmakers in 1910, and the national league pressured Congress until it passed the 1913 Webb-Kenyon Act, which banned the importation of all liquor in violation of state law. Dry proponents lauded this great victory. Horatio T. Laughbaum, superintendent of the Oklahoma league, even predicted that it might end the prohibition struggle.[30] In response, state and local liquor enforcement agents in Oklahoma City, Lawton, Guthrie, Perry, and other towns initiated seizures of interstate liquor shipments in the railroad yards.[31]

The dry advocates' enthusiasm cooled when opponents of Webb-Kenyon challenged its constitutionality in the federal courts.

President William Howard Taft vetoed the bill in 1912, believing it violated the Constitution's stipulation that Congress alone possessed the power to regulate interstate traffic. Oklahoma officials waited on Webb-Kenyon's legal fate before passing new enforcement legislation. Following a lengthy appeals process, the U.S. Supreme Court upheld the law in 1917, and seven states, Kansas, North Dakota, Georgia, Montana, Tennessee, Washington, and Oklahoma, passed laws banning the importation of all liquor.[32]

Thus Oklahoma's new liquor law of February 1917 made the importation or possession of liquor for any purpose other than scientific or medicinal illegal.[33] The "Bone-Dry Law," as it became known, provoked a negative reaction by a group that previously had remained silent on the liquor issue: the Roman Catholic Church. The church generally had not supported the prohibition campaign in the Sooner State, even though some clergy members in other states did join the Anti-Saloon League. The Catholic Total Abstinence Union had preached moderation or abstinence throughout the nation, but it and the church balked at prohibition. According to the guidelines of the Bone-Dry Law, the church's sacramental wine used during mass was not exempted from the importation ban, and this pulled the church into the prohibition fight.

The Catholic Church in Oklahoma was composed of isolated communities in a sea of evangelical pietistic Protestantism. Catholics comprised 2 percent of the territories' population in 1906, and were concentrated in the coal mining regions of east and southeast Oklahoma (Okmulgee, Coal, and Pittsburg counties) and a few northern and central counties, such as Osage, Noble, Kingfisher, and Oklahoma. The church possessed a strong immigrant presence, reflecting not only its parishioners' heritage (many coal miners were from Italy, Poland, and elsewhere in Europe), but also that of the Oklahoma clergy, sixty-one of the state's eighty-eight priests in 1907 were from Europe.[34] Culturally and ethnically, Oklahoma Catholics found themselves at odds with the native-born, white majority that constituted the mainstream, respectable element of society. The state's prolonged prohibition experiment furthered this alienation and marginalized the Catholic population.

The church's lack of support for prohibition was conspicuous, particularly because clergymen from several faiths (notably the Methodist, Baptist, Presbyterian, and Congregational churches) vigorously campaigned for the liquor ban as officers or trustees of the Oklahoma league. No Catholic clergymen served as league officers or trustees. The league also contained no Jewish, Episcopal or Lutheran clergymen, who, with their Catholic counterparts, comprised the liturgical political culture that generally did not endorse prohibition.[35]

Following the 1917 Supreme Court ruling on Webb-Kenyon, it was league superintendent and attorney Laughbaum who presented the bill that would become the Bone-Dry Law to Walter Ferguson of the Oklahoma Senate. Governor Williams threatened a veto, but the legislature's strong support for the bill (eighty-nine to seven in the house and thirty-two to five in the senate) and the intense pressure from the league convinced him to allow it to become law without his signature. During their talks, the legislature had debated a religious wine exemption, but Senator Ferguson refused such changes, presumably with Laughbaum's support.[36] That omission became obvious within a few months. In August 1917, a Santa Fe Railroad agent in Norman refused to release a barrel of sacramental wine consigned to Father John Metter of that city's Saint Joseph's Church. Metter, who had ordered the wine before passage of the new liquor statute, contacted Attorney General S. Prince Freeling to resolve this situation and to determine the provisions by which he might order wine in the future. He said he would discontinue religious services if his supply of sacramental wine ran out. Freeling responded that the Bone-Dry Law included no provision for such shipments; sacramental wine, like beer and whiskey, could not be brought into Oklahoma legally. The wine remained in the railroad's custody and the future of such shipments remained clouded.

Events took an embarrassing turn several days later. The Norman Santa Fe agent informed the attorney general that Cleveland County sheriff Ben Wheelis had confiscated the wine with a search warrant from Judge George C. Burke and that the wine had disappeared since. The railroad agent suspected (later confirmed by Governor Williams) that county officials, including Burke, had consumed the sacramental wine. The agent also testified that, minutes after seizing the wine, one of the county officers was "drunk as a Lord." A subsequent grand jury investigation produced insufficient evidence to prove who had removed the wine from the sheriff's custody and brought no indictments in the matter.[37] The Norman case was symptomatic of a recurrent problem in numerous Oklahoma communities under prohibition: officials consumed or resold seized liquor without consequence. The nature of the wine confiscated at Norman and the circumstances of its disappearance made the case particularly embarrassing.

The realization that the Bone-Dry Law prohibited the importation of religious wine alarmed the state's small liturgical population. Roman Catholic Bishop Theophile Meerschaert denounced the attorney general's ruling and vowed that the church would continue to use wine in its services in violation of the new law. Dean Frederick Bates of the Oklahoma City Episcopal cathedral sided with Meerschaert, stating that the prohibition of sacramental wine violated the principles of religious freedom. Reverend A. C. Dubberstein of Oklahoma City's Zion Lutheran Church and Reverend Oswald Helsing of that city's Unitarian Church gave similar statements of support for the Catholic position.[38] Each of those who rose to speak in defense of the Catholic Church represented a liturgical church, which generally did not support prohibition, and none were involved with the Oklahoma Anti-Saloon League.

In addition to its public criticism of the new law, the Catholic Church challenged it in the courts. In October 1917, Father Urbane De Hasque, Bishop Meerschaert's chancellor, attempted to ship a small amount of sacramental wine from Oklahoma City to Guthrie to test the Bone-Dry Law. The Santa Fe Railroad refused to transport the wine and De Hasque, in the name of the Catholic Church and with the support of the state's small Episcopal church, sued the company to compel shipment. The district court rejected the church's religious freedom argument and found in favor of the state and the railroad, but the Oklahoma Supreme Court overturned this ruling

in May 1918. It held that sacramental wine did not constitute intoxicating liquor and so was exempt from the provisions of the Bone-Dry
Law.[39] The state henceforth allowed importation of religious wine
into Oklahoma.

Following this ruling, the Catholic Church dropped out of the
public discussion of Oklahoma prohibition, though many parishioners likely ignored the ban. Because of the insular nature of Oklahoma's Catholic Church, little mention was made of such violations.
That they occurred can be inferred from national studies of prohibition that depict Catholics, with some exceptions, as regular consumers of alcohol as a beverage and as staunch opponents of prohibition.[40] Additional hints at the stance of Catholic communities
toward prohibition come from the small town of Okarche, northwest of Oklahoma City. The local newspaper made only indirect
mention of liquor violations, even though the region's population
was overwhelmingly German Catholic. Either Okarche experienced
few liquor violations, or the press and authorities largely ignored
such activity.

A 1917 incident supports the latter conclusion. Officials of the
nearby community of Okeene arrested a Kansas City man for soliciting orders for out-of-state liquor. The *Okarche Times* noted, "We
understand that quite a number in this vicinity gave him orders and
paid cash."[41] The editor portrayed this venture not as scandalous
but as a common occurrence with the unfortunate consequence of
arrest. Okarche's residents, like other Oklahoma Catholics, were
sensitive to the anti-Catholic sentiment common in the state's much
larger Protestant population and saw no need to fuel such animosity by emphasizing area liquor violations.

The Bone-Dry Law was part of a pattern of anti-Catholic sentiment that flourished in early twentieth-century Oklahoma. Groups,
such as the Guardians of Liberty and the Knights of Luther, formed
to foil alleged Catholic plots to overthrow the federal and state
governments.[42] Reflecting this attitude and mindful of the Oklahoma league's political influence, state legislators chose to ignore
the Bone-Dry Law's implications for religious wine, implications
they surely recognized because the issue had arisen previously.

In 1912, a federal court had declared the shipment of sacramental wine into former Indian Territory to be illegal unless the consignee attained a permit from the War Department; the U.S. Supreme Court subsequently ruled that the War Department had no authority to issue such permits, effectively banning such shipments. Bishop Meerschaert contacted Governor Cruce, who reassured him that state enforcement officers would not seize sacramental wine.[43] Federal officials provided similar assurances that they would not confiscate religious wine. Area railroad agents, unmoved by these pledges, balked at shipping sacramental wine into the area until the House of Representatives Committee on Indian Affairs announced a new policy to allow church-authorized shipments of sacramental wine into any "Indian country reservation."[44] This resolved the issue for a time.

The religious wine issue resurfaced in other dry states. In April 1916, Arizonans voted themselves dry, and the uproar over sacramental wine quieted only when the state attorney general promised no prosecutions against anyone transporting or possessing such wine. The state legislature of Kansas drafted a bone-dry law early in 1917, at the same time that Oklahoma lawmakers were considering such legislation. Signed into law in late February, the Kansas ban clearly exempted sacramental wine[45]; therefore, it can be argued that the Oklahoma legislature and Attorney General Freeling did not act from ignorance in failing to exempt religious wine.

Oklahoma's Bone-Dry Law prioritized the interests of pietistic evangelicals over those of liturgicals and the principles of religious freedom. Although some of the legislators who debated the 1917 Bone-Dry Law had not been in office when the issue arose in 1912, league attorney Laughbaum, the man who drafted the law, had been crafting state liquor bills since 1910. Laughbaum edited the league's *American Issue*, Oklahoma Edition, which reported Arizona's sacramental wine case in 1916. He kept in regular contact with the Anti-Saloon League of America's Wayne Wheeler, who testified before the Kansas legislature while it refined that state's bone-dry bill.

Oklahoma's pietistic denominations shared Laughbaum's insensitivity for the principles of religious freedom when they applied to the liturgical faiths. Although Episcopal, Lutheran, and Unitarian clergymen rose in defense of the Catholic Church, representatives from the large Baptist and Methodist churches and the other evangelical denominations did not. They continued to accept the Oklahoma league's leadership concerning the liquor question. The pietistic Oklahoma City Ministerial Alliance endorsed the Bone-Dry Law even after Laughbaum, the law's author, addressed them and explained that it banned sacramental wine also.[46] What the Bone-Dry Law controversy does illuminate is the growing rift between Oklahoma's liturgical and pietistic populations. The liquor stance of the former put it at odds with the numerically dominant pietists and alienated it from respectable, mainstream society.

The liturgical-pietistic split, however, does not completely explain Oklahoma's prohibition experience. Bootlegging persisted throughout the state, and the liturgical population was too small to account for more than a minor portion of this illegal liquor activity. Oklahoma liturgicals were a mere fraction of the population that fell outside the bounds of respectable society. Liquor men maintained a customer base that was large enough to support an extensive bootlegging network, even though this activity received less notice after the first years of statehood.

In the second decade of the twentieth century, liquor violations became commonplace and so received less public attention than they had previously. The conflict in Europe dominated the news, particularly after the United States joined the quagmire in April 1917. Oklahoma and the rest of the nation became caught up in the war. The state set up extensive military recruitment programs, liberty loan drives, and formed an Oklahoma Council of Defense to monitor the population for subversive activity. As elsewhere in the nation, the wartime attack on German culture undercut the cultural arguments against prohibition voiced by Oklahoma's German-American population.

Although liquor was no longer the dominant issue it had been previously, the illegal liquor industry remained vibrant throughout Oklahoma during the war years. Late in 1916, Guymon officials arrested a bootlegger in possession of thirty-five quarts of liquor. The following year saw the arrest of the soliciting Kansas City liquor man in Okeene, a grand jury investigation of Muskogee's vice industries in July, and Norman's embarrassing sacramental wine case in the fall. In 1918, Attorney General Freeling investigated liquor and gambling enforcement failures in Okmulgee, Muskogee, Creek, Tulsa, Rogers, Ottawa, Carter, Pottawatomie, and Grady counties.[47] Illegal liquor sales continued in Oklahoma after the First World War edged bootlegging reports out of many newspapers.

The war experience also sparked a flurry of federal liquor legislation, affecting dry and wet states. Congress passed the Lever Food and Fuel Control Act in August 1917, forbidding the use of grain in liquor distillation; adopted the Eighteenth Amendment the following December (to be submitted to the states); and passed the War Prohibition Act, which banned the manufacture and sale of liquor after June 30, 1919. Oklahoma's congressional delegation unanimously voted for the Eighteenth Amendment; they had supported national prohibition as early as 1914 when such legislation was first introduced.[48] These measures did not address the possession or consumption of liquor, but the proposed amendment banned the personal and commercial production of liquor.

These new pieces of legislation cast the liquor trade as unpatriotic, yet liquor continued to flow in Oklahoma. Fort Sill military police targeted area bootleggers, gamblers, and prostitutes, prompting this lament from an editor, "considerable liquor is still finding its way into Oklahoma, despite the federal and state antiliquor laws."[49] Late in 1918, Oklahoma's Assistant Attorney General R. E. Wood informed J. M. White, chairman of the Oklahoma Council of Defense, that druggists should be forbidden from selling Jamaica Ginger, Harter's Iron Tonic, Peruna, and several other patented medicines because alcohol was a key ingredient. As a result, the Council of Defense added liquor enforcement to its list of responsibilities.[50]

Liquor remained available during the war despite extensive efforts by enforcement agents. As in other aspects of the U.S.'s war home front, enforcement officials became increasingly bold with little consideration for basic liberties. Oklahoma City and other municipalities employed "axe squads" to raid, without court-issued warrants, rooming houses rumored to contain drinking and gambling.[51] Tulsa police seized one hundred gallons of Jamaica ginger in a July 1919 action, and bootleggers engaged federal officers in a gun battle during a raid on the Arkansas River northwest of that city. After the liquor men retreated, the revenuers seized a moonshine still that they determined had been in operation for more than a month.[52]

Patriotic arguments of wartime necessity had little impact on Oklahoma's liquor industry. In August 1918, Attorney General Freeling was informed that, "Such conditions as exist in Muskogee are not compatible with the full military efficiency of the Nation. I do not doubt that Muskogee is thoroughly loyal and patriotic, but it will not have proved so until it enforces the laws against prostitution and bootlegging more thoroughly."[53] In 1918, state investigators determined that liquor was readily available in Ardmore hotels and that predominantly rural Coal County contained at least one hundred liquor sources. Another report noted, "there are probably as many as one hundred places in the city of Tulsa where liquor can be purchased."[54] These flagrant violations of state and federal liquor statutes speak not only to the bootleggers' determination but also to the public's demand for liquor.

The situation bred frustration among enforcement officials and led to some excesses. In 1919, liquor officers killed several people returning from out of state. Armed but unidentified as peace keepers, the officers ordered the car to stop so that they could search its contents. The driver feared a holdup was in progress, sped up instead, and officers riddled the car and occupants with bullets. The *Tulsa World* asserted that this was not an isolated incident, "To date, the enforcement officers have inflicted greater damage on the law-abiding population that [sic] have the holdups and bank robbers."[55] The persistent efforts of bootleggers and the constant urgings of dry proponents led officers to ratchet up their own efforts, at times to the public's detriment.

The 1919 Volstead Act, which provided for the enforcement of national prohibition, took effect on January 16, 1920. Like the War Prohibition Act, it allowed for the possession of liquor purchased before the date it took effect. On paper, national prohibition brought joint enforcement by state and federal officials. In practice, Oklahoma's state and local enforcement officers gladly surrendered this headache to their federal counterparts, as did officials in Kansas and other states.[56]

Oklahoma prohibition remained problematic during the first two decades of the twentieth century because bootleggers, motivated by profit, found a consistent market for their product; many Oklahomans continued to consume alcohol after state, and later, federal statutes had banned it. The demand for liquor was sufficiently strong (and the potential for profit sufficiently great) that bootleggers found ways to circumvent the legal hurdles that the state created. Dry advocates in Oklahoma focused on the liquor men as the source of this demand, and undoubtedly the liquor men did take advantage of some Oklahomans who were addicted to alcohol. However, the scope of the illegal liquor industry in Oklahoma suggests that liquor men provided booze to more than just alcoholics.

Dry proponents, such as the Anti-Saloon League and the Woman's Christian Temperance Union (WCTU), ignored the state's large liquor-consuming population and targeted instead the liquor producers and suppliers. This was politically wise because the producers and suppliers represented a much smaller voting population than the consumers. Additionally, the league focused on destroying the old-time saloon; this strategy pitted Oklahoma professionals and merchants, who formed the core of respectable society (and generally avoided the saloons), against the state's laboring men, who operated at the periphery of respectable society or beyond and who tended to support the saloon in much greater numbers.

Oklahoma's tangled liquor codes further eroded effective enforcement, and the uneven application of those laws augmented this confusion. Jurisdictional questions and enforcement officials' trampling of civil liberties reduced conviction rates, and out-of-state liquor flooded into Oklahoma. The 1917 Bone-Dry Law addressed this issue and closed the personal-use loophole many bootleggers had employed. The Bone-Dry Law, by banning liquor imports, inadvertently spurred the growth of whiskey production in Oklahoma, as the increased mention of distilleries indicates. The patriotic arguments of the First World War also failed to dry up Oklahoma. Liquor remained available into the 1920s when federal officials assumed primary responsibility for liquor enforcement.

The league's appeal to Oklahoma's respectable middle classes did little to convince the laboring population that it should end its patronage of saloons, which had become a staple of working-class culture. These men continued to support the liquor industry even though it operated outside the law. As a result, Oklahoma prohibition between statehood and the onset of the national ban amounted to paper prohibition. Though the Oklahoma statutes defined the sale of liquor as illegal, it remained available throughout the period. The government attested to this by repeatedly tightening the prohibition code to block the efforts of the resourceful liquor industry. Despite these legal adjustments and criticism from dry advocates, bootleggers found the means to meet the demand for their product.

CHAPTER FIVE

Oklahoma Drys

The Shadow Government

Oklahoma dry advocates had outshone their wet counterparts in achieving statewide prohibition in 1907. They did not, however, rest on their laurels once the state banned liquor. The Oklahoma Anti-Saloon League, the flagship organization for prohibition supporters, remained intricately involved in state and local politics. It also monitored public officers to ensure they enforced the liquor ban. Recalcitrant officials drew the ire of the league, which targeted these same men for defeat during subsequent election campaigns. As bootleggers continued to test various aspects of the ban for legal weaknesses, league officials worked with the state legislature to strengthen the liquor codes. Results were mixed. Some league officers took the law into their own hands when they were discontented with the efforts of elected officials.

During the last years of the territorial period, the league had gradually perfected its organization and increased its influence on elected officials. Operatives drafted legislation such as the 1901 liquor bill, introduced by Representative F. M. Ferguson of Watonga. It provided for local option in Oklahoma Territory; that is, it would allow communities to ban the retail liquor industry from their midst.

The bill also set the annual liquor license at one thousand dollars, and prohibited saloons within a five-mile radius of any territorial school.[1] That bill failed to emerge from the Territorial House committee on intoxicating liquors, as did another bill, which would have banned liquor throughout the territory. However, the Oklahoma House did allow Reverend D. W. Keller to address legislators concerning this prohibition bill on behalf of the Logan County Anti-Saloon League.[2] In a separate action, league representatives lobbied the territorial government, albeit unsuccessfully, to ban saloons from all towns opened to white settlement after the summer of 1901.[3] The Oklahoma league's political activism initially produced only limited results, but its officers gained valuable political experience that they later used during the campaign for dry statehood.

By 1905 the league had representatives across Oklahoma Territory, and many of them were doctors, lawyers, and ministers. Under Superintendent H. E. Swan, the league worked locally to enforce existing liquor laws and lobbied the territorial legislature to block the passage of any new legislation that might allow saloon operations to expand. League activists campaigned against officials who failed to enforce legal restrictions on the use of liquor and filed charges against a justice of the Territorial Supreme Court who subsequently was removed. Swan, during his seven years as league superintendent, conducted more than one thousand representations and prosecutions against saloon operators in courts around the territory, and he gave over twelve hundred speeches before league supporters.[4]

Politically, the league not only achieved a statewide liquor ban in 1907 but also was influential in the first gubernatorial race. It assisted Charles Haskell in gaining the Democratic nomination to be Oklahoma's first governor; Lee Cruce also sought this nomination, and he enjoyed considerable support. Cruce personally supported prohibition but publicly took a moderate stance on the liquor question, making him less appealing to the league and other dry proponents in the Sooner State. With the aid of Oklahoma prohibitionists, Haskell, as the Democratic nominee easily defeated his Republican opponent, Frank Frantz, at the general election in

November. The new governor became a powerful ally of the league in its calls for effective enforcement of the liquor ban. Reverend Evander M. Sweet later described Haskell's election as "a great triumph for militant riteousness [sic]."[5] Haskell's support for the liquor ban during the constitutional convention and during his term as Oklahoma's first governor informally married the issue to the Democratic Party. This was a wise decision by the politically astute Haskell, who understood that the respected, middle-class elements of Oklahoma society were gravitating toward prohibition. This marriage also benefited the Oklahoma league, which gained considerable political influence through formal and informal access to the governor's office during Haskell's term and those of his Democratic successors.

The league remained politically influential following the adoption of statewide prohibition. Late in 1907, league secretary Reverend Thomas H. Harper and superintendent Edwin C. Dinwiddie went to Washington, D.C., to meet with President Theodore Roosevelt regarding selection of federal district judges for the new state. Former Oklahoma Territory attorney general W. O. Cromwell, a Republican, was a leading candidate for one of these posts, but, as Harper noted, "Cromwell was not acceptable to us. Cotteral was acceptable. Burwell also was acceptable. We did not try to dictate the appointment."[6] Harper's disclaimer aside, Roosevelt ultimately tapped John H. Cotteral to be the federal judge for the western district of Oklahoma. The eastern district judgeship went to John Campbell, who also met with league approval.

To promote its views and keep its supporters abreast of enforcement issues, the Oklahoma league began publishing a state edition of the national league's newspaper, *American Issue*, in September 1908 in Oklahoma City. League officers were not content with the adoption of the liquor ban and used this monthly publication to marshal support for strict enforcement of prohibition. Editorials urged supporters to get behind local and state candidates who demonstrated the will to do so; others urged readers to campaign and vote against those candidates who did not enforce the ban. In 1910, when prohibition critics succeeded in placing the liquor question on the ballot again, the state league used its edition of *American Issue* to rally supporters against the proposed local option measure. The editors informed readers of prohibition successes in Oklahoma and around the nation and countered arguments of the various wet organizations.[7]

During the early years of statehood, the Oklahoma league worked closely with the government to create effective enforcement of the state prohibition law. Sympathetic to the league, Governor Haskell appealed to the legislature in December 1907 for legislation that would give him broad powers to end the flagrant violation of prohibition around the state. Toward that end, he asked league attorney Horatio T. Laughbaum to draw up a bill to implement the constitution's prohibition clause. Laughbaum and Dinwiddie did so and then furnished legislators with briefs explaining the law.[8] Their work became the foundation for the Billups enforcement bill of 1908.

William E. "Pussyfoot" Johnson, the former federal liquor enforcement officer in Indian Territory who remained active in the national league, also claimed a portion of the bill's authorship. He described the Oklahoma league's political influence this way: "The Legislature seemed anxious to enact anything that was desired by the organized dry forces of the state."[9] The league's ties to powerful office holders, such as Haskell, and its political muscle during elections ensured it considerable input into the legislative process when law makers discussed liquor policy.

Laughbaum continued to author state and local legislation to address loopholes bootleggers found in the state's liquor codes. In 1909, he drafted a model liquor ordinance for Oklahoma cities and towns that the league distributed to its supporters.[10] When bootleggers abused the personal use clause in the state liquor codes to bring large quantities of liquor into the state, Laughbaum crafted legislation, which became law in 1911, to limit the amount of personal use liquor an individual could possess: one quart in places of businesses or recreation and one gallon in homes. He noted to supporters that the ingenuity of the bootleggers had forced him and the legislature to address this issue.[11] In 1915, when the Oklahoma Woman's Christian Temperance Union (WCTU) lobbied the legislature for a law requiring scientific temperance instruction in the state's public schools, Laughbaum arranged an audience with the legislature's liquor enforcement committees for union president Abbie B. Hillerman. Together, they coauthored the bill presented to the senate and the house.[12] Subsequently, when court decisions hindered the effectiveness of the 1917 Bone-Dry Law that he had written, the Oklahoma league sponsored amendments to address the issues raised in the courts.[13] In this way the league continued to shape state and local liquor codes well into the twentieth century.

Concern over the continued importation of liquor into the Sooner State led Oklahoma league representatives to join dry advocates from other states in Washington, D.C., in 1912. A congressional interstate commerce conference opened while the United States Senate debated the merits of a bill introduced a year previously by Representative Morris Sheppard of Texas and Senator William S. Kenyon of Iowa. This bill evolved into the Webb-Kenyon Act of 1913, which allowed dry states to ban the shipment of liquor across their borders. Several Oklahoma dry proponents were prominent at the 1912 conference, including the league's and state enforcement officer Fred S. Caldwell who drafted an early version of this bill.[14] Captain A. S. McKennon, vice-president of the league, also attended the conference as did H. H. Holman, a Wetumka banker who later joined the Oklahoma league board of trustees, and W. J. Milburn, an Oklahoma City businessman who subsequently served as league treasurer.[15] When asked to name Oklahoma delegates to the interstate shipment conference, Governor Cruce nominated all of those whom the league had suggested.[16]

Congressional passage of the Webb-Kenyon Act over President William Howard Taft's veto demonstrated the league's growing political influence in Washington D.C., and the league sent representatives back to the capital in December 1913 to lobby for national prohibition. The Committee of One Thousand, as this group was known, included a six-man delegation from Oklahoma. Four of them, Reverend E. O. Whitwell, Holman, Milburn, and Laughbaum, were influential in the Oklahoma league. Laughbaum gained greater national, and even international, prominence in the anti-liquor crusade when President Woodrow Wilson named him to represent the United States at the Fourteenth International Congress on Alcoholism in Milan, Italy, in 1913.[17] This national notoriety facilitated league operatives' access to public officials throughout the nation.

Back in Oklahoma, the league was not content to involve itself in the legislative process. It also folded itself into various levels of the state enforcement bureaucracy. In late summer 1908, Governor Haskell named Caldwell as special counsel to the governor concerning prohibition enforcement. The league noted its approval of one of its own, stating, "As he is a trustee of the Anti-Saloon League and one of its legal advisors, the appointment is very satisfactory."[18] For the next thirty months, Caldwell traveled around the state, investigating county and municipal officials suspected of failing to enforce the liquor ban. In April 1909, Haskell selected Laughbaum as special attorney for state law enforcement.[19] These appointments gave the league intimate knowledge of and influence over state enforcement policy.

Non-enforcement of prohibition at the local level remained a thorn in the side of dry Oklahomans. As discussed previously, local officials struggled to find the proper balance in enforcement amid competing pressure from dry advocates and from wet proponents. A league editorial equated those officials who did not enforce prohibition strictly with social radicals, stating bluntly, "The supreme danger confronting the American people of today is official anarchy . . . the officer who refuses to enforce the law is an anarchist ten thousand times worse than the red-shirted bomb-throwing savages from the slums of our cities."[20] Placed in the context of the period, this warning was designed to generate fear in some readers, particularly the middle class, which viewed labor organizations as anarchistic. President William McKinley had been assassinated nine years earlier by an anarchist, and radicals had been active in Europe attempting to topple the entrenched aristocratic monarchies there. The work of anarchists was a regular part of national and international news of which educated Oklahoma businessmen and professionals, alike, kept abreast. Public officials seeking election or reelection in 1910 also recognized the import of the league's accusation.

The league also held considerable sway in executive and judicial appointments. Governor Haskell publicly admitted that he consulted the league before naming judges to the state criminal court of appeals.[21] Haskell's successor, Cruce, also relied on league recommendations when appointing men to the Oklahoma judicial system. Late in 1912, T. E. Sisson, a minister from Tulsa recently elected to the Oklahoma league board of trustees, wrote to Cruce urging him to name a judge suitable to the league to the superior court for the Tulsa area to "break the back" of the local bootlegging industry.[22] Like Haskell before him, Governor Cruce, consulted the league concerning liquor enforcement. When informed that local officers were not enforcing prohibition, Cruce advised correspondents to contact the Oklahoma league, which would refer the matter to the state enforcement agency.[23] In this way, league officials not only kept apprised of enforcement measures but also played an integral role in the enforcement process.

The Cruce administration, like its predecessor, also accepted league input into the selection of liquor enforcement personnel. The governor bestowed commissions to local enforcement officers based on Laughbaum's endorsement and allowed Laughbaum a role in training these local officials.[24] When the Bryan County attorney asked Cruce to send a detective to gather evidence against liquor violators in that locale, Governor Cruce directed him to contact the Oklahoma league because it had names of private detectives it recommended for such work.[25] Attorney General Charles West also recognized the league's influence. In 1911, he urged Cruce to use the state bank commissioner in attacking those banks that allowed people to pay for shipments of liquor (from out of state) at their front windows. To add weight to his suggestion, West notified Cruce that the league's Reverend Dinwiddie supported this tactic.[26] From the governor's perspective, the resistance of the Oklahoma legislature to additional expenditures and its desire to limit the appointive powers of the governor made the Oklahoma league indispensable to effective liquor enforcement. However it also provided the ministers and merchants who directed the league — none of whom had been elected by Oklahoma voters — with a disproportionate amount of input into the administration of state and local government.

The Oklahoma league maintained a part of the enforcement apparatus during the administrations of subsequent governors. Early in 1915, Laughbaum contacted Governor Robert L. Williams asking him to resubmit Caldwell's name to the Oklahoma Supreme Court as a candidate for commissioner. To expedite this matter, Laughbaum told Williams, "I would suggest that you put it up to the Court that Mr. Caldwell's appointment to this position is not only your desire, but is backed by the Anti-Saloon League of Oklahoma."[27] In Laughbaum's view, at least, mention of the Oklahoma league with regard to appointments carried some weight with the supreme court. The following month, the governor's office contacted Laughbaum concerning the persistent problem of illicit liquor sales in drug stores.[28] James B. A. Robertson, governor from 1919 to 1922, also consulted the Oklahoma league on prohibition matters. In 1921, Robertson held a conference on law enforcement at the statehouse attended by ministers and members of the Oklahoma union. In addition to the governor's address, attendees listened as league superintendent Laughbaum and Josephine M. Buhl, president of the Oklahoma union, spoke on liquor enforcement issues.[29]

The executive branch of the state government, then, worked closely with Oklahoma dry proponents concerning liquor enforcement. When the state investigated the official liquor dispensary system's financial irregularities in 1909, the four-man investigating committee included George Conger, Oklahoma league superintendent, and Muskogee's Reverend W. S. Wiley, a prominent league trustee.[30] The presence of Conger and Wiley on the committee reflects not only Governor Haskell's close personal ties to the league but also his desire to satisfy Oklahoma's organized dry advocates that the investigation was thorough. Through these men, the league

gained the ear of the governor concerning prohibition enforcement policy and joined in the implementation of that policy.

The league also enjoyed well-placed connections locally. William J. Caudill, a league trustee from 1910 to 1914, was elected as
the clerk of the district court in Frederick. Judge C. T. Bird of Tulsa
helped organize local leagues around the state in 1907.[31] Reverend
Charles C. Brannon served both as a minister and as a federal liquor enforcement officer before and after statehood. The Methodist Episcopal Church of Oklahoma named Brannon as its trustee to
the Oklahoma league. Tulsa Methodist clergyman Sisson worked as
a local prohibition enforcement officer.[32] These men provided the
league with firsthand knowledge of liquor violations and interjected
league perspectives and strategies into liquor enforcement.

The ties between Governor Haskell and prohibition supporters
proved beneficial to the governor also. In 1908, President Roosevelt
attacked Haskell amidst rumors that the national Democratic Party
was considering Oklahoma's chief executive as its next national
chairman. Roosevelt and Haskell battled in the press for several
weeks, and the Oklahoma league came to the aid of their prohibition ally. Superintendent J. J. Thomson informed Haskell that Roosevelt had violated federal liquor policy while on a 1905 hunting
trip in the Big Pasture region of southwestern Oklahoma Territory,
which at the time was designated as an American Indian reservation
and thus under federal prohibition. Thomson told Haskell that the
Roosevelt party brought liquor with it into the Big Pasture area
where they camped and hunted for five days. Haskell publicly threw
this story back at Roosevelt in response to the President's disparag-
ing remarks and the quarrel soon quieted.[33]

Haskell was a vocal ally of the dry crusade. In 1908, he spoke
before the Oklahoma prohibition convention in support of the liquor ban and its enforcement. Describing the liquor interests in the
United States as "monopolies of greed and graft," he urged Oklahoma clergymen to involve themselves in politics so that the influence of the "good people of the United States" might be brought
to bear against the saloon men.[34] In 1910, Haskell addressed the
Southern States Anti-Saloon League Annual Convention in Atlanta,

Georgia. He criticized the federal government's continued collection of federal liquor license fees from residents of dry states such as Oklahoma.[35]

Not satisfied with merely influencing liquor policy, league officers occasionally took part in enforcement of the ban even if they had not received an official commission to do so. For example, in August 1908, Rev. Thomson joined federal officials in confiscating over forty gallons of liquor in Lawton.[36] Throughout the early decades of Oklahoma statehood, the league aided enforcement officers in collecting evidence against bootleggers, and Laughbaum's appointment as special attorney for state law enforcement facilitated that work. Late in 1909, Adair County attorney E. B. Arnold, on Laughbaum's order, seized ninety-one barrels of beer as contraband.[37] In 1913, Laughbaum traveled to the town of Cushing, in the oil field of the same name, to check on reports of flagrant liquor violations there. Appalled, he informed Governor Cruce of the situation, and Cruce referred his report to special enforcement officer Bert Tillotson for resolution.[38] However Laughbaum's enthusiasm for strict enforcement of the liquor ban created some difficulty among other enforcement officers; Caldwell grumbled to Governor Haskell that Laughbaum was overstepping the bounds of his appointed position as an enforcement field worker for the state.[39]

The league also encouraged the formation of local enforcement leagues to help officers gather evidence against and convict prohibition violators and those officials whom dry proponents viewed as lax in their duties. Oklahoma City residents formed such a group, the law-and-order league, in early 1900, shortly after a local anti-saloon league had organized there. Mayor Henry Overholser criticized the law-and-order league's methods as excessive, drawing charges that he was an anarchist opposed to sound law enforcement. Community leaders in El Reno, Lawton, Stillwater, and Cashion also formed law-and-order leagues in the early years of the new century to monitor the efforts of elected officials.

Further, the Anti-Saloon League organized these local groups around Oklahoma Territory to allow community residents an active role against the saloon industry. In 1905, the Oklahoma City law and order league formed a committee to address the city council concerning liquor violations. Specifically, the league was disturbed that saloons remained open past midnight and that drunken girls reportedly were seen within these establishments.[40] Similar leagues provided authorities with evidence of liquor violations and pressured those officials to act on this information. Some monitored saloons to identify patrons and passed this information to county attorneys. A few leagues published the names of these people in local newspapers to shame residents into avoiding these establishments. Some of these groups hired detectives to enter saloons and collect evidence against proprietors. To facilitate this, the Oklahoma Anti-Saloon League established a referral system of detectives who were unknown in the community and were willing to testify in court.

Law-and-order leagues were also formed in Indian Territory, in support of the few federal officers in that region. McAlester residents formed such a league in 1906 and the Muskogee commercial club did so the following year.[41] Officers in these organizations tended to be merchants or professional men, often ministers. The leagues provided these middle-class men the means to involve themselves directly in the enforcement process and to monitor their elected officials.

Following Oklahoma statehood and statewide prohibition, law-and-order leagues sprang up in numerous communities because law enforcement officials became swamped with liquor violations. Prominent men in the southwestern Oklahoma town of Altus, upset at the continued operation of pool halls that illegally served liquor, formed such a league in 1908. Similar groups formed in Sulphur, Andadarko, Bartlesville, and elsewhere.[42] By 1915, at least thirty Oklahoma communities, including the state's principal cities, had formed law-and-order leagues or equivalent clubs. Typically, men prominent in a community called a meeting at which they organized a league and elected officers to the various committees. Officers of the Oklahoma Anti-Saloon League supervised this organizing process in towns around the state.[43]

These law-and-order leagues strove to improve liquor enforcement at all levels of state and local government. The Anadarko league petitioned Governor Haskell to refuse parole for two local bootleggers serving time in prison. Members feared these men would return to the liquor trade in Anadarko. The Apache law enforcement league submitted a petition to Governor Cruce to sign legislation making the sale of liquor a felony.[44] The rapidly growing oil boomtown of Tulsa, sporting numerous saloons and roadhouses, belatedly formed an enforcement organization. In 1914, citizens there formed the Independent Law Enforcement Club to combat area bootleggers. This club contacted Cruce and Attorney General West, claiming that area liquor men had organized an extralegal combine or trust to better control local officials and to divide the profitable liquor trade among them.[45] Although some law-and-order leagues attended to other enforcement issues as well, most focused their attention on the most frequent violation of the law in their communities: the sale of alcohol as a beverage.

The influence of local religious leaders was unmistakable in some leagues. The Muskogee law-and-order league reorganized in 1908 under the supervision of the local Baptist minister and Oklahoma Anti-Saloon League trustee, Wiley. A resolutions committee called for the formation of a permanent executive committee, a legislative committee, a committee on law enforcement, a membership committee, and a finance committee. Each of these committees included at least one Muskogee minister. The city's Baptist, Methodist Episcopal, Southern Methodist, and Presbyterian churches were active in the league, which characterized its work as a "crusade for law enforcement." By 1910, city clergymen had collected one thousand dollars for a detective to gather evidence against elected officials who failed to enforce prohibition.[46] Preachers also held offices in the leagues of Alva, Collinsville, Eufaula, El Reno, and elsewhere. The prominent role played by ministers in these leagues, and the rhetoric they used, gave the prohibition enforcement campaign a markedly religious tone.

That these merchants and professionals were active in organizing these leagues is not surprising because they represented the community's leading residents. Several leagues even listed physicians among their officers. The Altus men who spoke at the meeting to organize that town's law-and-order league in 1908 were community leaders. In 1911, the league in the northeastern Oklahoma town of Miami petitioned Governor Cruce to commission a special enforcement officer. To impress upon the governor the respectable nature of their organization, several of the signatories listed their occupations; these included the Ottawa County attorney, an Ottawa County judge, a private attorney, two merchants, and a real estate agent.[47] Notably absent from this and similar petitions are the names of wage-earning men, such as carpenters, miners, and roughnecks from the oil fields. The middle-class men who joined the leagues viewed the saloon from outside and did not appreciate its value in working-class culture.

The Oklahoma government welcomed these popular enforcement efforts. Governors Haskell and Cruce relied heavily on the national league and its local law-and-order leagues to satisfy public demands for stricter enforcement despite the legislature's fiscal conservatism. Cruce, responding to complaints from Reverend L. Q. Hargraves of Copan that several illegal saloons operated freely there, advised him that the legislature had tied his hands by restricting enforcement funding. He urged Copan residents to involve themselves in the prosecution of liquor laws, adding that he would deputize local citizens of good standing as enforcement agents. When the Bryan County attorney requested that Cruce supply a detective to be used against saloonists, Cruce again stated that the legislature had provided no funding for this and advised the attorney to contact the Oklahoma league regarding the matter.[48] Concerning enforcement problems in the small community of Packingtown, Cruce contacted Oklahoma league superintendent H. L. Sheldon, asking, "Will you please have your men investigate this matter, and take steps toward correcting any existing evils?"[49]

The law-and-order leagues, like the Anti-Saloon League, often were unsuccessful in ending the profitable liquor trade. Particularly in the state's growing oil fields and mining districts, bootleggers found a ready customer base for their wares, regardless of the legal risks. Liquor remained plentiful in oil towns, such as Cushing, Kiefer, and Ardmore, as long as the oil boom continued. The mining camps of northeast Oklahoma supported such a vibrant liquor industry that state authorities intervened in 1916 to break it up; similar interventions by the state in other counties produced limited results. Officials and dry proponents often complained that voters in some regions routinely reelected to office men who failed to arrest or prosecute bootleggers.[50]

In some locales, bootleggers aggressively resisted enforcement efforts. The liquor industry operated outside the bounds of the law and thus attracted some unsavory men, willing to take extreme measures to protect their source of income. Bootleggers injured or killed enforcement officers on several occasions. Many residents who complained to the governor about bootlegging in their area withheld their name for fear of reprisals from local liquor men. This violent defense of the liquor industry prompted angry demands from some dry advocates that elected officials do more to stop this activity.

Oklahoma, then, contained both a population determined to end the liquor trade and a population — bootleggers and their customers — who favored the continuation of that trade. Elected officials had to check the political winds of the local populace when enforcing the liquor ban. Lax enforcement and the sometimes violent resistance by bootleggers encouraged some Oklahoma dry proponents to support the measures of extremists. In 1913, John Harold Scott of Oklahoma City, an initiate of an organization called the Silent Brotherhood, sent Governor Cruce the following announcement: "Official warning to law breakers, predatory crooks, grafters, political and business sharks within the city and state of Oklahoma whose law shall be maintained as demanded and required by the Constitution." Scott went on to threaten all law breakers with divine damnation.[51] Much of this lawbreaking was tied to the city's expansive liquor industry. Although Scott never detailed the Silent Brotherhood's role in law enforcement, clearly he saw this as its major concern, and the organization's existence indicates dissatisfaction with efforts by public officials. The latter made concerted, but temporary, efforts to clean up the city from 1913 to 1915.

The inability or refusal of some local officials to strictly enforce the liquor ban and the voting public's willingness to return such men to office year after year remained a source of frustration for the Oklahoma league. Regarding such officials, the league assured supporters, "If they refuse, neglect or fail to enforce the law, recourse can be had in court and also at the polls."[52] In reality, however, the league's influence in some local electorates remained limited. Under state enforcement officer Caldwell, several local officials were dismissed, but others remained who did not enforce the law. Governor Haskell estimated in early 1909 that liquor enforcement was adequate in 75 percent of the state's counties; but he failed to specify his definition of adequate.[53] Reports from newspapers and concerned citizens indicate that liquor enforcement was more problematic than the governor stated.

In addition to its role in liquor enforcement, the Oklahoma league remained active in election campaigns, seeking to fill state and local offices with men of dry sentiment and striving to sustain its influence over seated officials. Shortly after statehood, superintendent Sweet vowed that the league would actively campaign for legislative candidates who supported prohibition.[54] League leaders in Oklahoma City announced that they would join with the local civic league to offer a slate of candidates in the 1909 municipal elections.[55] The following year, the league urged supporters to nominate candidates who championed the dry cause and to vote for those candidates at the primary and general elections. It announced the names of candidates who were soft on enforcement, such as judge H. Doyle of Oklahoma's northern district criminal court, and urged voters to support their opponents instead. This prompted other justices of the court to accuse the Oklahoma league and superintendent Conger of demagoguery.[56] The Oklahoma league's influence on Oklahoma politics was not boundless, as evidenced by the nomination of Cruce for governor on the 1910 Democratic ticket. The league had endorsed William H. Murray for the chief executive seat in the state because the other candidates, including Cruce, supported the resubmission of the liquor question to a popular vote.[57] Despite this setback, the league worked closely with Cruce on liquor policy. League speakers also continued to canvass the state in support of dry candidates and against wet candidates during the early decades of Oklahoma statehood.

Between elections, the Oklahoma league used its political clout to pressure elected officials to shape their policies according to league guidelines. In 1913, Laughbaum contacted Governor Cruce urging him to persuade the attorney general to prosecute to the fullest extent those cases then in the district courts against liquor joint operators and the owners of the property on which the joints operated. Cruce agreed to do so.[58] The following year, Laughbaum complained to Cruce that the Alexander Drug Company, as the liquor wholesaler for drug stores throughout Oklahoma, was indiscriminately selling large amounts of alcohol to druggists. He threatened to introduce legislation to choke off all sources of liquor in Oklahoma, including that for medicinal use, if Cruce did not rein in Alexander Drug.[59] Laughbuam's willingness to make such a demand of the governor speaks volumes on the league's political muscle in the Sooner State.

The league made its presence felt in local government as well. In 1914, Caldwell, no longer a state enforcement agent, but still a member of the Oklahoma league board of trustees, filed an affidavit calling for the recall of Oklahoma City mayor Whit M. Grant as a result of his inability or refusal to reduce vice in the city. Caldwell submitted his petition, containing 125 signatures, on behalf of the Central Hundred, an Oklahoma City civic organization pledged to end bootlegging and gambling in the capital city. In response to this threat on his job, Mayor Grant named a new police chief and stepped up vice enforcement. A series of raids soon netted the arrest of one hundred liquor men. Governor Cruce placed Attorney General West, in charge of vice conditions in Oklahoma City and named Caldwell as a special attorney to aid West in prosecuting bootleggers. The stepped-up vice campaign by the police calmed Oklahoma City reformers, and the movement to recall Mayor Grant ended.[60] In subtle and not so subtle ways, then, the Oklahoma league pressured elected officials to enforce prohibition strictly.

Despite the league's claims of prohibition reducing crime and drunkenness, enforcement remained a contentious issue in Oklahoma during the period before national prohibition. Laughbaum, as league attorney and then as superintendent, toured the state, urging his audiences to involve themselves in liquor enforcement. He was able to rally that portion of the population committed to prohibition, but ultimately his and others' efforts failed to sway those committed to continuing the liquor industry.

CHAPTER SIX

Dry Oklahoma

The Class Nature of the Movement

In studying efforts to ban liquor in the early twentieth century, it is tempting to explain dry organizations as composed of narrow-minded, wild-eyed ministers attempting to legislate morality and return the United States to a romanticized past dominated by religion. Such a portrayal is partially accurate, particularly in rough-and-tumble early Oklahoma, but it fails to tell the entire story. Christian lobbyists possessed considerable influence in Washington, D.C., and in several state capitals during the second half of the nineteenth century; they remained influential as the new century opened, and also gained the support of less religious professionals and merchants concerning the liquor question. The Anti-Saloon League of America actively courted these middle-class voters, stressing social and religious reasons for closing the saloons. The league achieved prohibition at state and later national levels where previous organizations had failed, because its base of support stretched beyond the church pews.[1]

In Oklahoma in particular, clergymen played a prominent role in the prohibition campaign; they shaped the liquor debate and pursued aims that went far beyond the wishes of most supporters. The majority of dry proponents belonged to the middle classes; they were merchants and professionals, leaders in their communities who believed the saloon to be a blight on society that possessed no redeeming social or moral value and must be destroyed. Although the Woman's Christian Temperance Union involved middle-class women in the liquor reform movement, these women, in keeping with accepted gender roles, generally deferred to the ministers, lawyers, and merchants who led the Oklahoma league. The league claimed to speak and act for all who supported prohibition, and the women of the union accepted this, though sometimes grudgingly. Oklahoma's Prohibition Party, small and ineffectual outside a few communities, never challenged the league for leadership of the anti-liquor movement.

The union had preceded the league, however, and was easily the most visible and influential anti-liquor group in the area in 1900. It had organized in both territories by 1890, establishing local unions in the eastern communities of Muskogee, Tahlequah, Atoka, Vinita, Wagoner, Claremore, Prior Creek, and Poteau during the last decade of the century.[2] By 1904, the union had local groups in such Indian Territory towns as Bartlesville, Phillips, Sterrett, Howe, Tuskahoma, Antlers, Grant, Edwards, Calvin, Spiro, Quinton, Ravia, and Purcell.[3] In keeping with its emphasis on education, the union set up temperance day programs in the area American Indian schools, funded a special evangelist to local American Indians, and launched *Our Helper*, the territorial union newspaper in 1903.[4] Chelsea and Tulsa union members served coffee at polling places on election day; Muskogee, South McAlester, and Ardmore unions held religious services in jails, distributing temperance literature and fruit to prisoners.[5] This activism gained notoriety for the union, though its impact on the liquor issue is dubious because drinking remained common despite the federal liquor ban in the region.

The Oklahoma Territory union also joined the struggle against liquor during the late territorial period. It organized a school of methods in Norman by 1901 to train local union members. Supporters came from the Tecumseh, Earlsboro, Oklahoma City, El Reno, Chandler, Perkins, Guthrie, Stillwater, Noble, and Neal Dow unions to hear speeches by activists, attorneys, and clergymen.[6] The Oklahoma union also began its own newspaper, *The Oklahoma Messenger*, shortly before statehood. Like its counterpart to the east, this union emphasized education and persuasion over coercion as the surest way to end liquor consumption. Despite this focus on moral suasion, the unions from both territories also endorsed a coercive prohibition law for the future state of Oklahoma.

In 1905, when the federal government considered both single and twin statehood for the region, the Indian Territory union urged all members to write the congressional committee on territories and plead for prohibition statehood whether Congress formed one or two states from the territories. The union also applied pressure locally: The Tulsa County union sent a committee to convince the *Tulsa World* editor to remove a liquor advertisement from his newspaper. Shortly after the constitutional convention opened late in 1906, the *Tulsa Union* formally petitioned that body to adopt a prohibition clause.[7] Union members did not let up after the convention closed but looked toward the September 1907 prohibition referendum with great anticipation. The two territorial unions merged to form the Oklahoma union in 1907, and this body designated September 17, 1907, "as a day of fasting and prayer to Almighty God, that he lead the men of Oklahoma and Indian Territories, to vote for the Home."[8]

The union's invocation of the home was in keeping with contemporary gender attitudes. The WCTU targeted political issues related to women's traditional domestic role in society, even though its activism drew members into the male realm of politics. This adherence to the domestic ideal underscores the union's moderate, middle-class perspective. More radical women's groups rejected the notion that women's activities should be confined to accepted feminine issues. The union, instead, worked within traditional gender roles, while at the same time pushing the boundaries of those roles through its political lobbying.

The Tulsa union's reference to God and religion also reinforced traditional gender roles. As the new century opened, the congregations of several denominations were predominantly female, leading ministers to worry about the feminization of American religion.[9] The religious census taken in Oklahoma in 1906 and 1916 reported a majority of women in the region's prominent denominations: Methodist; Presbyterian; Congregationalist; and Baptist churches.[10] These female majorities reinforced religion's perceived feminine nature. Despite the preponderance of women in congregations, they did not hold leadership positions; the vast majority of clergy were men. The very name of the WCTU, belying its religious perspective, accepted the leadership of the ministers and other men who directed the Oklahoma league in much the same way that union members accepted the leadership of clergymen and male elders in their churches.

The union, in addressing the liquor issue, worked closely with local clergymen and the league. When prohibition opponents brought the question up for a vote again in 1910, members joined the political fray. The Tulsa union placed editorials in area newspapers and, supported by local ministers, held a parade in the city the day before the election.[11] The Alfalfa County WCTU sponsored street meetings in Cherokee and at several rural sites directed by clergymen. League officers, such as Reverends H. E. Swan and J. J. Thompson, and attorney Horatio T. Laughbaum, regularly spoke at the union's annual state convention.[12] The Oklahoma WCTU was a force in the war on liquor but increasingly deferred to the Oklahoma league during the latter territorial period.

Following adoption of statewide prohibition, some Oklahoma unions involved themselves in enforcement issues, but their efforts in this area did not match those by the league. Members of a local union attended court in Nowata to remind enforcement officials that they were under scrutiny, and the Newkirk union recommended the local sheriff to Governor Lee Cruce as a state-employed detective.[13] More often than not, the WCTU coordinated this work with that of the league or left enforcement to the authorities and local league representatives.

The union, although committed to the liquor ban, also devoted considerable time and resources to various other social causes. In this respect, it differed markedly from the single-issue league. Local unions endorsed Sunday closing laws for all businesses, children's curfews, city beautification projects, the formation of humane societies, an anti-smoking campaign, and women's suffrage. The multifaceted reform program of the WCTU encouraged its members to yield to the men leading the Oklahoma Anti-Saloon League on the issue of liquor prohibition.[14]

The political connections of league officers contributed to that organization's primacy in the Oklahoma anti-liquor campaign. Captain A. S. McKennon, who was a member of the Dawes Commission, president of the Indian Territory Church Federation for Prohibition Statehood, and later vice-president of the Oklahoma league, incorporated calls for a liquor ban into the final treaties between several American Indian tribes and the federal government. He was part of the delegation that met with President Theodore Roosevelt and convinced him that Oklahoma statehood, though dominated by the Democratic Party, should go forward, citing the prohibition clause in the proposed state constitution as evidence that the region merited statehood. Reverend Evander M. Sweet, secretary of the federation and later superintendent of the Oklahoma league, knew Charles N. Haskell personally, and this relationship produced dividends at the constitutional convention in 1906–1907.[15] Reverend Edwin C. Dinwiddie, Oklahoma league superintendent during the 1907 campaign, personally knew several members of Congress from his previous work as a lobbyist. He also worked closely with Oklahoma legislators and coauthored the Billups enforcement bill with Laughbaum[16]; Laughbaum later penned the Bone-Dry Law of 1917. The Oklahoma WCTU continued to support prohibition as part of a broad platform of goals, but its efforts in shaping the liquor ban pale in comparison to those by the Oklahoma league.

The Oklahoma league supplanted the WCTU as the standard bearer in the crusade against liquor, claiming to represent all opponents of the saloon industry. It also enjoyed better funding than the union did. The league's close ties to evangelical religious denominations, which it cultivated by placing ministers in several of its offices and encouraging all denominations to name representatives or trustees to the Oklahoma league, led many churches to financially back the league to the exclusion of other organizations, such as the Oklahoma union. One WCTU member complained that this practice hindered the union's effectiveness, but the practice continued.[17]

That these women surrendered leadership of the prohibition campaign to the Anti-Saloon League is not peculiar to Oklahoma. Nationally, the WCTU, which was the most prominent temperance organization under Frances Willard, gave way to the Anti-Saloon League of America after the turn of the century. This transition aided the prohibition campaign because many voting men resented the inroads union members had made into the male sphere of politics.[18] This changing of the temperance guard might be described as the masculinization of the anti-liquor campaign. Although the league directed some of this appeal to manly virtue toward church-going men, it also made secular gender-based arguments to professionals and merchants.

One constant during this transition was the middle-class nature of the reform movement. The WCTU contained some professional women — teachers, principals, college professors, administrators — and wives of clergymen or businessmen. Businesses promoted temperance as part of the scientific efficiency campaign sweeping U.S. industry at the time; they gladly supported the union's endeavors.[19] The Oklahoma union was similar to the national organization: Mrs. Lilah D. Lindsey, activist in Tulsa County and Oklahoma state unions, had taught school and was married to a Tulsa businessman. Mrs. George Mowbray and Mrs. C. W. Kerr, early organizers of the Tulsa union, were married to Methodist and Presbyterian ministers, respectively. Abbie Hillerman, president of the Oklahoma union at the time of statehood, was an attorney.[20] These middle-class women had little appreciation for the perspective of the saloon's working-class clientele.

Like the WCTU, the Oklahoma league was a middle-class organization, and this shaped its approach to the liquor question. It did not seek to recreate the societal attitudes of an imagined golden past. Rather, the league was a forward-looking organization, hoping to improve society through a ban on liquor. Specifically, it sought to remove the old-time saloon, which it charged with spawning such unsavory activities as gambling, prostitution, and violent crime, from the U.S. landscape. These arguments carried weight with middle-class voters. They did not frequent saloons and learned of these nefarious activities secondhand or from league reports, often ascribing the traits of a few saloons to the entire industry.

The Oklahoma Territory league and the Indian Territory Church Federation for Prohibition adopted the organizational structure of the national league. Offices included president, vice president, secretary, treasurer, and superintendent. The last office held the most influence and generally directed the local league's activities and coordinated them with those of the national organization. Beginning in 1903, the national league instructed all state and local leagues to allow each religious denomination expressing interest in league work to select representatives to a board of trustees.[21] This body served as a conduit of information from the Oklahoma Territory and Indian Territory leagues to local supporters, such as evangelical religious denominations, and as a means by which those groups could make their wishes known to league officers.

The territorial leagues formed local and county leagues also. Anyone willing to sign a pledge against the saloon could join. This structure provided the league with support from members of the WCTU, the International Order of Good Templars, the Prohibition Party, and other dry organizations. Standard procedure was for the league to create an executive council of pastors from all supporting churches and representatives from various religious temperance societies. This body directed local campaigns, such as promoting local option referendums (in wet districts) and monitoring area saloons for violation of current liquor codes. Each local league sent representatives to a county league, directed by a superintendent.[22] These local leagues became prominent in liquor enforcement through their surveillance and campaign activities. Noticeably absent from these organizations were wage earners, even though working-class men had been central to earlier temperance movements, such as the Washingtonians.

Instead, middle-class professional dominated the leadership of the Oklahoma Anti-Saloon League. Three of its five original officers (J. W. Sherwood, Thomas H. Harper, and Swan) were clergymen as were seven of the eighteen trustees. Harper and Swan were ministers in Oklahoma City Congregationalist churches. Two trustees were doctors and one was a judge.[23] The presence of these middle-class professionals among the leadership of the Oklahoma league gave it instant credibility among respectable society and influenced the perspective of the league toward the saloon industry. Neither these men nor their friends frequented the saloon. If they drank liquor at all, they did so in their homes or in private clubs. Viewing the saloon from a distance, they saw no redeeming qualities in it and accepted the accounts of violence in some saloons as representative of activities in all.

Structurally, the national league, with which the Oklahoma league was affiliated, was rather autocratic. National leaders issued directives to state and local leagues, and the latter provided funding and staffing for league projects.[24] This relationship existed in the Sooner State as well, but the Oklahoma league demonstrated some independence. Although the national league made its presence felt when superintendent Purley A. Baker came to Oklahoma and re-organized the Oklahoma league in 1904, state officers exercised a measure of discretion at other times and adjusted their activities and speeches to the interests of the state. Even though Laughbaum owed his position as legislative superintendent, and later super-intendent, more to the national league than to the Oklahoma orga-nization, he enjoyed considerable autonomy once in office as when he crafted prohibition enforcement legislation for the state. The interaction between the state and national leagues produced a mix of authoritarianism and local independence.

The dual nature of this relationship becomes evident when ex-amining events following the national league's recall of Rev. Din-widdie from Oklahoma in 1907. Despite his resignation from the national league, the Oklahoma league retained the popular Din-widdie as superintendent until 1908. Late in 1907, on the Okla-homa league's behalf, he went to Washington and lobbied Congress for federal legislation that would prohibit the ongoing liquor traffic into Oklahoma. The following year he surrendered his position in the Oklahoma league and left the country to promote temperance in England.[25]

The Oklahoma league remained closely associated with the national league despite the Dinwiddie affair. The national organization continued to provide significant financial aid to the struggling state league. Superintendent Baker paid another visit to Oklahoma and went on a brief speaking tour to raise $3,000 for the league and reduce its debt incurred during the 1907 campaign to a manageable figure. He again reorganized the Oklahoma league, emphasizing its affiliation with the national league and named Dr. George D. Conger of Ohio as the new state superintendent.[26]

The league brought the benefits of large-scale organization, fundraising, and experience in state politics to the ministers of Oklahoma in their battles against the nonrespectable saloon. Although clergymen generally opposed the liquor industry before the league's appearance, the league provided them with the organizational apparatus to reach a much wider audience. The league also attracted support from non-religious middle-class men. These businessmen, attorneys, and other professionals shared with the clergy a strong distaste for what they saw as the coarse saloon culture.

Leadership of the Oklahoma league remained fluid after statehood because the national league regularly changed out the state superintendent. Reverend Sweet of Muskogee replaced Dinwiddie in 1908 but held the post only until Baker's visit the following January. His replacement, Reverend Conger, came to Oklahoma from Illinois, where he had served as league assistant superintendent for the Chicago region. He retained the top post in Oklahoma's league for two years before moving on to the superintendency of the Washington state league. In his place came Reverend H. L. Sheldon who also had served in the Illinois league. Sheldon remained one year, moving on to the Oregon league in 1912. Oklahoma league leadership stabilized when Oklahoma City's Laughbaum, league attorney since 1906, succeeded Sheldon in the top post. He held the position of state league superintendent until 1932.[27] Even during the early years of frequent change, the leadership of the Oklahoma league remained consistently middle class. Wage earners held no state or local offices in the league and played no role in formulating league strategies. Either wage earners rejected invitations to join the organizations (league records make no mention of such a rebuff) or the league ignored the working class.

The leadership of the Oklahoma league had greater allegiance to the national league than to the state organization. Conger and Sheldon did not remain in the state long enough to establish state ties to rival their associations with the national leaders. Laughbaum was Oklahoma league attorney and legislative superintendent when he became state superintendent in 1912, but he was still a recent immigrant to the region, having moved to Oklahoma City from Ohio six years previously.[28] His Ohio roots acquainted him with the leadership of the national league because many officers hailed from Ohio. The national league, by filling the superintendency with men whom it had trained as professional lobbyists, not only standardized and increased the effectiveness of the state organizations but also maintained ties to and some influence over state leagues such as that in Oklahoma.

The Oklahoma league leadership, although differing with the national league on policy issues at times, generally shared with that body a middle-class perspective of the liquor issue. The Oklahoma league and the local law-and-order leagues were comprised of men from strong evangelical and middle-class backgrounds. They accepted the stereotype of the saloon as a well spring of crime without merit. Not surprisingly, several Oklahoma Protestant conferences and synods endorsed the league's efforts.[29] The league shared with these religious boards not only an antipathy toward the saloon but also some personnel. Laughbaum served as a member of the Presbyterian Church's Temperance Committee. Reverend Sweet was pastor in Methodist Episcopal South churches in Tulsa, Muskogee, and later Lawton. Reverend Harper, league treasurer and a member of the headquarters committee member from 1908 until 1913, was an Oklahoma City Congregational minister. The annual state conferences of the Presbyterian, Baptist, Methodist, Southern Methodist, Congregational, Friends, and Christian churches elected members, often ministers, to the Oklahoma league as trustees to convey their views to the league and the latter's messages and directives to their congregations. The league became the political arm of these churches, as they strove to end public drinking.

The league's exact composition is difficult to determine because only a few local membership rolls remain. However the Oklahoma league listed its state officers and trustees between 1908 and 1916 and often included their religious affiliation. The state officers held the majority of seats on the ten-member headquarters committee. Members of the Presbyterian and Methodist churches held several offices throughout this period, followed by smaller representations by the Baptist, Congregational, and Christian churches. None of the officers belonged to the Roman Catholic, Episcopal, Lutheran, and Jewish faiths.[30] The prominence of Southern Methodist Church affiliation among the league's leadership is understandable because it was the second largest denomination in Oklahoma (60,263 according to the 1916 religious census). Members of the Southern Baptist Church, which reported the largest following in the state at 87,028, held no league offices during much of this period and never more than two in any given year.

The prevalence of Presbyterians among league leadership is noteworthy because the membership of the largest Presbyterian denomination in Oklahoma was less than one fourth the size of the Southern Baptist denomination and ranked seventh in the state overall. Despite the relatively small number of Presbyterians in Oklahoma, at least three of the ten officers in the Oklahoma league listed their religious affiliation as Presbyterian between 1909 and 1916. Laughbaum, occupying the all-important position of state superintendent from 1912 on, was Presbyterian. Viewed in a national perspective, the presence of Presbyterian ministers in the Oklahoma league is less surprising because members of that denomination were active participants in the prohibition crusade throughout the nation.

The Congregational church also held influence in the Oklahoma league disproportionate to the size of its congregation in the Sooner State. Although the league's headquarters committee rarely contained more than one Congregationalist, the small membership of the state's Congregational churches (3,419 in 1916) makes noteworthy the presence of its clerical and lay members in league leadership positions. Oklahoma's total churched population in 1916 was 424,492. The Congregationalists, then, comprised less than 1 percent of the state's religious population, yet consistently held one of the top offices in the Oklahoma league.[31]

Clergymen from the various denominations discussed previously were prominent among the officers and particularly the trustees of the Oklahoma league. Ministers occupied more than half of the offices in the Oklahoma league in most years and increased their representation on the board of trustees until, by 1916, more than two-thirds of the board were clergymen. Oklahoma's evangelical religious denominations took seriously the work of the Oklahoma league, and the league enjoyed considerable access to these denominations.[32] These paragons of respectability set the tone of the liquor debate and portrayed their opponents as something other than constructive members of their communities. The lack of wage earners among the league's leadership gave this organization a decidedly middle-class voice.

The absence of Catholics, Episcopalians, Jews, and Lutherans among the league officers and trustees also is understandable because these denominations possessed no strong evangelical movement and generally opposed prohibition or remained silent on the issue. Membership in the latter three faiths remained quite small in early twentieth-century Oklahoma. By contrast, Oklahoma's Roman Catholic population was sizable (47,427 members in 1916). Bishop Theophile Meerschaert of Oklahoma's Roman Catholic diocese publicly advised the moderate use of liquor but opposed its prohibition. Given the anti-Catholic sentiment present in the state's evangelical denominations and the fact that most Catholics nationwide did not support prohibition, the absence of church members from league offices is not unusual.[33] Members of these liturgical denominations generally did not support prohibition in most parts of the nation, including Oklahoma. Participation in the league reveals the clearest split between what Paul Kleppner has termed the

pietist (evangelical and salvationist) and ritualist (liturgical) political cultures in the late nineteenth and early twentieth centuries.

Also of note, no women served in leadership positions in the
Oklahoma league. This was not standard practice around the nation; women held some offices, though always an extreme minority,
in other state leagues and as delegates to the national league. The
early prominence of the WCTU in the anti-liquor campaign in the
territories stands in stark contrast to the Oklahoma league's exclusively male leadership. Again, the union's acceptance of middle-
class roles for women explains its willingness to surrender direction
of the prohibition movement to men, often clergymen.

One last observation regarding the Oklahoma league leadership involves race. As was the norm in most regions containing a
notable black population, religion split along racial lines in Oklahoma. The Southern Baptist Convention was exclusively white as
were the smaller Free Baptist, Free Will Baptist, General Baptist,
and Primitive Baptist churches. The National Baptist Convention
represented the state's black Baptist churches. These churches contained 42,408 members, making it the fourth largest congregation
in Oklahoma. Given the strong presence of ministers and elders
among the leadership of the Oklahoma league, the absence of any
members from the state's fourth largest denomination is strik-
ing. The smaller African Methodist Episcopal and Colored Methodist Episcopal churches (7,250 and 5,541 members, respectively, in
1916) also received no mention in league publications and correspondence.[34] The league sensed that inclusion of blacks in its hier-
archy would hinder rather than help its political fortunes. Race was
a charged issue in early Oklahoma (as evidenced by the hurried
adoption of Jim Crow legislation in 1908 and the implementation
of voting restrictions against blacks and others in 1910). Further,
league officers, to varying degrees, internalized the racist attitudes
that produced Oklahoma's Jim Crow and disfranchisement laws. As
a result, league literature avoided direct statements on the issue of
race and liquor in Oklahoma.

The league's ties to white, evangelical churches cemented it to
respectable elements of Oklahoma society. The Oklahoma Ter-

ritory league originated in a church (Oklahoma City's First Baptist Church in 1899), and ministers formed the Indian Territory Church Federation for Prohibition during their 1904 meeting in the Muskogee home of Reverend T. F. Brewer. In 1907, with statehood imminent, the ministers convened again in Brewer's parlor and decided to merge with the Oklahoma Territory league.[35] The Oklahoma league was not an organization of radical reformers operating on the fringe of society. It was prominent in the state and in most communities, and it provided the means by which the supporting religious denominations attained significant influence in state and local politics in early Oklahoma.

The league's respectable and centrist nature is reinforced by the prominent positions league officers held in their churches. The league recruited such men to enhance its standing in the community, and the various denominations sent well-known, respected men to the league because they valued the league's work. Reverend Marion Porter, Oklahoma league treasurer from 1903 until 1923, was a presiding elder in the Enid district of the Methodist Episcopal Church in 1905.[36] Reverend W. J. Moore, a member of the league board of trustees from 1912 until 1918 and of the league's headquarters committee from 1920 until 1925, was chairman of the Southern Methodist Church Sunday school board. Reverend Charles L. Brooks, named to the league board of trustees in 1915, was presiding elder of the McAlester district conference of Oklahoma's Southern Methodist Church and was selected in 1920 as the secretary of the board of church extension for the Southern Methodist Church based in Louisville, Kentucky.[37] Turning to league officers from Oklahoma's Christian churches, Reverends D. A. Wickizer, J. M. Monroe, and A. L. Spicer each served as state corresponding secretary to the American Christian Missionary Society. Wickizer was a league trustee, whereas Monroe and Spicer served on the headquarters committee.[38] Oklahoma's Southern Baptist and Presbyterian churches also selected men of note to the state league. Reverend J. M. Clark, served on the league board of trustees and as the superintendent of evangelism and home missions for the Oklahoma Presbyterian Church.[39] Reverend J. B. Rounds, who later served on the league's headquarters committee and as a trustee, was president of the Baptist young persons conventions in 1907 and 1908. Reverend W. S. Wiley, a member of the league board of trustees from 1909 until 1918, was the first education secretary for Oklahoma Baptist University and later served as state field secretary for the Sunday school board of the Southern Baptist Convention.[40] Reverend E. D. Cameron, a league trustee from 1913 to 1916, succeeded Wiley as education secretary for Oklahoma Baptist University.[41] These men held important religious positions, which gained them the respect of their communities; their positions in the league conveyed respect to that body also.

Many of the ministers involved with the Oklahoma league also were prominent in secular activities and organizations. Reverend Harper sat on the Oklahoma City school board and attended the statehood convention as a delegate from Oklahoma County.[42] Reverend Wiley helped to draft the local platform of the Democratic Party in Muskogee.[43] Reverend E. O. Whitwell, a member of the league headquarters committee from 1909 until 1918, ran for Congress in 1913.[44] Reverend J. E. Disch, Oklahoma league treasurer from 1914 until 1917, chaired the Oklahoma County election board and later the Washington County Anti–Horse Thief Association.[45] The reputation of these men extended beyond church congregations.

League officers, like Reverend I. Frank Roach, held influential state positions. Secretary for the Oklahoma league and a member of its headquarters committee from 1916 until 1922, Roach worked for the Oklahoma council of defense during the First World War. Governor Robert Williams created state and county defense councils in August 1917 to support the war effort by organizing and promoting loan drives and by rooting out subversives around the state. Reverends Frank Barrett and H. H. Hulton, members of the league headquarters committee during the war, also toured the state speaking for the council of defense. Barrett served on the Oklahoma County council of defense as well.[46]

An atmosphere of intolerance formed in Oklahoma during the war as its residents sought to demonstrate their state's loyalty to the

U.S. cause by squelching any dissent, which was often the work of state and local defense councils. Suspicion of those new to the nation and those possessing immoderate political views continued after the shooting ended in November 1918. When, in the following summer, Governor James B. A. Robertson created a state commission to Americanize Oklahoma's small immigrant population, it included Reverend G. I. Gordon, a former league trustee.[47] His appointment demonstrates the Oklahoma league's weight in state government and its sympathy toward the Americanization program.

The league's influence extended to other political arenas. In 1919, Governor J. Robertson formed a three-man commission to investigate a short-lived coal miners' strike. Reverend Roach was a member, as was judge W. L. Eagleton, whom the league had warmly endorsed earlier for one of Oklahoma's district courts. The third member of the commission, John J. Gerlach, had ties both to the league and the Oklahoma council of defense. The commission's report was unsympathetic toward the strikers, stating that work conditions in the mines were good, though dangerous. They concluded that the strike was unjustified.[48] As members of Oklahoma's respectable, middle-class society, the commission had little understanding of and appreciation for the life and work experiences of the miners. Robertson's selection of these three, to the exclusion of any working-class men, speaks to the governor's view of organized labor; and his bias against working-class groups was not unique among Oklahoma office holders.[49] By contrast, the presence of league officers in these secular positions augmented their prestige and tightened the league's hold on the moral high ground in its crusade against liquor.

Those Oklahoma league officers and trustees who were laymen also held respectable, middle-class positions in their communities. Dr. A. Grant Evans, a league trustee from 1909 until 1912, was active in the Oklahoma City Young Men's Christian Association and served as the second president of the University of Oklahoma. The Oklahoma state Sunday school association elected Laughbaum to lead its temperance department and to chair of the temperance Committee of the synod of Oklahoma Presbyterian Church,

U.S.A.[50] Wetumka banker H. H. Holman, an Oklahoma delegate to the 1913 Committee of One Thousand and a league trustee during the war, had been a senator in the first state legislature. He also served on the Hughes County council of defense during the war. Oil man W. J. Milburn, also a member of the Committee of One Thousand and subsequently league treasurer from 1918 to 1919, served a term in the Oklahoma House of Representatives.[51] Attorney H. S. Braucht, league vice president from 1909 until 1910 and a trustee until 1918, briefly served as the Kay County attorney.[52]

C. L. Stealey, Oklahoma league president from 1909 until 1920, organized the Oklahoma Cotton Growers' Association in 1920 and served as general manager of that 52,000-member body for the next six years.[53] Five doctors held leadership positions in the league, including Dr. Thomas P. Howell of Davis, active in the state Democratic Party and a member of the state Methodist education board, and Dr. J. G. Street of Oklahoma City, active in the Oklahoma division of the united Confederate veterans.[54] Through these men, the league gained a respect that stretched well beyond religious circles.

Nor was the prominence of Oklahoma's league officers limited to the Sooner State. Dr. Evans was provisional secretary and organizer of the Oklahoma state branch of the Social Center Association of America. Among its national officers, this organization counted Josiah Strong and Louis D. Brandeis in 1912.[55] In 1915, Governor Williams named Dr. Cameron as a delegate to that year's southern commercial congress and chose the league's Reverend J. W. Mosely and Laughbaum as Oklahoma representatives to the southern sociological congress.[56] These men circulated with some of the nation's leading reformers. Like other progressive reformers of the period, they sought to improve society, locally and throughout the state. The destruction of the old-time saloon and the liquor industry that supported it seemed a certain means to accomplish their goals.

The Oklahoma league operatives were respected, middle-class leaders in their communities. In Muskogee, for instance, several ministers were active in the state league, including Reverends Asa P. Beal, D. R. Martin, and O. C. Bronston of the Methodist Episcopal churches; Reverend Brooks of the Methodist Episcopal Church, South; and Reverends Wiley and Cameron of the Southern Baptist churches. This organization reflected the middle-class perspectives of its members. Notably absent were wage-earning men and labor organizations.

Muskogee's working class did not show much interest in local league affiliates. In 1907 the Muskogee Commercial Club voted to create a local law and enforcement league. Many of the officers of these leagues were active in the state league as well. Reverend Wiley presided over the Muskogee law enforcement league and Reverend Beal sat on the membership committee. In all, the eighteen members of the various committees included six ministers and one doctor. These men pledged themselves to work toward "civic rite-ousness."[57] None were working-class men, though Muskogee wage earners were active in causes that directly affected their livelihood during this period.

In November 1908, 106 of Muskogee's public works employees presented a signed petition to Oklahoma labor commissioner Charles L. Daugherty urging him to investigate violation of the eight-hour law as it applied to public workers. None of these 106 men participated in or supported the Oklahoma league or its local affiliate, the Muskogee law-and-order league.[58] Similarly, the list of officers for the Oklahoma state conference of Bricklayers and Masons International Union of America contained no names associated with the Oklahoma league.[59] In Oklahoma's second-largest city, wage earners lent little support to the liquor crusade, and vice versa, the liquor crusaders demonstrated little interest in working-class issues. Oklahoma was not an anomaly in this as the prohibition campaign pitted middle-class reformers against working-class groups throughout the nation in the early twentieth century.[60]

The middle-class merchants and professionals of the Oklahoma league conducted the prohibition campaign, seeking to better their society locally and regionally by destroying the retail liquor industry. They saw no redeeming value in the old-time saloon. The Oklahoma league, which overtook the WCTU as the leading dry proponent after the turn of the new century, epitomized the class-based nature of the anti-liquor crusade. Men of position in their churches and communities served as the face of the league. Oklahoma's early governors relied on this organization to supplement their meager enforcement staffs, granting the league considerable influence throughout the state. The league's social cachet led to the appointment of operatives to posts having little to do with liquor enforcement. They served on state labor dispute commissions and national sociological and commercial committees. They were active in political parties locally and at the state level and held elected offices. Religious organizations selected league men for instructional and administrative positions within their denominations. These men were a part of the respectable element of mainstream Oklahoma society that opposed the less standard working-class elements of society.[61]

Oklahoma's liquor industry was not synonymous with radical politics, but the two shared the disparagement of the respected middle classes. In contrast to many of the issues that divided people along class lines, the differences over prohibition did not arise from economic considerations but from cultural ones. The liquor issue pitted a middle-class culture, championed by the Oklahoma league, against a working-class saloon culture. The respected merchants and professionals who supported the liquor ban, viewed the saloon as a source of numerous sins and social evils. Oklahoma wage earners saw the saloon, legal or illegal, as a place to socialize and recreate. This class-based cultural conflict was at the root of the liquor debate.

CHAPTER SEVEN

Wet Oklahoma

Liquor Men and the Saloon

The men of the Oklahoma Anti-Saloon League sought to remove the liquor industry from the state's economic and cultural landscape, and the saloon keepers fought to keep liquor flowing freely. Saloons were for-profit ventures; area liquor men engaged in this traffic to make money. This fact was lost on prohibition supporters as they groped for a solution to the liquor problem. Bootleggers ignored those cultural impulses that turned dry proponents against the saloon or reasoned that the liquor trade's opportunities for profit outweighed such considerations. Although some women sold liquor, most saloon keepers and bootleggers were men. Men also dominated organized efforts to defeat prohibition in Oklahoma.

Liquor had been both illegal and readily available in Indian Territory in the last decades of the nineteenth century. Frank James's Long Branch saloon dispensed liquor to early Vinita residents. Bill Sennett's Coyote saloon at the junction of the Arkansas and Cimarron rivers was the first business in the territorial town of Sennett. In the rural areas surrounding territorial Tulsa, bootleggers visited communities at night, shouting to residents that they had whiskey to sell. Near Henryetta, a man sold whiskey to thirsty miners from his log cabin, three hundred yards from the Whitehead No. 2 mines. He announced the arrival of each shipment by firing into the air three times, a signal area drinking men understood.[1]

Some liquor men accumulated large fortunes in the trade. Al Simco bought Hines Beer in Kansas City for $729 a lot and resold the same amount in Indian Territory for $1,100, earning $100,000 in a short time. William Creekmore reportedly amassed a million dollars from bootlegging before his federal conviction in 1915. Dating back to the early territorial period, liquor men brought whiskey up from Texas on pack mules along what became known as the Whiskey Trail. This narrow path stretched north from Gainesville, Texas, roughly following the current route of Interstate 35, across the Red River and through the Arbuckle Mountains into the Chickasaw lands. The Arbuckle portion of this trail became notorious for numerous liquor thefts. Some early Oklahomans placed the Whiskey Trail farther east, from Denison, Texas, past Okmulgee, and north to Coffeeville, Kansas. Still others asserted that the Whiskey Trail began at Ft. Smith, Arkansas, and ran southwest into the Choctaw lands, terminating at the town of Kiowa near McAlester. These divergent accounts suggest that several trails into Indian Territory bore liquor traffic, leading locals to refer to each as "the Whiskey Trail."[2]

In this lucrative trade, enterprising liquor men quickly bounced back from setbacks such as arrest by federal authorities. After release from jail, they begged nickels and dimes until they accumulated twenty-five cents. With this they bought half a pint of alcohol in Arkansas, poured it into a pint bottle and filled it with water. Slipping back into Indian Territory, bootleggers sold the watered-down whiskey to blacks working in the eastern river bottomlands and thus quickly built back their liquor trade.[3] Selling liquor required only slight start-up costs. Anyone willing to risk arrest and possessing sufficient intelligence could try his or her hand at the trade.

The region's limited number of federal officers prevented effective enforcement of the liquor ban and encouraged some officials to abuse their power. Federal marshals around McAlester regularly stopped travelers and charged them with transporting liquor. Those arrested could pay a one-hundred-dollar fine on the spot or challenge the charge in a Ft. Smith, Arkansas, court. Many chose to pay the fine rather than travel out of their way to face an uncertain verdict. Enforcement officials benefited financially if the accused challenged the fine, because the government paid them for transporting prisoners to court regardless of the case's outcome. Many officers supplemented their meager salaries in this way, and some planted whiskey on unsuspecting travelers to generate additional revenue for themselves and to demonstrate their diligence in their job.[4] This tactic became sufficiently common that some travelers reacted violently if an officer demanded to search their wagons or saddle bags. This practice presaged similar corruption problems during statewide and national prohibition.

Shortly after Oklahoma Territory formed in 1889, licensed saloons dotted the business sections of numerous towns. Oklahoma City's saloon district (Hell's Half Acre) became notorious. The territorial capital of Guthrie sported forty-four saloons shortly after the first land run. Establishments, such as the Reaves Brothers Saloon, Pady Shea's Saloon, the Blue Bell Saloon, and the Same Old Moses Saloon, were not marginal businesses. Territorial government offices were even located above the Same Old Moses. Tom Mix, the cowboy actor, once worked at the Blue Bell.[5] These saloons were not hidden in dark alleys; they were a vital part of the local community.

The retail liquor industry became prominent throughout the region. Saloons opened in Lawton on its establishment in 1901; ultimately ninety-six saloons operated in that territorial community, though its population totaled only 5,562 at statehood. Lawton's ratio of saloons to residents — one to fifty-eight — was much larger than that of major U.S. cities criticized as wet; for example, temperance groups sought to limit the number of saloons to one per five hundred residents in Milwaukee, Wisconsin. Shawnee, adjacent to the Seminole Nation, contained sixteen saloons in the 1890s, though its population totaled only 3,462 in 1900. At statehood, Shawnee contained 10,955 people and thirty saloons.[6]

Saloons became commonplace in smaller territorial communities as well. The proportion of saloons to population in Sayre and Granite was less than one to two hundred. Lexington, along the Canadian River dividing Indian and Oklahoma territories, contained fewer than twenty-five hundred residents during the territorial period, yet supported eleven saloons. The tiny community of Ralston, bordering the Osage Reservation, contained ten saloons before statehood. Kingfisher (population 2,214 in 1907) contained sixteen saloons; Woodward (population 1,500 in 1907) contained nine; Enid (population 10,087 in 1907) contained nineteen; Marshall (population 400 in 1903) contained five saloons. The saloon became a fixture throughout the territories. The high number of saloons in large and small communities alike belies not only the availability of liquor but also the saloon's accepted position in these early towns and cities. Several small towns along the border between Oklahoma and Indian territories relied so heavily on the saloon industry for their economic well-being that they virtually disappeared during dry statehood.[7]

The saloon's physical appearance, which was influenced by legal statutes, was distinctive. Typically, large picture windows facing the street flanked the front door. Local officials often stipulated that a saloon's interior and its occupants be visible to passersby. Proprietors displayed varieties of whiskey, brandy, and wine in these windows to entice customers. Many saloons contained two bars, one at which whiskey was served and one at which wine was sold. Mirrors surrounded the wine bar and screened it from the rest of the room. Saloons contained no furniture because territorial law forbid chairs in them, though patrons could rest a foot on the brass rail attached to the front of the bar near the floor. Proprietors displayed still more bottles of liquor behind the bar. A side or rear entrance was designated for black patrons, who tended to gather separately in the saloon's rear.

Many saloon operators provided gambling facilities in a rear room, connected to the saloon front by an arched doorway. Common games included roulette, craps, faro, klondike, keno, and poker, which often warranted its own room for greater privacy. An employee watched over or conducted each game, making the

Men gather at a Ponca City saloon, circa 1900. The territorial government banned chairs from saloons to discourage extended stays by patrons. Also note the absence of female customers.

saloon a significant employer in a small community; a saloon employed as many as thirty men in these capacities.[8] During a community's early years, saloons, like other businesses, resided in more makeshift structures. In newly settled towns, many early saloons were nothing more than tents, and wooden planks lain across barrels served as a bar.[9]

Most saloon patrons were adult men. As one Oklahoman recalled, "Not many women drank in those days and the ones who did never drank in public."[10] By most accounts, few men under the age of twenty-one entered saloons, though there was no identification check required. Someone who claimed to be of age was considered thus, unless the proprietor was acquainted with the young man and knew otherwise.[11]

Illegal liquor varied from its legal counterpart in price and source. In the 1880s, liquor men sold whiskey at two dollars per pint bottle. A Savanna area merchant purchased whiskey from outside the territory and resold it at a profit to augment his grocery sales.[12] In this way, then, respected community members also involved themselves in the clandestine liquor industry during the territorial period. Availability also influenced the price of liquor. In 1890s-Guthrie, a mug of beer sold for a nickel, which was about the same price as a glass of water. Bottled beer sold for thirty-five cents in Perry saloons. El Reno's illegal all-night saloons sold beer for fifty cents per bottle. A saloon in the small town of Burnett offered its patrons beer at twenty-five cents for a glass or mug, and whiskey at fifty cents for a pint bottle.[13]

Other factors also influenced the price of liquor. El Reno's saloons saw an unusual amount of business in 1901 because many men came to register for land drawings in Caddo, Kiowa, and Comanche counties. The construction of a rail line to Lawton brought working men to the El Reno saloons, heightening liquor demand and price. Prices also varied according to the customers' ability to pay. A former bootlegger recounted that he sold whiskey to Cherokee Indians for ten dollars per quart on days when they received money from the government.

Some saloon customers did not pay immediately. The Burnett saloon offered lines of credit to sixty-one people in 1902. Several of these were quite lengthy, suggesting that some patrons were engaged in farming or other endeavors that did not provide a regular income. The rural nature of this small Pottawatomie County community reinforces this supposition. The saloon, whether large or small, was a male institution; only one of the Burnett saloon's sixty-one customers was female. Burnett, like the saloon located there, would cease to exist after statehood.[14]

Statewide prohibition reduced the price of liquor late in 1907. Whiskey in Tulsa joints fell from twenty-five to fifteen cents per drink, and some establishments offered customers two drinks for a quarter. These falling liquor prices suggest that Oklahomans initially reduced their consumption when it became illegal or that they stockpiled liquor before the ban took effect. The price of beer rebounded and then dropped again in the autumn of 1910 to fifteen cents per bottle (or two bottles for twenty-five cents) in anticipation of that year's referendum on prohibition.[15] The newspapers' mention of prices indicates a continued availability of liquor in dry Oklahoma. In many communities, however, the liquor men could not openly engage in this trade anymore. The liquor industry persisted in the Sooner State, but it was no longer a part of the respected commerce of main street.

To avoid public scrutiny and arrest, bootleggers often selected odd, seemingly innocent sites from which to sell their product. In the oil boomtown of Cleveland, one of the best known sources of liquor was a partially completed building near the railroad tracks. Liquor men stashed their contraband in this structure, and men strolled by throughout the day to purchase whiskey and beer. Near Okmulgee, a bootlegger concealed his liquor in a brush-filled area and for twenty-five cents allowed customers to suck as much liquor as they cared from a straw protruding from the bushes. In Muskogee, small-time liquor men sold liquor by the drink on the streets from flasks they carried in their coat pockets. As several of these bootleggers were black, local authorities adopted the habit of confronting any black man who wore a long coat (an early twentieth-century example of racial profiling). An Oklahoma City cab driver sold liquor to passengers and other motorists from an ice box he had installed in his cab.[16]

Bootleggers devised various means to conceal their wares. A woman near Prague hid whiskey in bundles of baby's clothes that she washed in a stream each day. While at the stream, she delivered the whiskey to waiting customers. A woman in the Osage Nation carried whiskey bottles suspended on long strings from a belt beneath her long loose skirts. Having prearranged payment, she strolled into the nearby woods and on encountering one of her customers, reached beneath her dress and cut the string allowing the bottle to quietly fall to the ground with no break in her stride. Other bootleggers hid pints of whiskey in watermelons, hollowed-out saddle horns, horse collars, or steel wagon and automobile axles. (A hollow axle held several gallons of liquor.)[17]

But the liquor trade also attracted danger. The middle-class champions of prohibition viewed the old-time saloon as a center of violence and crime, and some of the liquor establishments lived up to this image. Perry's liquor district, known locally as Hell's Half Acre, frequently served the Doolin-Dalton gang during the early territorial years. Asher, Avoca, Wanette, Earlsboro, and Keokuk Falls early on became known as dangerous saloon towns. Refusing a drink in these communities was grounds for violence, even gunplay. Early Shawnee became known for its drunken brawls; Violet Springs gained the moniker "City of the Dead" when it designated a portion of its graveyard for those killed in saloon altercations; fighting was commonplace in Lexington's saloons and often spilled into the streets, making them nearly impassable.[18]

The town of Corner became one of the most notorious for crime. Situated at the junction of the Chickasaw and Seminole nations and Pottawatomie County at a bend in the Canadian River, Corner was little more than three saloons in the river's bottom lands. Its secluded location made it a regular stop for the Doolin-Dalton gang and other outlaws. During the 1890s, an area doctor treated hundreds of men injured in Corner saloon fights, and fifty murders occurred at the three establishments. On one occasion, a patron shot a man standing on top of his cotton gin during a flood, merely to watch him fall into the water. When a new owner took possession of the Old Corner Saloon in 1900, he hired two Texas gunmen as protection. The saloons at Corner, symbolizing the lawless West, were the type of dangerous magnets for criminal activity that Oklahoma's Anti-Saloon League and other dry proponents hoped to close forever.[19]

Of course, Oklahoma's less infamous saloons also saw violence. In the late territorial era, Woodward received a jolt that convinced it to close all liquor establishments. Jack Garvey's was a prominent saloon, featuring an orchestra, gambling, and drinks. In 1904, Jack Love and Temple Houston, having lost a land decision to attorney Ed Jennings, shot him dead while he sat at Garvey's. A jury acquitted Houston and Love of all charges because Woodward residents decided to direct their wrath against all saloons. Ministers circulated petitions to prevent the renewal of liquor licenses, and Woodward became completely dry before statehood as a result.[20]

But even after Oklahoma became dry, saloon violence continued. The Hump, an illegal roadhouse located near Drumright along
the border between Creek and Payne counties, provided its staff
and patrons quick escape should enforcement officials from one
county or the other come calling. Situated in the booming Cushing
oil field, the Hump sported a bulletproof gun turret in the center
of the main barroom from which an armed guard deterred both
potential thieves and eager enforcement officers. Following unsuccessful efforts by local authorities, state and federal officials closed
it permanently and bulldozed the structure to prevent its reopen-
ing. In so doing, they found several human skeletons beneath the
roadhouse.[21]

Sapulpa, in the Glenn Pool oil field, also saw its share of saloon
violence. Several shootings took place on Main Street, and the local
jail proved too small to accommodate the number of drunks arrested nightly. At Kiefer, gunplay and knife fights became common.
The promise of high wages in the oil patch attracted young laboring
men: Women and children were scarce; many workers were single,
and those who were married initially refused to bring their families
to the lawless region. Kiefer did not calm until some of the oil
workers risked bringing their families to the region. "With the 'respectable women' came a demand for law and order. . . . When the
Bowery's worst offenders opposed the 'civilizing' of their community, Kiefer's more respectable citizens formed a vigilance committee and drove them out of town."[22] The issue of respectability lies at
the heart of the struggle between Oklahoma wets and drys. The
latter, partially as a result of the antics of some saloon patrons in such
wide-open towns as Kiefer, captured the mantle of respectability in
that struggle and painted the saloon and its defenders as nonrespectable and as a hindrance to progress both nationally and locally.

Despite the notoriety that the Oklahoma saloons gained with
the general public, many area saloons were relatively peaceful places
operated by reasonable people. Clinton's first Sunday school classes
were in a local saloon. Early residents of Keokuk Falls, one of the
infamous border towns, asserted that their community's wild reputation was overblown; most people were law abiding, and saloon

men often taught Sunday school.[23] Although during the prohibition fight, area clergymen and the Oklahoma league stressed the dichotomy and competition between the church and the saloon, the two cultural institutions were not irreconcilable in the early years of these communities.

Saloons, in fact, often fell short of the violent reputation dry proponents attributed to them. The Burnett saloon saw little raucous activity. An El Reno journalist described the saloon as a "drowsy unoffensive little place where the majority of people drank moderately."[24] The image of the coarse, greedy saloon operator also was inaccurate. Bartlesville saloon man Ernest Lewis was popular locally, known for his friendships, even with many who disliked his occupation, and as a friend to the poor. He died from wounds suffered during a liquor raid by overzealous federal marshals. The liquor industry, then, was less nefarious than its opponents might have suggested. It was an integral part of local communities, such as McAlester, where area residents occasionally paid for music lessons with ten-gallon cans of White Mule whiskey rather than money.[25]

Several Oklahomans also challenged the assertion that prohibition reduced excessive drinking. Though El Reno supported twenty-two saloons in the 1890s, one resident asserted that the town contained more drunks under prohibition than it had during the territorial days. A former grocer in the Osage Reservation also argued that people drank more during statewide prohibition than they had in the territorial days.[26] Such arguments were lost on the middle-class reformers of the Oklahoma league, the Oklahoma Woman's Christian Temperance Union (WTCU), and similar dry organizations.

Part of the battle for wet advocates was overcoming the reputation for violence that several notorious saloons created and that reformers attributed to all liquor establishments Oklahomans were anxious to shed their region's violent territorial image, and some saw prohibition as a means to this end.[27] Dry proponents argued that the saloon was inherently violent, though the evidence suggests otherwise. Liquor was a normal part of life in many communities, and some liquor men held places of standing in their towns before prohibition. Dry organizations, ignoring this, portrayed all saloons as breeding grounds for crime and immorality and all saloon operators as harmful to societal progress. Despite evidence to the contrary, the Oklahoma league enjoyed considerable success in painting the entire liquor industry as antagonistic toward organized religion and hence, nonrespectable.

When liquor sales in Oklahoma became illegal, many saloon operators moved into other lines of work or left the state. Guthrie's Henry Braun, local agent for the Pabst Brewing Company and manager of several area breweries and saloons, closed his liquor businesses and focused on his various Oklahoma ice plants. J. B. Leech, an Edgewood saloon operator, opened a grocery store in Comanche after statehood. Bush N. Bowman closed his five saloons in Guthrie, Blackwell, and Perry and opened a cigar and billiard parlor in the latter community. Jim Williams, a Guthrie saloon keeper, worked in a saloon in Denver, Colorado, for a year before returning to Guthrie as a police officer and restaurant owner.[28] August Ille converted his saloon into a hardware store. Moses Weinberger, owner of seven Guthrie saloons, sold his saloon equipment for a pittance and went into the transfer business. Those men that were respected members of local communities left the liquor industry at the end of 1907, and because the demand for liquor remained high after prohibition took effect, others, perhaps less respectable, moved into these ventures.[29]

Prohibition turned over the liquor business to less respectable people or prompted previously respectable people to engage in activities now deemed illegal. Peter Eischen and his family were well-established members of the small German community of Okarche, receiving regular mention in the local society news, and their business, Eischen's Saloon, was a prominent part of the main street business district. When liquor became illegal, the Eischens purchased a billiard table and opened a pool hall where their saloon had been. Dry proponents suspected many such pool halls of selling liquor, though the Okarche press made no mention of liquor violations at Eischen's.

Following the repeal of national prohibition in 1933, Oklahoma legalized the sale of drinks containing 3.2 percent alcohol or less. Eischen's son Nick and grandson Jack opened a beer bar known as the Tap Room, which to this day is one of the oldest bars in Oklahoma.[30] The demand for liquor in Okarche continued despite prohibition, and those who attempted to meet that demand engaged in a business that produced frowns among the respectable elements of greater Oklahoma society.

The liquor question was about respectability. Most respectable citizens, those who owned significant property and were long-standing members of their communities, viewed the saloon with growing disdain. The Oklahoma league and its dry supporters played on this sentiment, contrasting their supporters — ministers, merchants, prominent farmers, and professionals — with those of the area's various short-lived wet political organizations. The dry forces, which were the picture of respectability according to the league, were pitted against an army of outlaws, drunks, and those in the pay of or duped by the corrosive liquor industry. Supporters of the wet organizations in Oklahoma saw themselves as respectable members of society also, but theirs was a minority message that the league and other dry advocates buried in a flurry of literature and speeches calling for the end of the nonrespectable saloon.

The Citizens League, the Sons of Washington, the German-American Association, and the Businessmen's League each took on the Oklahoma league in the first two decades of the new century. The brief existence of these wet groups belies their organizational limitations and explains their failures against the Oklahoma league. They did not possess the league's staying power. Several of these organizations shared members: men who campaigned against constitutional prohibition in 1907 under one banner and sought to repeal the ban in 1910 under different banners. Despite this overlapping membership, these groups cooperated in a limited way only. They presented various arguments against prohibition: It would hurt the state economy; it would cost more than the state could afford; it would infringe on people's personal liberty. These were legitimate criticisms of the liquor ban, but they did not resonate with Oklahoma voters.

The leaders of the organized opposition to prohibition in the territories and early state tended to be businessmen and professionals, such as Isaac B. Levy of Guthrie, Z. T. Burton of Tishomingo, William D. Cardwell of Oklahoma City, and Dr. John Threadgill of Oklahoma City. They were poorly coordinated and often stained by the league as cronies of the liquor industry, though Threadgill, in particular, lent a social legitimacy to the wet cause.

The first prominent wet organization to form in the region was the Citizens League. Levy, a banker and territorial house representative from Guthrie, and Enid real estate agent J. P. Goulding formed the league in May 1907. They campaigned actively against prohibition before the September referendum that year, leading dry proponents to criticize their group as a mere front for the liquor industry. Independent of the Citizens League, attorney Burton and W. F. Gilmer of Durant formed a Durant-based anti-prohibition organization in the summer of 1907. Following the September 1907 vote in favor of prohibition, the Durant group disappeared and the Citizens League sought but failed to convince the Oklahoma attorney general that the prohibition clause was illegal. The Citizens League also dissolved within a year.[31]

Part of the problem with the Citizens League was that they conceded much to the Oklahoma league. It accepted the latter's arguments that the saloon was a social evil, though Levy's group argued that this evil should be controlled and regulated rather than banned. The Citizens League saw little redeeming value in the regulated saloon beyond its contribution to public revenues. This approach separated the group from the saloon customers who, by their very patronage, demonstrated that they did not share this disdain for the saloon. Ultimately, this disconnect between patrons and the Citizen's League the latter's attempts to turn out wet voters for the 1907 prohibition referendum.

The wet cause was hurt further by the Oklahoma league's charges that prohibition critics were mere foot soldiers for a corrupt liquor industry that cared more for its own profits than for economic development and progress in the state. This message drowned out the Citizens League's warnings that prohibition would increase crime and other social ills, predictions that were born out after 1907 and in the nation as a whole after 1920.

After the Citizens League disappeared, another wet group formed. In July 1908, Threadgill, J. M. Haley, and Lewis Eichop of Oklahoma City organized the Sons of Washington. They campaigned across the new state seeking signatures on a petition to get the liquor question placed before voters in a second referendum. The organization's also opposed the controversial liquor dispensary system established in 1908, hoping that its closure would turn more Oklahomans against prohibition.[32]

By October of 1908, the Sons of Washington claimed to have organizations in each town and city, though its statewide membership was only 20,000 by September 1909. Oklahoma City attorney Cardwell served as the organization's secretary, and its active members included two state legislators. The Sons of Washington campaigned against the dispensary system in 1908 and then refocused their efforts in 1909 on collecting signatures on a petition for a second vote on prohibition. The Sons of Washington's legislative committee petitioned an uncooperative Governor Charles Haskell to resubmit the liquor question to voters. Haskell delayed until 1910 when the Oklahoma Supreme Court ruled that he must accept the petition and schedule a second referendum.[33] Following the 1910 liquor vote, the Sons of Washington, like the wet organizations before it, vanished from Oklahoma's political landscape.

The powerful Oklahoma league outmaneuvered the Sons of Washington, as it had other wet proponents. The Sons of Washington leadership, although composed of middle-class professionals, did have some ties to wage earners in the state that damaged its image among the middle class. For example, attorney Cardwell prosecuted Oklahoma City area businesses that illegally blacklisted workers.[34] This "friend" of labor and secretary of the Sons of Washington was the principal author of the local option amendment that voters rejected in 1910.

The Sons of Washington were not alone in the prohibition fight, either. Aiding them in the 1910 campaign against prohibition were the German-American Association, the Oklahoma High License and Local Option Association, and the Oklahoma Business Men's League. The latter claimed 30,000 members and representation in all counties of the state during the height of the 1910 campaign.[35] These organizations enjoyed brief durations with the exception of the German-American Association.

The German-American Association dated back to 1897 when delegates from nine northern Oklahoma Territory counties resolved to oppose prohibition and lynching and to support equality before the law. It campaigned against statewide prohibition in 1907 in those communities that contained notable German populations, arguing that the liquor ban infringed upon personal liberties.[36] This approach distinguished the association from the Citizens League and the Sons of Washington, which emphasized prohibition's negative economic consequences. The German-American Association threw its support behind the Sons of Washington in 1910. President Henry Braun and the association resolved that prohibition created hypocrisy (because officials could not enforce it), made criminals of good people, targeted the poorer elements of society, robbed Oklahoma of the tax revenue from liquor establishments, and infringed on the inherent rights of individuals.[37]

A vocal part of Oklahoma politics, the association's political clout was limited to the few primarily rural counties where most of the German-American population resided. The 1910 federal census puts Oklahoma's total population at 1,657,155, its German-born population at 10,089, and its German stock population (those whose parents were born in Germany) at 17,510. Most of the state's 27,599 German Americans, representing 1.7 percent of Oklahoma's total 1910 population, resided in Alfalfa, Garfield, Grant, Kay, Kingfisher, Logan, Noble, and Payne counties.[38]

Oklahoma's German population saw prohibition as part of a larger nativist campaign against immigrants and the children of immigrants. The Oklahoma league criticized German-American Associahtion members as foreigners who refused to become U.S. citizens, and the Presbyterian churches of Oklahoma equated "all German-Americans with gamblers, bootleggers, and anarchists."[39] In this way dry proponents effectively discounted German cultural arguments that liquor consumption was a vital part of their European heritage. The league insisted that association members must abandon this aspect of their German culture to become full-fledged U.S. citizens. Such pronouncements made Oklahoma's German-American population acutely aware that mainstream society considered its culture beyond the bounds of respectability.

Criticism of and attacks on German Americans in the state escalated following the United States declaration of war against Germany in April 1917. State authorities ordered the closing of German schools and residents even burned German books. A Collinsville mob lynched Henry Rheimer because he had vocally supported a local German school that the community had closed. The police chief cut down Rheimer before he died, and the incensed citizenry vowed to prosecute him for expressing pro-German sentiment. The Oklahoma Council of Defense fed this animosity, vowing, "A blank wall and a firing squad may soon be the remedy for pro-Germanism in Oklahoma in the few sections where it exists."[40] This virulently anti-German mood squelched wet arguments that defended beer drinking as fundamental to German culture. Personal liberty arguments against prohibition also rang hollow; officials and citizens trampled civil liberties in Oklahoma and throughout the nation during the repressive war years and after.

The German-American Association and the various other wet organizations active in Oklahoma during the early twentieth century also suffered from the perception that they were mere fronts for a vested liquor interest that sought to increase its profits at society's expense. The Anti-Saloon League portrayed the German-American Association and the Sons of Washington as tools of the brewers and Braun's position as a regional wholesaler for Pabst did little to counter this image. Dry advocates charged out-of-state brewers with funding Oklahoma's anti-prohibition campaigns. Governor Haskell, in a speech supporting prohibition, claimed that St. Louis breweries had poured $30,000 into the 1907 campaign to keep prohibition out of the Oklahoma constitution. The league stated that the brewers spent even more money in Oklahoma during the 1910 campaign on prohibition.[41] The wet cause suffered from the perception that it was self-serving, whereas the dry cause successfully portrayed itself as altruistic.

The wets' 1910 defeat did not end efforts to resubmit the liquor question to Oklahoma voters. The Local Option Association formed in 1911, the Business Men's Protective League in 1913, and the United Civic Association in 1914, each seeking resubmission of the liquor question to the ballot.[42] None succeeded in bringing the question before Oklahoma voters again. As it had with previous organizations, the Oklahoma league painted these groups as fronts for the nonrespectable liquor industry. Oklahoma voters did not consider local option again until after the repeal of national prohibition in 1933.

Dry advocates' success in Oklahoma can be attributed to superior organization. The Citizens League, the Sons of Washington, the Business Mens' Protective League, and the United Civic Association existed briefly with little continuity or cooperation between, and none was a match for the Oklahoma league, which painted each group as the reincarnation of earlier organizations and as a front for a sinister liquor interest. The German-American Association enjoyed longevity, but its base of support in Oklahoma was quite small relative to the total population. Its social standing eroded still further during the First World War as it became a lightning rod for criticism of German culture.

Another hindrance to the wet cause was the sudden death of Threadgill in 1915. Physician, banker, owner of the Hotel Threadgill in Oklahoma City and a prominent Republican in the territorial legislature, he lent an air of respectability to the wet cause. He was a major general in the Oklahoma Confederate Veterans Association and belonged to the International Order of Odd Fellows, the Shriners, and the Knights Templar. From this position of social prominence, he publicly charged the Oklahoma league with demagoguery and misleading voters, though he described the ministers who promoted league doctrine as sincere men who believed they were telling the truth. This rather delicate criticism was one of the few attacks on the religiously based league. Most wet leaders did not enjoy Threadgill's social and political cachet and so did not dare to address the league so bluntly. Until his death, Threadgill provided the wet campaign with a respectable face. By comparison, the Oklahoma league coordinated the efforts of all anti-liquor organizations in the area after 1900 and kept clergymen at the forefront of its work.[43]

In the contest for respectability, the wet forces could not compete with the religiously affiliated league. The links that prohibitionists drew between the wet organizations and bootleggers — the least socially acceptable portion of the liquor industry — damaged the local option cause. Although the wet cause enjoyed some measure of respectability during the territorial period, it lost this ground shortly after statehood. The Oklahoma league's message, that it spoke for respectable Oklahomans and that opponents of prohibition endorsed the violent criminality associated with the saloon, overwhelmed any counter arguments from Oklahoma's ununited wet organizations.

CHAPTER EIGHT

The Oklahoma Liquor Question as a Class Issue

The profit motives that drove the liquor industry did not drive its customer base. Men entered saloons or purchased liquor on the streets for recreational purposes. For some, drinking alcohol was a part of the ethnic heritage they had brought with them from Europe. Oklahoma's immigrant population, however, constituted less than 10 percent of the total state population between 1900 and 1920. If these had been the only people consuming alcohol, area liquor men quickly would have gone broke or would have severely limited the size of their operations. The highly competitive nature of Oklahoma's liquor industry indicates that many saw opportunities for wealth because a large retail liquor market existed. This market comprised ethnic populations and the region's large working class. Miners working in the coal fields of southeastern Oklahoma or in the zinc and copper mines of northeastern Oklahoma and the roughnecks working in the Cleveland, Glenn Pool, Cushing, and Healdton oil fields supported saloons so faithfully that officials were unable or unwilling to enforce the liquor ban in those regions. Laboring men across the professions viewed drinking as a basic part of working-class culture.

Conversely, the Oklahoma Anti-Saloon League and its supporters were predominantly middle-class merchants and professionals. They tied their campaign to organized religion, particularly the evangelical faiths, and presented their efforts as a struggle between religion and the nefarious saloon, making support for prohibition a litmus test for respectability in Oklahoma. Wage earners demonstrated their opposition to prohibition by continuing to patronize illegal saloons. Liquor men, less concerned with cultural matters than with turning a profit, understood that a significant part of their customer base was working class and thus targeted regions containing concentrations of laborers. Much of this illegal commerce was undocumented. Enforcement officers, however, indicated that bootlegging and later moonshining were particularly problematic in mining districts, in the aforementioned oil fields, and among at least some itinerant agricultural workers.

Wage earners represented a significant part of the regional population long before statehood. Miners opened the first coal mines near McAlester in 1870, serviced soon after by the Missouri, Kansas, and Texas Railroad. By 1899 twenty-two coal mines operated in the Choctaw and Chickasaw lands of Indian Territory, many owned by railroad companies. The expanding mines and rail yards attracted a growing workforce.[1]

These wage earners possessed a strong proclivity for drinking. The Poteau area became raucous in the late 1880s when railroad workers brought the St. Louis and San Francisco and the Kansas City Southern lines through the region. The construction crews were "eager customers and free spenders" for area gamblers, bootleggers, and prostitutes.[2] Bootleggers sold liquor to black farm laborers in extreme eastern Oklahoma during the later territorial years. The Collinsville smelters and brick plants drew large numbers of wage earners, who supported a vibrant liquor traffic, particularly at the dance halls. In the small western community of Mountain View, which supported four saloons, one store, and one blacksmith, prosperity depended on construction of a nearby rail line, which brought wage earners to town.[3] Liquor also became a prominent commodity among the mining districts of Indian Territory. Area liquor men had identified their customer base: where large work gangs went, saloons or bootleggers followed.

Wage labor remained plentiful after statehood. The new government, seeking to improve the state's infrastructure, commissioned further railroad construction. One newspaper reported that, with the possible exception of Texas, Oklahoma led the nation in rail construction in 1912. That year, work crews laid nearly two hundred miles of track by September, and the corporation commission estimated that they would add another two hundred by year's end. Crews built new lines or extensions of existing lines from Wagoner to Miami in the northeast, from Henryetta to Oklahoma City across east central Oklahoma, from Beaver to the western end of the panhandle, and from the central region of the state to the western community of Cheyenne. All told, workers laid more than five hundred miles of rail in Oklahoma in the first five years following statehood.[4]

The young state's growing population and its booming mine and oil industries pushed railroad construction and liquor consumption higher. In 1913, workers built lines from Henryetta to the surrounding mining camps, from the Kansas border to Tulsa, and west from Ardmore through the Healdton oil field to Byers, Texas. The following year, workers extended a branch rail line into the Cushing oil field. In 1915 talk began of building an interurban rail line between Tulsa and the town of Cushing.[5] Wage earners flooded into the state not only to construct these rail lines but also to operate and maintain the state's growing rail network. They became regular customers of area liquor men.

Oklahoma's coal industry, though dangerous, also remained active after statehood. Despite the introduction of the United Mine Workers union and federal regulation of the Indian Territory mines in the late 1890s, coal mining remained a hazardous profession. In 1905, a mine explosion near Wilburton buried fifteen miners; in 1908 an oil lamp explosion entombed thirty men near Haileyville, only one of whom survived. In 1912, an explosion in the Sansbois mine killed seventy-three, the state's most devastating work accident to date.[6] Miners also endured less publicized injuries on a regular basis. Men and boys lost eyes, broke or severed limbs, and lost their lives as a result of faulty materials, inexperience in using those materials, or geographic factors over which they had little control. The violent nature of their workplace, where they spent the better part of most days, encouraged these workers to tolerate a level of saloon violence that alarmed middle-class reformers.

Mining was also an important part of the economy outside the southeast portion of the state. By 1912, the United Mine Workers had formed a local organization at Midway, northwest of Shawnee. Significant sources of coal were developed in Nowata County, in the northeast. Surface coal mining operations commenced near the northeast Oklahoma communities of Blue Jacket, Collinsville, Dawson, Tulsa, Broken Arrow, and Pryor. Coal was but one of the minerals extracted from the area; lead and zinc mining began near Peoria in the 1890s. After the turn of the century, lead and zinc operations began near the northeastern towns of Quapaw and Miami, in the Arbuckle Mountains and near Ardmore in south-central Oklahoma, and in the Wichita Mountains near Lawton in the southwest. In each of these areas mining communities formed, and, not coincidentally, several of these regions became notorious among liquor enforcement personnel for continued liquor violations. In 1912, the state mine inspector reported that Oklahoma's mining population had grown to more than 12,000.[7]

Officials recognized the close association between miners and the liquor industry during the territorial period. In 1907, federal liquor officer William E. "Pussyfoot" Johnson raided a village post office in the southeast based on reports that it was distributing liquor to area mine workers. He destroyed sixty bottles of Boranica, a type of liquor popular with miners. The following spring, authorities in Durant boarded a train and arrested a miner in possession of twenty-five pints of whiskey; fellow miners had paid him to transport the whiskey from Texas.[8] Another drink of choice for coal miners was Choctaw beer, an inexpensive, low-quality, and low-alcohol-content beverage common in Oklahoma before and after statehood. Many in the mining camps believed beer to hold medicinal properties that would improve one's health, whereas others argued that choc beer was more palatable and safer than the local water supply. Area women brewed or purchased much of this beverage while the men worked beneath ground. In addition, area bootleggers sold whiskey shipped into the region on the Muskogee, Kansas and Texas Railroad.[9] Liquor consumption was a standard feature of life in the mining districts, one which enforcement officers attempted to control if not eliminate.

Federal officials became acutely aware of illegal liquor activity in the mining districts of Coal and Latimer counties. In 1906, officers collected several hundred gallons of beer in a raid at the tiny community of Gowen. The *Coalgate Courier* reported in 1907 that raids at Lehigh and Coalgate netted one thousand and 200 gallons of liquor, respectively. These amounts were considerably less than that confiscated during operations in Tulsa and Oklahoma City, though the relatively meager populations of Gowen, Lehigh, and Coalgate suggest a much higher per capita consumption. Liquor raids also brought complaints of selective enforcement, "In Wilburton the Choctaw beer and cider joints are spasmodically raided while other concerns who sell the real stuff are never molested."[10]

Despite this attention from enforcement officials, liquor violations continued in the mining districts. State enforcement officer Fred S. Caldwell notified Governor Charles Haskell late in 1908 that Coalgate, population 3,255 in 1910, contained twenty-two establishments that had paid the federal liquor tax during that year in open defiance of state law. Lehigh, with a population of less than 2,500 people, contained ten such establishments.[11] On paydays at the mines in the Jack Fork Mountains, liquor men off loaded their product at a nearby abandoned railroad stop and then distributed the liquor by pack mule to area mining camps.[12]

Latimer County's mining districts also supported bootlegging. A September 1910 county criminal court docket contained forty cases, of which twenty-seven involved liquor violations. Officials gained convictions in only eight of these and held over the remainder on a continuance, prompting an editor to conclude that the authorities largely ignored prohibition. Another newspaper declared that the flagrant violation of liquor codes had created a state of emergency in the area. Charges of uneven enforcement arose again because some liquor peddlers suffered arrest, whereas others continued their operations unfettered.[13]

The presence of illegal liquor did not trouble these mining communities. The Oklahoma league blamed a local judge who had posed the first legal challenge to the search and seizure clauses of the prohibition statutes. Despite this criticism, voters repeatedly reelected the judge. An area newspaper asserted that 98 percent of people sought to evade the liquor ban, adding that the public sympathized with the liquor men against enforcement officials. This situation — a local populace that sided with the bootleggers — was worrisome and confusing to the league's middle-class constituency.[14]

The wet sentiment evident in the coal fields of the southeast might be attributed to the cultural traditions of the area's immigrant population. Miners came from Italy, France, Poland, and elsewhere in Europe to work the mines, and many viewed liquor consumption as a part of their cultural heritage. This ethnocultural explanation for liquor opposition breaks down, however, when examining other regions of the state that saw considerable bootlegging, such as the mining district of Ottawa County in northeast Oklahoma. Liquor violations there became acute after statehood as the lead and zinc mines expanded and more wage earners moved into the region. Unlike the coal fields of the southeast, however, Ottawa County contained a small foreign-born and foreign stock population, less than 5 percent of the total in 1910 and 1920.[15]

Despite Ottawa County's minor immigrant population, officials encountered extensive liquor operations in local mining camps. A Miami resident wrote to Governor Lee Cruce about the area bootlegging in 1911, but liquor violations continued, leading Cruce's successor, Robert L. Williams, to admit that prohibition could not be enforced in Ottawa County. County residents continued to press Governor Williams for a solution. A Miami attorney blamed the county's mining camps for the bootlegging and asked the governor to investigate local enforcement efforts. He urged Williams to not appoint anyone from the mining camp populations, "a large part of whom are not in sumpathy (sic) with the enforcement of the prohibition and anti-gambling laws."[16] Eventually, the county commissioners collected sufficient evidence against the sheriff to charge him with failing to enforce the liquor ban in the mining camps of Commerce, Cardin, Picher, and Lincolnville. The trial court transcripts note that each of the camps contained unconcealed liquor establishments.[17] The local population accepted these illegal enterprises and reelected officials who did not act against them. Liquor, whether legal or not, was integral to working-class culture in early Oklahoma; and, contrary to prohibition studies that pit a wet urban United States against a dry rural population, the worst liquor violations in Ottawa County occurred outside the prominent towns among makeshift mining camps.

Furthermore, liquor remained available in Oklahoma mining communities through the First World War. Late in 1919, when state coal miners joined a nationwide coal strike, Governor James B. A. Robertson sent troops in to force open the coal mines and sent investigators to assess conditions in the coal fields. The latter reported that most of the illegal Choctaw beer joints had closed when the troops arrived, but at least one remained open at Hartshorne throughout the labor action. The detectives described John Petee, whiskey peddler to the miners, as a dangerous agitator who posed a threat to state and national governments.[18] Reports such as this buttressed dry advocates' claims that liquor not only inhibited worker productivity and a man's ability to provide for his family but also produced radicals labeled as un-American in the years after the war.

Whereas the railroads and coal mines drew many workers to early Oklahoma, other endeavors also attracted wage earners to the area. Major dam-building projects began near Muskogee in 1907 and near Ft. Gibson in 1913, each of which required a host of laborers. The U.S. entrance into the First World War halted such infrastructure projects, but these resumed at the war's conclusion when the state proposed an extensive system of improved roads and highways. The legislature called for construction of a bridge over the Canadian River linking Oklahoma and Canadian counties, a bridge spanning the Arkansas River near Ft. Gibson, and road-building projects in Tulsa, Okmulgee, Bryan, and McCurtain counties.[19] These projects also required large numbers of workers; men who, by and large, became regular customers for bootleggers.

The liquor men also followed Oklahoma's booming oil industry. Although most wells required only two men to maintain them, the vast number of oil derricks in the Glenn Pool, Cushing, and Healdton oil fields, and in the smaller fields of Muskogee, Osage, Pawnee, Nowata, and Okmulgee counties, drew numerous wage earners. Before statehood, nearly 250 oil wells operated near Kiefer, which was notorious for its illegal saloons. Two hundred wells surrounded the small boomtown of Mounds. Oklahoma wells were highly productive. Those in the relatively small Boynton field yielded 2,500 barrels of oil daily in 1915, and the various wells in the Cushing field produced 300,000 barrels per day.[20] This impressive production created a corresponding need for storage and transportation facilities, which in turn attracted more laborers.

The construction of oil storage tanks and pipelines drew still more wage earners to the oil fields. Nomadic work crews formed rural camps that followed the progression of the pipeline across the state. Competing oil producers built separate lines to transport their crude to refineries in the east or along the gulf coast. In 1906, construction began on an oil pipeline from Indian Territory to Port Arthur, Texas, and three years later the Prairie Oil and Gas Company began building an oil pipeline from the Glenn Pool and Muskogee fields to Baton Rouge, Louisiana.[21] These projects required a large labor force. Because the work was not steady, it attracted single men who could afford periods of unemployment. Those married men who came to Oklahoma as drillers, tankers, or pipeline workers (cats) often left their families behind to shield them from the vice and violence of the boomtowns until they established themselves.

Many oil workers received a chilly reception from local residents. Few people not engaged in the vice industries mixed with them. The mobile pipeline camps not only kept the cats close to their job sites but also away from area townspeople. Bootleggers shadowed the pipeline crews, setting up crude shanties or tents from which to dispense their stock. Pipeline crews typically comprised several dozen men who cleared brush, dug the ditch for the pipe, and moved nine hundred pound lengths of pipe into place. The work was arduous and the conditions often trying. One former pipeline worker recalled the misery of laying pipe through a mos- quito- and snake-infested swamp in southern Oklahoma, "A man could slip down in the mud and before he could get up six men would have walked all over his face."[22] The dangerous nature of their work made these men more accepting of the coarse saloon culture than were the merchants, ministers, and other professionals who supported the Anti-Saloon League.

Although oil field jobs paid relatively high wages, workers often could not save much money. Serious injuries, requiring extensive work absences, were common, and injury insurance was inconsis- tent. The high cost of goods and services in the oil boomtowns also sapped workers' savings. A former roughnecker recalled that, though daily wages ranged between twelve and eighteen dollars, he was able to send little back to his family. Area stores charged fifteen dollars for shoes, thirty dollars for work boots, ten dollars for work pants, five dollars for a shirt, and a night's stay in a boarding house cost two dollars or more.[23] Arguments by prohibitionists that the liquor industry robbed workers of their hard-earned wages carried little weight with oil workers who paid such exorbitant prices for basic necessities.

So it was that liquor was a basic component of life for these oil workers. As one man recalled, "Fighting and getting drunk were part of the job then."[24] Another man recounted that he worked twelve-hour days, midnight until noon, on the oil derricks, "we couldn't get all the oil off of us and everything we ate or handled smelled and tasted like crude oil. If it hadn't been for plenty of whiskey we probably wouldn't of [sic] made it, and we stayed half- drunk all the time."[25] Liquor for these men was both a coping mechanism and recreational drink.

Fights and killings were commonplace in the numerous liquor joints of the oil patch. One oil driller described Kiefer as lawless and the roughest town in the state, noting that prohibition had little impact there. Whiskey and violence were commonplace. During his two-year stay in that community, local authorities found the bodies of more than twelve murder victims.[26] Oil towns, such as Kiefer, provided a solid customer base for the enterprising bootlegger, but they also provided an environment of violence that dry proponents generalized to the entire liquor industry when campaigning for prohibition. Vice conditions in Kiefer were typical of other oil towns as well. One man told Governor Williams in 1915 that nearly all of the cities and towns of the oil fields sported liquor joints.[27]

For example, Sapulpa, which was in the Glenn Pool oilfield, contained small ethnic populations, traditionally identified as prohibition opponents. The region's liturgical religious populations — Roman Catholics, Episcopalians, Lutherans, or Jews — also were small. The area did contain a large number of wage earners, many of whom worked in the oil fields, for the railroads, or as farm laborers. These workers frequented area liquor joints and kept Sapulpa's liquor industry robust. In 1912, the Oklahoma league charged that the oil town "has been made up of a population, the majority of whom are opposed to prohibition and the enforcement of law."[28] The league recognized early on the connection between the working class and the illegal liquor industry.

The general public also was well aware that liquor men served a working-class clientele. A Bristow resident warned Governor Cruce in 1913 that bootleggers and gamblers would take over Creek County if the state abolished the state liquor enforcement office. A Sapulpa newspaper reported a 1915 spike in area liquor activity as drilling in the nearby Cushing oil field picked up. Another noted that renewed enforcement efforts in Cushing and Drumright had had little impact on liquor violations there, though Sapulpa remained the liquor nexus.[29]

Prohibition divided wet Sapulpa along class lines also. In 1915, thirty-three residents signed a petition to Governor Williams requesting state assistance against area liquor and gambling establishments. To demonstrate their respected positions in the community, many petitioners identified their occupations: eight as merchants, four as attorneys, four as religious ministers, three as oil businessmen, two as contractors, and one each as a newspaper editor, a physician, a hotel manager, and a marble works manager. The occupations of eight petitioners were not listed or were unreadable. Except perhaps for the marble works manager, these men were merchants and professionals, that is, solid members of the middle class. Their perspective on the liquor question coincided with that of dry organizations, such as the Oklahoma league.[30]

Sapulpa's defiance of the liquor ban was emblematic of the situation in other oil communities. Responding to numerous reports of liquor violations in booming Cushing, Governor Cruce admitted that he was perplexed at how to improve conditions there. His successor, Williams, also conceded that liquor enforcement in the oil fields of Creek, Muskogee, Osage, and other counties was less effective than elsewhere. The Hog Shooter oil field of Washington and Nowata counties and Nowata's Alluwe oil field and coal fields also attracted an inordinate amount of liquor activity. Increased oil drilling in the Healdton oil field prompted increased liquor violations there in 1915.[31]

The spirit of sacrifice during the First World War and arguments that the liquor industry hampered the United States' war effort had little effect on bootlegging among Oklahoma's oil workers. In 1917, Tyrone officials arrested two Prairie Oil and Gas Company employees, sent to construct oil storage tanks, for bringing six quarts of liquor with them. The oil towns of Ardmore and Wirt also witnessed blatant and persistent liquor violations in 1918.[32]

Further, the postwar period brought no abatement in oil patch liquor activities. Early in 1919, the Payne county attorney informed Governor Robertson of liquor violations in the oil town of Yale. A Healdton resident notified the governor that recent municipal elections had retained officials unsympathetic to prohibition and, as a result, liquor was widely available. The following summer, a Cushing minister complained to Robertson that a bootlegging network operated there. Other Cushing residents sought to play down violations in their community by asserting that conditions remained much worse in nearby Oilton.[33] Bootlegging remained sufficiently commonplace in the Healdton field that area dry advocates petitioned Governor Robertson for state intervention in 1921.[34] The Ardmore and Healdton bootleggers, like their counterparts in Sapulpa and

Cushing, found ways to elude the authorities and continued their trade because the oil workers provided a ready market for their product. The breadth of the wet sentiment in these towns is evidenced by the election and reelection of officials who failed to enforce the liquor ban.

As wildcatters opened new oil fields in Oklahoma in the 1920s, bootlegging spread to these regions also. The Tonkawa region experienced a minor oil boom in 1921. An oil camp named Three Sands sprouted nearby with no police or jail but numerous saloons. The oil men hired a saloon operator as camp sheriff. He forced all competing saloons to pay him to avoid police raids. The town of Seminole, in the central oil field of the same name, quickly gained a reputation for drunkenness and violence in the 1920s. Brawls, shootings, and intoxication were the order of the day. In Cushing, Ardmore, Three Sands, and Seminole, the flow of liquor followed the flow of oil despite national prohibition.[35]

Ethnic and religious explanations of the split over prohibition break down in the Oklahoma oil patch as well. Few immigrants worked in the oil fields, and most of Oklahoma's small German population resided in the distant north central counties. The state's liturgical religious populations also were not concentrated in the oil fields. The oil patch and the state's growing cities, which were both problem areas for liquor officials, had large working-class populations. The liquor men recognized this and dug in their heels against enforcement efforts in these regions to maintain their profitable trade.

Although officials focused on the association between oil workers and liquor, they recognized that other wage earners also ignored the liquor ban. In 1909 federal authorities raided several long-standing stills in the Jack Fork Mountains that supplied whiskey to the lumberjacks of southeast Oklahoma. Liquor men also targeted the state's large itinerant farm labor population, which followed the cotton and corn harvests across the state in autumn and the wheat harvest in late spring. In 1913, a minister in the southwestern town of Frederick informed Governor Cruce that area liquor men staged dances in the work camps each Saturday night at which they sold liquor to the cotton-picking crews.[36] These workers, like those in Oklahoma's mines and oil fields, held liquor consumption to be acceptable despite the admonition of local ministers and merchants.

Organizations associated with Oklahoma wage earners did not endorse prohibition but only rarely were they willing to risk broader goals by openly challenging respected society's support for the liquor ban. In October 1910, one such statement appeared. The *Working Man*, a Lawton Socialist newspaper, asserted that the working class could carry the vote against prohibition. "And it should be carried by that class because it means jobs. Do not vote your brother out of a job. It is up to the working men of Comanche County and Oklahoma to make an organized effort to defeat prohibition this fall."[37] This defense of the liquor industry in the name of jobs is curious in a publication with the subheading "Workers of the World Unite." The *Working Man* did not support other industries in the name of jobs, and the editorial does not state that brewers, distillers, or retailers were particularly generous toward their employees. Oklahoma Socialists tailored their message to their readers' attitudes to broaden their support. The working classes of the Lawton area wanted legal liquor, and this publication found the means to justify opposition to prohibition. Other Socialist publications spoke in favor of prohibition. The *Woods County Socialist* urged readers to vote for dry candidates, and the *New Century* stated that voters should bolt from the Democratic Party because it contained booze peddlers.[38]

Still other labor organizations were less definitive on prohibition. The Oklahoma Farmers' Union did not mention the liquor issue at its 1906 convention, though prohibition was a lively political topic in the months before the state constitutional convention in Guthrie. The union's nominee to the convention endorsed statewide prohibition, but the organization's newspaper ran beer advertisements into the fall of 1906. As the convention opened in December, it editorialized that most Oklahomans were opposed to both drunkards and prohibition and advocated the "safe middle ground" of regulated saloons over an absolute liquor ban.[39]

The Farmers' Union maintained its wet position as the first liquor referendum drew near in late summer 1907. Its publications argued that each man should choose to resist the temptation of liquor and that prohibition robbed men of that choice. It also printed an editorial by Isaac B. Levy, chairman of the anti-prohibitionist Citizens League.[40] Following the 1910 referendum, the Farmers' Union resumed its earlier silence on the liquor question. Prohibition and its enforcement received no mention at the 1914 Oklahoma Farmers' Union convention, though these were contentious issues in many sections of the state.

Oklahoma's cities contained large working-class populations, and, not coincidentally, strong liquor operations as well. Several Lawton unions joined to sponsor a large Labor Day celebration in 1909. Despite the liquor ban and a local judge's ruling that the city's many liquor establishments be closed, bootlegging remained so common that the city collected licensing fees from its illegal saloons. Shawnee also contained a large number of wage earners; the city's labor organizations were sufficiently prominent that they announced a joint effort in 1905 to build a labor temple as the headquarters of all labor movements in the territories. By this time, Shawnee's reputation as a saloon town was widely acknowledged.[41] Similarly, Oklahoma City, Muskogee, and Tulsa contained large working-class populations, drawn by jobs in the manufacturing and service industries. The wage earners, in turn, attracted bootleggers to these cities.

Laborers' defiance of prohibition was a product of their different experience of the liquor ban from that of the respectable middle class. State and local officials did not enforce the liquor ban evenly, and at times this uneven enforcement took on a class bias. In 1908, the state liquor dispensary ordered local agencies to sell medicinal beer only in packages of twelve bottles or more because it determined that beer possessed health benefits only if consumed over an extended period of time. As refrigerators and ice boxes were rare among wage earners, this caveat allowed middle-class and upper-class men to purchase medicinal beer, whereas the working class went without.

A few officials bluntly stated their skewed application of liquor codes. A Muskogee judge lectured drunks in his courtroom, noting that, "no one except a rich man and one in good health should drink liquor."[42] Oklahoma's prohibition statutes at this time banned the sale or provision of liquor but said nothing of simple possession or consumption. Nevertheless, this judge in one of the state's largest communities put wage earners on notice that they could expect to be prosecuted for possessing or consuming liquor despite the court's more lenient approach toward those of a higher social status. Similarly, a Watonga man complained to Governor Cruce that local officials prosecuted poor bootleggers but not the town's "moneyed men."[43] These examples reflect the reality of liquor enforcement in early Oklahoma. Enforcement officials, as established members of their communities, were personally acquainted with the area's prominent men. Officers treated such respectable people differently than they did common oil workers, miners, or itinerant farm laborers arrested on liquor charges.

Federal officials, however, demonstrated less favoritism toward locally prominent men when enforcing the liquor ban. In 1912, as the courts considered whether federal or state and local jurisdiction held in eastern Oklahoma, a newspaper reported that several men urged an end to federal jurisdiction in the region, noting, "And it is not the bootleggers who are behind this movement, but many business and professional men who like to keep cold ones on ice in their refrigerator at home and who want their toddy night and morning."[44] These respectable citizens recognized a clear distinction between federal liquor enforcement, which was relatively evenhanded, and that conducted by state and local officials, which gave greater consideration to one's social status.

When sheriffs and police chiefs did arrest some locally prominent men on liquor charges, the courts dealt with these men quite differently than others. A Nowata judge sentenced a convicted bootlegger to a three-hundred-dollar fine and ninety days in jail but gave the young man, described as belonging to "one of the best families in the city," the option to leave town rather than serve jail time.

Ardmore officials arrested Dr. J. M. McRae for illegally prescribing liquor, the first doctor in the state to be arrested for such an offense. He subsequently was acquitted of the charges.[45]

Nationally prominent men also received preferential treatment regarding prohibition. In 1912, federal authorities charged Robert G. Valentine, commissioner of Indian Affairs, with introducing whiskey on American Indian lands. Valentine had led a hunting trip into Osage County for oil men seeking leases in the area. Reportedly, the party drank and gambled extensively while on this excursion.[46] Valentine's prosecution demonstrates federal officials' commitment to evenhanded enforcement. However the investigation did not seek prosecution of the oil men on the trip, though federal statutes prohibited the possession of liquor in the area. The investigation's timing, well after the hunting trip took place, suggests a less urgent approach to enforcement than was adopted when prosecuting pipeline workers or storage tank builders.

Middle-class social clubs, such as the Eagles and the Elks, also received preferential treatment from the authorities. The state courts ruled that the Oklahoma City Eagles club could purchase liquor from out of state. In 1910, an Oklahoma City judge ordered officials to return liquor seized from a local Elks lodge because the Elks broke no laws in providing liquor to members while at the club.[47] Members of these clubs typically were middle class because most working-class men could not afford the dues and did not know any members willing to sponsor them. Enforcement officers did not bother social clubs but actively pursued those establishments patronized by wage earners.

The double standard in liquor enforcement was not unusual. Socially prominent men who engaged in other vice activities also received preferential treatment from officials. Shortly before Christmas in 1912, Muskogee authorities raided a high-class party at which both liquor and prostitutes were present. A newspaper reported that officers took home six "society sports" in an automobile pending a hearing. A local businessman paid their bonds, and speculation was strong that these prominent men would not appear in court and so would forfeit their bonds.[48] This treatment of well-to-do offenders differs markedly from the experience of wage earners who encountered the authorities while selling, purchasing, or consuming liquor.

All of this indicates a willingness to vary liquor enforcement according to social status. Respectable members of the middle class and area laborers experienced the liquor ban in different ways: the former saw it as a reasonable effort to end a violent liquor culture; the latter viewed it as a subjective law that targeted those of meager means while overlooking similar activity by prominent men.

The class-based nature of the liquor question in Oklahoma was reinforced by the composition of dry organizations. The spokesmen for the Oklahoma league were merchants and professionals — ministers, doctors, attorneys, and teachers — who sought to impose their definition of propriety, and of manhood itself, on men of the lower classes. They refused to acknowledge that the saloon was integral to working-class culture. Not surprisingly, wage earners resisted such attempts to control their behavior; they continued to patronize the liquor men long after prohibition took effect in 1907, confounding the middle-class campaign to kill the saloon.

But this was not just the case in Oklahoma. The connection between liquor consumption and male working-class culture in the United States dates back to the antebellum period. New York City taverns provided wage-earning men with a place to recreate and socialize among men of similar economic stations and forged a distinct working-class male identity, which included consumption of large quantities of alcohol and violence against strangers who entered a group's neighborhood.[49] Drinking in local taverns became a common form of recreation for nineteenth-century U.S. wage earners, a practice continued into the next century. Oklahoma wage earners shared with urban laborers a lack of recreational opportunities and job security, which threatened the male wage earner's role as family provider. Socialist Party activist Oscar Ameringer asserted that the living conditions of Oklahoma tenant farmers were worse than those Upton Sinclair described in *The Jungle*.[50] Oklahoma's lower-class men sought relief from their dreary existence, as their counterparts elsewhere had for decades, in local saloons.

Middle-class reformers, members of respectable society, saw no redeeming value in the saloon. They focused on the boomtown saloons and portrayed the violence there as inherent to all saloons. Certainly some saloons were quite dangerous. Patrons risked serious injury in a brawl and death if a fight escalated. The violent reputations — few reformers witnessed these crimes firsthand — of these establishments galvanized middle-class support for prohibition. Those with good sense knew to avoid saloons, though the unsuspecting sons of respectable families might venture into these places and find themselves the target of criminals or the unintended victims of a saloon brawl.

From the point of view of oil workers, miners, or other laborers, however, most saloons were quite calm; and the risk of injury in the most violent saloon was no greater than at the job site. Roughnecks handled heavy machinery on uncertain wooden derrick frames and narrow oil-covered ledges daily. A fall from one of these might maim or kill. One man stated that accidents were so frequent in the oil fields that most workers spent two out of every ten months in the hospital.[51] Coal miners faced a constant risk of mine collapse or explosion. Fifteen died in a 1905 Latimer County mine blast; a 1908 explosion entombed twenty-nine miners in Pittsburg County; a 1912 mine explosion in the Sansbois Mountains left seventy-three miners dead and twenty-five more seriously injured.[52] On a more mundane, daily level, these workers used heavy equipment that could mangle limbs or damage vital organs. Long hours of work increased fatigue, which led to accidents and violent quarrels. For these men, the dangers of the saloon were comparatively less.

Unappreciated by middle-class dry proponents, liquor establishments held some worth for wage earners. Turn-of-the-century sociologists, in studying Chicago saloons, described them as providing important social functions for working-class men. Wage earners escaped their dark, cramped, dingy dwellings for the bright lights and conviviality of the local saloon. Saloons in New York and Worchester, Massachusetts, served those cities' laborers similarly. The clientele of these urban saloons was distinctly working class because middle-class men tended to drink at home, in private clubs, or at expensive hotels.[53]

Early Oklahoma's laboring populations — oil workers, miners, itinerant farm laborers, brick layers, teamsters, and others — endured equally deplorable living conditions; for example, oil pipeline workers and farm laborers slept in make-shift camps as they followed the harvests or pipeline construction. The local liquor joint, which was often no more than a tent hurriedly erected near a work camp, offered a diversion from this dismal life and so became a staple of working-class culture. Few merchants and professionals ventured into the oil patch and mining districts, let alone the remote camps of pipeline and farm workers. Respectable members of the community who wanted to drink did so in their homes or in private social clubs and so had no real experience with the wage earners' way of life.

But the Oklahoma dry advocates recognized the strong ties between working men and the liquor establishment. The Oklahoma Woman's Christian Temperance Union (WCTU) asserted in 1907, "Saloon keepers say their largest support comes from the men of labor." Two years later, the union reminded supporters, "The liquor industry, as you know, draws its support and power largely from the wage-earning class."[54] The Oklahoma league noted, "The liquor business is the workingman's worst enemy, but those engaged in it pretend to have a great interest in the laborer."[55] These dry supporters overlooked private liquor consumption by the middle and upper classes, focusing instead on the destruction of the saloon as a social institution because of the problems inherent at that institution. Likewise, state and local enforcement officials devoted special attention to the boomtowns of the oil patch, mining communities, and itinerant work camps and largely ignored liquor consumption at private clubs or parties.

Oklahoma's German population, although acknowledging its opposition to prohibition for cultural reasons, also conceded the relationship between liquor and working men. In 1919, one of the state's German newspaper editors quoted an anti-prohibition speaker who noted that, although he did not drink liquor, "I am nevertheless against prohibition because I believe that the worker is entitled to his beer."[56]

Although many historians of prohibition have emphasized ethnicity as a prime determinant of a person's liquor stance, the ethnocultural argument breaks down in Oklahoma, a state containing a small foreign population and a minor liturgical (Roman Catholic, German Lutheran, Episcopalian, Jewish) population. Defiance of prohibition was strong in the oil fields, regions with few ethnic populations and no overrepresentation of liturgicals. The demographic characteristic shared by the enforcement problem areas, that is, mining districts, oil fields, and the growing urban regions, was a large wage-earning population.

This is not to say that the ethnocultural argument is incorrect. Immigrants and Catholics in Oklahoma frequented saloons, and the German-American Association was integral to the organized opposition to statewide prohibition. However the ethnocultural argument fails to explain the depth and variation of the resistance to prohibition in Oklahoma. Considerable opposition to prohibition, far in excess of the state's scant immigrant population, existed in the Sooner State, both at the election polls in 1907 and 1910 and in the illegal saloons, which maintained a lively business despite the state and national liquor bans. Prohibition was a cultural issue, which evolved from class and ethnic and religious sources. Support for the liquor ban was strongest among merchants and professionals who had no time for the saloon; opposition or resistance to the ban was strongest among wage earners who valued drinking establishments as a haven from their daily grind.

Conclusion

As the 1920s began, liquor enforcement changed significantly though in many ways the results were the same. On January 16, 1920, the Volstead Act took effect and the manufacture and sale of liquor became illegal throughout the United States. Federal agents in Oklahoma and throughout the nation encountered difficulties similar to those with which Oklahoma officials had previously wrestled. Effective prohibition enforcement necessitated a dramatic increase in police powers that most U.S. citizens refused to accept, and many communities sheltered bootleggers because members did not view liquor running as a serious crime.

M. C. Binion, in charge of federal liquor enforcement in Oklahoma, reported in December 1920 that his men had destroyed at least five hundred gallons of corn whiskey and wine and five thousand gallons of corn mash in the previous four months. Nevertheless, he estimated that Oklahoma contained more stills per square mile than any other state in the union and that two more went into operation for every one that his men confiscated. In 1922, Governor James B. A. Robertson told the Oklahoma City Rotary Club that prohibition was a failure in the state because liquor was available in all seventy-seven Oklahoma counties, even though most of the seventeen hundred McAlester penitentiary inmates were liquor offenders. Most local officials were conscientious, he asserted, but liquor was produced faster than they could find and confiscate it. Frustration at their inability to stop the flow of liquor and the violent response of some bootleggers led federal, state, and local officials to respond in kind. In 1921 a deputy from Picher killed a Kansas woman when he fired on a taxi that he suspected to be a bootlegger car.[1]

Seeking a solution, officials expanded enforcement powers, but this generated protests and legal challenges. In 1923 the state prohibition director ordered the seizure of property leased to bootleggers. The criminal court of appeals reined in enforcement efforts when it ruled that officers must have prior knowledge of liquor activity before applying for a warrant to search a building. In 1924 the attorney general informed a member of the state legislature that his proposed bill to make the purchase (in addition to the manufacture and sale) of liquor a criminal offense would violate the state constitution.[2]

The Anti-Saloon League of America also remained active in Oklahoma in the 1920s, though its political influence had declined somewhat. In the second decade of the century, Horatio T. Laughbaum and others had worked to tighten prohibition enforcement. Following the adoption of the national ban, the league continued to send money into the Sooner State, but it increasingly moved away from active liquor enforcement. Instead, it flooded the state with speakers who stressed the need for strict enforcement by local, state, and federal officials. Between the summers of 1920 and 1921, the league spent $19,493.15 on speakers' salaries in the Sooner State. The national league generally spent more in Oklahoma than it collected in dues and contributions during this decade. For 1923, the deficit reached $7,496.47, more than fifty times greater than the shortfall in any other state. The lone year in which the national league collected more than it spent in Oklahoma was 1927. Its expenditures in the state did decline, from $34,591 in 1923 to $6,570.11 in 1928, though this is more a function of the league's slipping national prestige and funding than a shift in its Oklahoma strategy.[3]

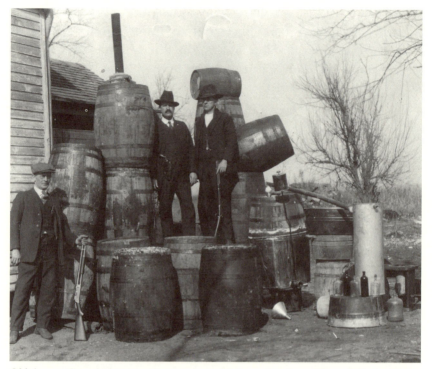

Oklahoma County peace officers pose with barrels of confiscated liquor at an illegal distillery in the 1920s. In 1921, Governor James B. A. Robertson noted that stills could be found in every county in the state. Notice the firearms the officers carry on such raids.

Support for the league and for prohibition remained stronger in Oklahoma during the 1920s than elsewhere in the nation. Although subscription revenues declined as the decade progressed, Oklahoma consistently ranked at or near the top of league subscription tallies as late as 1928. Likewise, the liquor ban remained more popular in the Sooner State than in the nation at large. A 1926 national newspaper poll revealed that 19 percent of respondents endorsed prohibition, 50 percent supported modifications to the liquor ban, and 31 percent desired its repeal. Oklahoma newspapers reported different results. *Oklahoma City News* and *Muskogee Times-Democrat* readers split almost evenly between the three positions; but the *Frederick Leader* reported 83 percent in favor of prohibition, the

Officers knock in barrel heads and dump liquor into the gutter in Oklahoma City, circa 1921. Despite such publicized raids, liquor remained available throughout the prohibition period in Oklahoma's cities and its rural districts.

Ardmore Ardmorite 57 percent for prohibition, the *Blackwell Tribune* 57 percent for prohibition, the *Durant Democrat* 63 percent for prohibition, and the *Ada News* 65 percent for prohibition.[4]

The liquor question also affected the 1928 presidential campaign. In Oklahoma and several other southern states, opposition to Alfred Smith's candidacy reached hysterical levels as rumors spread that he would initiate a Roman Catholic takeover of the United States. In Oklahoma, where the prohibition debate had further exiled Roman Catholics from mainstream society, a Smith presidency represented a sharp departure from the norm. Smith's vocal opposition to the liquor ban confirmed fears that he threatened the state's dominant cultural traditions. The middle-class white Protestants who directed state politics and set the standard for respectable behavior tacitly accepted or promoted such sensational stories of Catholic plots and wrongdoings.

Oklahoma's public officials reflected this dry sentiment into the

1930s as calls to end prohibition mounted nationwide. At the 1932 Democratic National Convention, a majority of delegates urged the immediate termination of the Volstead Act. Oklahoma delegates would not go this far, supporting instead an amendment to the Constitution to repeal the Eighteenth Amendment. State Republicans expressed greater support for the liquor ban, voting at their national convention for submission of an amendment to modify rather than repeal the Eighteenth Amendment.[5]

Oklahoma's support for prohibition not only was inconsistent with the growing national opposition to the liquor ban but also flew in the face of the continued liquor violations throughout the national prohibition years. In the year before June 1925, enforcement officials in the state arrested 1,777 people and seized 5,399 apparatuses involved in the production of liquor. Only eight states reported more seizures and thirteen reported more arrests, even though twenty states had larger populations than Oklahoma. For the year ending June 30 1928, officials initiated 1,668 liquor cases. During the following year, officials began 1,556 prosecutions. These numbers pale when compared to those of New York, the state leader in such cases, but are considerably higher than the figures reported for Iowa (357 and 232 cases in these years), a state with a similarly sized population. In January 1930, federal officials brought liquor conspiracy charges against 102 state defendants, many of them Pottawatomie County officials. They allegedly extorted protection money from illegal saloon operators in return for immunity from arrest.[6] These findings do not indicate greater hypocrisy in Oklahoma concerning the liquor issue, as much as they highlight two committed populations: one that strongly supported the League and prohibition and another that continued to buy liquor in violation of the ban.

The inability or unwillingness of local, state, and federal officials to curb the illegal liquor trade in the oil patch and the coal fields produced a growing frustration among many dry proponents. Although the Oklahoma league had formed local law-and-order leagues to assist public officials in the 1910s, a new organization entered the enforcement fray after 1920. The Ku Klux Klan,

Oklahoma County peace officers pose in a 1920s saloon, possibly during a raid. Saloons continued to operate in many Oklahoma communities despite state and national bans on liquor sales.

reformed nationally in 1915, entered Oklahoma in early 1921 and soon became active in attacking bootleggers and a host of other groups that it deemed un-American. The Oklahoma Klan certainly targeted blacks who refused to accept the precepts of white supremacy, and its attacks on the Roman Catholic and Jewish faiths during this period also are well-documented. In Oklahoma and neighboring states, the Klan also launched a moral crusade against vice activities (including the liquor industry) that public officials seemed unable to quash. A Stonewall newspaper published this warning from the Klan: "Bootlegging, gambling, etc. must stop, and this element can cease to operate or find more healthful surroundings elsewhere."[7] The Klan issued similar warnings to Pawhuska, Ardmore, Cherokee, McCurtain, and Idabel liquor men.

Many middle-class residents endorsed and welcomed the Klan's efforts. Ministers in the oil town of Ardmore and the mining town of Hartshorne asserted that the Klan was the only hope of ending law violations there, and the *Ada News* editorialized that criticism of the Klan would end if it succeeded in closing the Ardmore vice industries.[8]

Amidst this public acceptance of vigilantism, Klan activities spread throughout the state. The Sapulpa Klan, operating in the Glenn Pool oil field, formed permanent law enforcement bodies that resembled the law-and-order leagues of the previous decade. In the Healdton oil fields, Klansmen engaged in a gun battle with a reported bootlegger that resulted in several deaths and the arrest of, among others, the Klan's Reverend Leon Julius of Healdton. Similarly, a Muskogee group called the Riders of the Night whipped a local bootlegger and threatened another in an effort to discourage liquor sales. The Pryor Klan hired several men to attack and beat a local businessman reputed to be a bootlegger. The Okmulgee and Tipton Klans conducted liquor raids in those communities, arresting bootleggers and confiscating or destroying stills. The Klan also sent public warnings to officials in Tulsa, Ardmore, Healdton, Hobart, and Pittsburg counties to enforce vice laws in their districts or face ouster proceedings. The Tulsa Klan, with a claimed membership of five thousand in 1923, conducted its own raid of a bootlegger meeting and dumped several hundred gallons of liquor.[9]

The early twentieth-century Oklahoma Klan was not a marginal organization. Highly respected by mainstream society, numerous community leaders became members and officers in the Klan. Governor Robertson asserted in 1922 that most of the state's county attorneys and sheriffs and half of its Protestant ministers belonged to the organization. The Klan encouraged this religious affiliation, urging each local chapter to appoint an ordained minister of the gospel as its Kledd or chaplain.[10]

The Klan also attracted secular professionals. According to the Drumright Lions Club, the local Klan leadership included attorneys and real estate brokers. The Durant mayor led a Klan march through his town in 1922. Dr. J. A. Walker, a dentist, served as the cyclops of the Shawnee Klan. The mayor and chief of police in El Reno belonged to the Klan. John Foster, a Cushing banker, directed the local Klan. Edwin DeBarr, vice president of the University of Oklahoma, was the Grand Dragon of the Oklahoma Klan. An independent newspaper described Klansmen statewide as "high grade individuals, a selection from the mose [*sic*] substantial element of the state, morally, intellectually, and financially."[11]

As the 1920s progressed, the Klan inherited the league's role in liquor enforcement, but they went further than the league in attempting to stamp out bootlegging. Like the league, the Klan was a respected organization, dominated by middle-class men. The sketchy membership information for the two groups indicates that few people belonged to both. C. Grant Landon was an exception. A member of the Oklahoma City school board and of the Oklahoma league headquarters committee, Landon subsequently became Exalted Cyclops of the Oklahoma City Klan. In that capacity, he selected men to the local whipping squad, which meted out punishment to those engaged in bootlegging and other vice trades.[12]

The connection between the league and the Klan was much more ideological than personal and reflected the middle-class perspective of their respective members. Both organizations saw bootleggers as fundamentally immoral and hence un-American. Both were dissatisfied with official prohibition enforcement efforts, and this led them to form their own enforcement groups to aid and monitor elected officials. Nevertheless, Oklahomans continued to drink. The desire for liquor remained sufficiently strong throughout the first three decades of the twentieth century that men risked fines and imprisonment to provide it. Frustrated, dry advocates sanctioned the extreme measures of the Klan. The hooded order's failure to end bootlegging in Oklahoma damaged its reformer image and contributed to its decline in the region after 1925.

As the 1930s began, prohibition remained in effect throughout the nation, but opposition to and violation of the liquor ban continued to grow. The economic crisis of the period convinced some that liquor should be legalized to provide jobs in breweries, distilleries, and bars. The Wickersham Report of 1931 confirmed what many had witnessed firsthand: prohibition did not prohibit the production and sale of alcohol. The following year, a *Literary Digest* poll demonstrated that 73 percent of U.S. citizens supported the repeal of the Eighteenth Amendment. The issue continued to divide Oklahomans. Although wet forces gained steam and formed such groups as the Oklahoma Modification and Repeal Association, the league and the state Woman's Christian Temperance Union (WCTU) continued to defend the liquor ban as beneficial to the state and nation.[13]

In March 1933, newly elected President Franklin D. Roosevelt and a Democratic Congress quickly moved to roll back prohibition. A new law adjusted the Volstead Act to allow for the sale of 3.2 percent beer. (As national prohibition receded, Oklahoma' liquor ban remained in place, and so 3.2 percent beer remained illegal in the Sooner State). Next, they began crafting a new amendment to repeal the Eighteenth Amendment, arguing that liquor sales would bolster the depressed economy and that liquor taxes would contribute to state and federal budgets.

Oklahoma officials were much more measured in discussing repeal. Governor William H. Murray vetoed a bill to put the Twenty-First Amendment before Oklahomans in a referendum in 1933 on a legal technicality. When the thirty-sixth state (Utah) ratified the repeal amendment in December of that year, Oklahoma's ratification debate became unnecessary, and Murray and other state politicians avoided the treacherous political waters between the wet and dry camps.[14]

Amidst the rising tide of wet sentiment nationally, Oklahoma politicians carefully moved to amend state prohibition. To avoid recriminations from either the wet or dry camps, the legislature put a referendum before voters: the question of legalizing 3.2 percent beer in Oklahoma. Dry advocates organized in advance of the vote, but encountered difficulty in generating money to finance their campaign. Oklahoma wet proponents matched the dry efforts, and, in July 1933, the 3.2 referendum passed 224,598 votes to 129,582. The victorious wets, however, did not assume full political control of the state. Respectable, middle-class Oklahomans' opposition to the working-class saloon scuttled for the next two decades various attempts to legalize all liquor.[15]

The issue of respectability offers a more complete understanding of prohibition in Oklahoma. Nineteenth-century evangelicals had set the standards of respectable behavior in the United States, but by the early twentieth century, other middle-class groups adopted these values as well. They disdained drinking, smoking, swearing, and gambling, labeling such activities as vices.[16] This middle-class standard of respectability faced stiff challenges in early Oklahoma.

To add to the problem, the territories contained a diverse population at the turn of the twentieth century. Racially, the region was overwhelmingly white, but it contained a burgeoning black population and an American Indian population that, although declining in numbers, bequeathed to the state an enduring cultural heritage. Oklahoma also was diverse religiously, as the Methodist, Southern Methodist, Southern Baptist, Presbyterian, and Roman Catholic churches each drew many supporters. Early residents engaged in a variety of economic endeavors that affected their social status. Some farmers prospered, whereas many did not. Merchants and professionals became prominent residents of the towns and cities. The railroad, mining, and oil industries attracted wage earners to the region. The diverse nature of society and culture in the state's early years unnerved some socially prominent people and convinced them that Oklahoma needed societal and cultural standards that mirrored their own concepts of respectable behavior. Prohibition was a mechanism by which these community leaders imposed their criteria on the state's eclectic population.

Scholars examining the Progressive movement describe its leaders as respected and prominent members of their communities. The campaign against liquor was not an anomaly but an integral part of larger reform efforts.[17] In early Oklahoma, respectable community pillars sought to blot out the saloon industry because they saw it as nonrespectable, that is, without redeeming value. By contrast, liquor consumed in the home or in private clubs, although still frowned upon by the most extreme prohibitionists, was largely ignored during the dry campaign.

Oklahoma's middle class strove to achieve respectable status. Criticisms by outsiders that former criminals and economic failures had founded the state intensified the desire to clean up the region's radical and lawless image. Merchants and professionals sought to present their state as the model of respectability and patriotism.[18] Prohibition became the centerpiece of this moral canon as liquor had been a central part of the untamed territorial past. Those who opposed the liquor ban fell outside the bounds of respectable society. The liquor issue became a litmus test in determining one's social standing.

A brief sample of public and private comments by prohibition supporters illustrates the emphasis they placed on issues of respectability and social status. One dry publication criticized saloon keepers, stating, "They themselves know they are not of respectable standing and character in the community."[19] Reverend Edwin C. Dinwiddie, speaking on behalf of the Oklahoma Anti-Saloon League in 1907, urged, "the betterment of citizenry of the new state to stand shoulder to shoulder for statewide prohibition."[20] Complaints to state officials of lax local enforcement also stressed hierarchical distinctions within society. A Skiatook resident's comments to the governor are typical: "The whiskey-men simply control the town and the better element have given up in despair."[21] Muskogee officials, temporarily believing prohibition to be a dead letter in 1908, went so far as to distinguish between liquor establishments' clientele, "The officials will see to it that the joints which fail to pay the (liquor) license and other places where the disreputable are allowed to congregate are suppressed."[22]

Early Oklahoma's Protestant ministers claimed the mantle of respectability for the dry cause. Businessmen and professionals also sought to close the saloon, arguing that it stunted the economic growth of local communities and the future state because it reduced productivity and siphoned the working man's income from more vital and respectable purchases at stores selling dry goods, hard wares, and so on. A few business-minded men countered that a licensed saloon provided greater benefit to the state than illegal saloons. Wet advocates, however, had no effective response to the Oklahoma league's charges that prohibition would improve the moral condition of the population.

The league, in focusing on the unsavory saloon, pitted religious institutions against an industry that they claimed countenanced a host of illegal activity. The crass image of the saloon, which was accurate for some notorious saloons, but inaccurate when describing many others, disgusted merchants, doctors, lawyers, teachers, and other respectable community leaders. Many of these had spent little time in a saloon. The league and other dry organizations tapped into their revulsion to stamp the entire industry as inherently corrupt, dirty, and parasitic, as evil. Brewers, distillers, and saloon operators did little to counter this criticism. The liquor industry did not attempt to clean up unsavory activities until after the prohibitionists had built a strong foundation of political support using such arguments.

To understand more clearly the concept of respectability, one must also look at those populations that remained beyond its parameters. Racial minorities comprised a portion of this population. American Indians might achieve respectability by negating their cultural heritage, learning English, adopting Christianity, and pursuing gainful employment or purchasing property. Among the eastern American Indians, this process was far advanced by the turn of the century because members of the Five Tribes had intermarried with European Americans for generations.[23] Many American Indian leaders during the early statehood years were prominent land owners and businessmen. By contrast, traditionalists remained separated from respectable white society. Chito Harjo and his followers rejected white society so completely that they ignored their allotted land claims. Unwilling to assimilate into white society and culture, they remained beyond the par of respectability.

The few European immigrants to Oklahoma also fell outside respectable society; they brought with them customs, such as the tendency to drink in public liquor establishments on Sunday, that were radically different from those of multigenerational U.S. citizens. Although this activity was acceptable to the residents of the state's few immigrant communities, it generated disapproval from the surrounding native middle-class population.

The black population of the territories encountered difficulty in achieving respectability as a result of white racial attitudes, particularly prevalent in the eastern portion of the new state. The urge to segregate the population, black from white, was so strong at the state constitutional convention that only the fear of President Theodore Roosevelt vetoing the document kept the popularly elected delegates from writing Jim Crow provisions into the state constitution. Officials enacted such legislation once the new government formed. Blacks might achieve respectability within the black community but generally not beyond. In all-black towns, such as Boley, the small black middle class produced community leaders who opposed the liquor industry for reasons similar to those expressed by the white middle class, though the former buttressed these reasons with a desire to keep white law enforcement authorities from entering their towns. Many believed that blacks could not be assured due legal process by white authorities given the rash of lynchings in the twentieth century.[24]

Religion also shaped standards of respectability in early Oklahoma. The liturgical population (Roman Catholics, Episcopalians, some Lutherans, and Jews) held relatively liberal views on the use of alcohol, but as noted previously, pietistic evangelicals (particularly Southern Baptists and Methodists) far outnumbered liturgicals and were more sharply critical of liquor consumption. Evangelical leaders, serving as officers in the Oklahoma Anti-Saloon League, determined that the only respectable stance toward alcohol was absolute avoidance. Roman Catholics remained an extreme minority in the state, concentrated in a few counties and possessing a strong immigrant flavor. Anti-Catholic sentiment was strong in Oklahoma by the First World War.[25] The traditional animosity that prominent evangelicals felt toward the church stained Catholics and other liturgicals as less than respectable members of society.

The split between pietists and liturgicals over the liquor question reinforced the latter's inferior social status in twentieth-century Oklahoma.

These various nonrespectable groups, although diversifying and enriching early Oklahoma culture, enjoyed significantly less influence in the establishment of broad societal norms. Established members of local communities — professionals, such as ministers, lawyers, teachers, engineers, and local business owners — held greater influence in determining model behavior because of their education and the stable nature of their positions. By contrast, the working classes, whether rural or urban, enjoyed less economic security and were more likely to be uprooted in search of employment. Many in the middle classes saw liquor as detrimental to the future of their community. Legal liquor sales would foster political corruption, place white women in danger from the drunken leers of black men, continue the downward spiral of the American Indian population, and hinder efforts to shed the state's wild image of drunken cowboys and saloon brawls. Because the saloon was associated closely with wage earners, middle-class Oklahomans sought to destroy this nonrespectable institution that, from their perspective, lacked any redeeming social qualities.

Thus the campaign for and against prohibition was a contest between competing standards of respectable behavior. By making the saloon illegal, the respectable middle classes went far toward imposing their standard on the entire state population. Prohibition brought to the dry cause some who previously had not held strong feelings on the topic, but who supported the enforcement of the law. Working-class men viewed the saloon as a socially vital establishment. They did not feel that they neglected their manly duties when they frequented such places. Oklahoma's immigrant and liturgical populations were so small as to have little impact on this discussion of respectability beyond a few scattered communities. The wage-earning population, however, was larger, and the saloon was as central to working-class culture in Oklahoma as elsewhere in the United States. The Sooner State's middle class, by contrast, saw the saloon as fostering violent crime; some held that merely going to a saloon robbed a man of his manhood because money spent there limited his ability to provide for his family financially.

Oklahoma's dry proponents, particularly clergymen and women, worried about the close association between liquor and manhood, seeking instead to define masculinity according to a man's level of devotion to familial responsibilities. The WCTU provided the means for women to effect change in this behavior of men, and the league gave Christian clergymen an influential voice regarding the saloon. As the league eclipsed the WCTU after 1900, the prohibition campaign took on a more masculine demeanor. The league saw to this, promoting itself as the church in action, and urged men to lend their support to this manly endeavor. If WCTU activism upended middle-class gender roles, the league righted the societal ship by placing middle-class men at the forefront of the prohibition movement.

By the mid-twenties, a middle-class culture of respectability supplanted the working-class culture that had pervaded early Oklahoma society. Middle-class professionals and businessmen marginalized the liquor industry but could not kill it. A working-class liquor culture continued to exist at the cultural and societal fringes. Violation of the liquor statutes continued, and enforcement remained irregular. In 1959, Governor J. Howard Edmondson began to enforce prohibition strictly, and nonrespectable Oklahomans demonstrated their continued influence by voting down prohibition in that year's referendum. Respectables retreated tactically, accepting legal liquor but only if sold in sealed containers. The sale of liquor by the drink was not legalized until 1986, reflecting the influx of outsiders into the state more than a change in long-standing cultural attitudes. Respectable society grudgingly accepted these setbacks as working-class culture no longer posed a serious challenge to the state's entrenched middle-class standards of respectability. Consumption of alcoholic beverages, particularly in public, remains an unacceptable behavior for many upstanding citizens.

As Oklahoma enters its second century of statehood, the vestiges of prohibition remain. The campaign to prohibit liquor came in the state's infancy. That fact, combined with the longevity of the liquor ban, affords this cultural phenomenon continued influence on the state's political and social composition. A dominant dry culture has shaped the liquor codes to stigmatize the liquor industry. Bars and saloons are relegated to fringe districts in many towns and cities. Liquor stores operate under strict guidelines, such as making their interiors sufficiently visible from the street that passersby can easily see all customers inside. Beverages with alcohol content greater than 3.2 percent cannot be sold on Sundays, holidays, or on the various election days held in the state annually. Beer containing more than 3.2 percent alcohol cannot be sold chilled.

These regulations have not destroyed the liquor culture. The liquor industry persists in Oklahoma, serving that portion of the population that distances itself from respectable society. Illegal liquor also remains discreetly available. Thus two Oklahomas have evolved, one that is respectable with a strong evangelical influence. This population sets the standards of propriety in the state. The second population rejects those standards, or more appropriately, ignores them and lives according to its own moral code. This rebellious population is more likely to patronize liquor establishments and consume illegal drugs, particularly marijuana, if they can do so inconspicuously. The heritage of prohibition has created a duality in the state: a daylight culture that is visible and vocal and a nocturnal culture that is less prominent but no less resilient. These competing cultures coexist uncomfortably in Oklahoma and continue to shape liquor policy and society into the twenty-first century.

Notes

Introduction

1. Jon M. Kingsdale, "The 'Poor Man's Club': Social Functions of the Urban Working-Class Saloon," *American Quarterly* 25, no. 4 (October 1973): 472.

2. Paul Kleppner, *The Third Electoral System, 1853–1892: Parties, Voters, and Political Cultures* (Chapel Hill: University of North Carolina Press, 1979); Richard Jensen, *The Winning of the Midwest: Social and Political Conflict, 1888–1896* (Chicago: University of Chicago Press, 1971).

3. U.S. Department of Commerce, Bureau of the Census, *Special Reports, Religious Bodies: 1906 Part I, Summary and General Tables* (Washington, D.C.: Government Printing Office, 1910), 252–54.

4. U.S. Department of Commerce, Bureau of the Census, *Special Reports, Religious Bodies: 1916 Part I, Summary and General Tables* (Washington, D.C.: Government Printing Office, 1919), 210–12.

5. U.S. Department of Commerce, Bureau of the Census, *Fourteenth Census of the United States, 1920: Population,* 3 (Washinton, D.C.: Government Printing Office, 1923), 812.

6. Pamphlet distributed by the Oklahoma Anti-Saloon League, Prohibition Files, Frederick S. Barde Collection, Oklahoma State Historical Society, Oklahoma City, (hereafter cited as Barde Collection). In the 1907 referendum, 46.3 percent of those considering prohibition voted against it. In 1910, 45.4 percent voted against it. The league's tabulations are confirmed in Victor E. Harlow, *Oklahoma: Its Origins and Development* (Oklahoma City: Harlow Publishing Corporation, 1935), 310.

7. On early Oklahoma's working class, see Nigel Anthony Sellars, "Oil Wheat

and Wobblies: The Industrial Workers of the World in Oklahoma, 1905–1930" (PhD diss., University of Oklahoma, 1998).

1. Liquor and Liquor Policy in Territorial Oklahoma

1. Walter LeGrand, "The Temperance Movement in Oklahoma" (master's thesis, Oklahoma Agricultural and Mechanical College, 1948), 1.

2. *Cherokee Phoenix and Indian Advocate (Tahlequah)*, December 7, 1833; *Pauls Valley Enterprise and Valley News*, July 26, 1906; Arrel Gibson, *The Chickasaws* (Norman: University of Oklahoma Press, 1971), 198.

3. LeGrand, "The Temperance Movement in Oklahoma," 7.

4. Jeffrey Burton, *Indian Territory and the United States, 1866–1906: Courts, Government, and the Movement for Oklahoma Statehood* (Norman: University of Oklahoma Press, 1995), xix.

5. LeGrand, "The Temperance Movement in Oklahoma," 6.

6. Burton, *Indian Territory and the United States*, 216, 202–203, 73, 241, 230–31.

7. Burton, *Indian Territory and the United States*, 251.

8. Burton, *Indian Territory and the United States*, 244.

9. Blake Gumprecht, "A Saloon on Every Corner: Whiskey Towns of Oklahoma Territory, 1889–1907," *Chronicles of Oklahoma* 74, no. 2 (Summer 1996): 151–56.

10. Gumprecht, "A Saloon on Every Corner," 157–59.

11. Jimmie Lewis Franklin, *Born Sober: Prohibition in Oklahoma, 1907–1959* (Norman: University of Oklahoma Press, 1971), 6; *El Reno News*, November 11, 1900.

12. LeGrand, "The Temperance Movement in Oklahoma," 30, 31.

13. LeGrand, "The Temperance Movement in Oklahoma," xviii.

14. LeGrand, "The Temperance Movement in Oklahoma," 24.

15. Ethel Katherine Knox, "The Beginning of Perry Oklahoma" (master's thesis, Oklahoma Agricultural and Mechanical College, 1937), 55.

16. LeGrand, "The Temperance Movement in Oklahoma," 17–18; Franklin, *Born Sober*, 10.

17. *Daily Oklahoman (Oklahoma City)*, April 16, 1908.

18. Mary Ann Blochowiak, " 'Woman with a Hatchet': Carry Nation Comes to Oklahoma Territory," *Chronicles of Oklahoma* 59, no. 2 (Summer 1981): 134; Mildred B. McFarland interview with Phamie Elizabeth Sheldon, August 13, 1937, Edmond, Oklahoma, in Grant Foreman, ed., *Indian Pioneer History Collection* 101 (Works Progress Administration Project S-149, 1937–1938): 259 (hereafter cited as Foreman, *Indian Pioner History Collection*); Mildred B. McFarland interview with Mrs. Bonnie Doxsie Terry, July 29, 1937, Edmond, Oklahoma, in Foreman, *Indian Pioneer History Collection* 112, 95.

19. Blochowiak, " 'Woman with a Hatchet,' " 135–36.

20. Blochowiak, " 'Woman with a Hatchet,' " 138–39.

21. Franklin, *Born Sober*, 14.

22. Blochowiak, " 'Woman with a Hatchet,' " 140–44.

23. Blochowiak, " 'Woman with a Hatchet,' " 146–49.

24. Robert Smith Bader, *Prohibition in Kansas: A History* (Lawrence: University of Kansas Press, 1986), 142, 153.

25. W. F. Wilson, comp., *Wilson's Revised and Annotated Statutes of Oklahoma, 1903*, (Guthrie, Okla.: State Capital Co., 1903), 481, cited in Franklin, *Born Sober*, 5.

26. *Kingfisher Free Press*, January 4, 1900.

27. LeGrand, "The Temperance Movement in Oklahoma," 28–29.

28. J. C. Roberts, Attorney General, and C. H. Woods, Assistant, *Report of the Attorney General of the Territory of Oklahoma*, (Guthrie, Okla.: State Capital Company, 1902), 26–36; Jimmie Birdwell interview with George Plummer, July 19, 1937, Oklahoma City, in Foreman, *Indian Pioneer History Collection*, 107: 374.

29. Oklahoma, *Oklahoma Reports, Volume X: Cases Determined in the Supreme Court of the Territory of Oklahoma at January 1901 and Previous Terms and not Published in Former Volumes*, (Guthrie, Okla.: State Capital Printing Company, 1901), 547–55.

30. *Daily Oklahoman*, January 24, 1900.

31. *El Reno News*, February 15, 1900.

32. *El Reno News*, July 28, 1900.

33. *Chickasha Daily Express*, September 17, 1900.

34. *El Reno News*, November 1, 1900.

35. Franklin, *Born Sober*, 8.

36. *Stillwater Gazette*, January 31, 1901; Oklahoma, *Journal of the House Proceedings of the Sixth Legislative Assembly of the Territory of Oklahoma, Beginning January 8, 1901, Ending March 8, 1901*, 183–84; *Indian Journal (Muskogee)*, August 2, 1901.

37. *Daily Oklahoman*, May 4, 1906, cited in Franklin, *Born Sober*, 10.

38. (Sayre) *Headlight*, November 8, 1906, cited in Franklin, *Born Sober*, 10–11; LeGrand, "The Temperance Movement in Oklahoma," 20–21.

39. *Muskogee Times-Democrat*, September 8, 1906.

40. Frederick A. McKenzie, *"Pussyfoot" Johnson: Crusader — Reformer — A Man Among Men* (New York: Fleming H. Revell Company, 1920), 67.

41. McKenzie, *"Pussyfoot" Johnson*, 73.

42. McKenzie, *"Pussyfoot" Johnson*, 68–70.

43. *Muskogee Times-Democrat*, November 7, 1906.

44. McKenzie, *"Pussyfoot" Johnson*, 95–96, 98.

45. McKenzie, *"Pussyfoot" Johnson*, 82.

46. *Muskogee Times-Democrat*, March 25, 1907.

47. McKenzie, *"Pussyfoot" Johnson*, 81–82.

48. McKenzie, *"Pussyfoot" Johnson*, 85–86.

49. McKenzie, *"Pussyfoot" Johnson*, 82, 88, 91–92; *Muskogee Times-Democrat*, September 15, 1906.

50. *Muskogee Times-Democrat,* January 12, 1907.

51. *Muskogee Times-Democrat,* August 2, 1906; *Muskogee Times-Democrat,* February 27, 1906.

52. *Muskogee Times-Democrat,* May 16, 1907.

53. *Muskogee Times-Democrat,* September 14, 1907; *Muskogee Times-Democrat,* September 24, 1907.

54. *Muskogee Times-Democrat,* September 5, 1907.

55. McKenzie, *"Pussyfoot" Johnson,* 86.

56. *Muskogee Times-Democrat,* October 9, 1906.

57. *Muskogee Times-Democrat,* May 24, 1907; *Muskogee Times-Democrat,* September 30, 1907.

58. *Muskogee Times-Democrat,* February 4, 1907.

59. *Muskogee Times-Democrat,* October 4, 1907.

60. *Muskogee Times-Democrat,* October 7, 1907; *Muskogee Times-Democrat,* October 9, 1907; *Muskogee Times-Democrat,* October 12, 1907.

61. *Muskogee Times-Democrat,* October 17, 1907; McKenzie, *"Pussyfoot" Johnson,* 105–106.

62. *Muskogee Times-Democrat,* October, 22, 1907; *Muskogee Times-Democrat,* November 1, 1907.

63. Jay R. Dew, "Moral Reform for the 'Magic City': Temperance in Guthrie, Oklahoma, 1889–1907," *Chronicles of Oklahoma* 77, no. 4 (Winter 1999–2000): 411–12.

64. *Norman Transcript,* April 27, 1894; *Blackwell Morning Tribune,* October 17, 1932.

65. *Stillwater Gazette,* May 2, 1901; *Stillwater Advance,* October 9, 1902.

66. U.S., Department of Interior, William M. Jenkins, *Report of the Governor of Oklahoma to the Secretary of the Interior, 1901* (Washington, D.C.: Government Printing Office, n.d.), 84–85.

67. *Stillwater Advance,* August 22, 1901.

68. John Fortson, *Pott Country and What Has Come of It: A History of Pottawatomie County,* (n.p.: Pottawatomie County Historical Society, 1936), 24; U.S. Department of Commerce, Bureau of the Census, *Thirteenth Census of the United States, 1910: Population*: 3 (Washington, D.C.: Government Printing Office, 1913), 481.

69. *Stillwater Advance,* March 21, 1901; *El Reno News,* June 7, 1900; Bureau of the Census, *Thirteenth Census of the United States, 1910: Population*: 3: 482.

70. Virgil Coursey interview with R. L. Wilcox, October 25, 1937, Altus, Oklahoma, in Foreman, *Indian Pioneer History Collection,* 75: 279; interview with Caroline Brown Cornels, n.d., Sayre, Oklahoma, in Foreman, *Indian Pioneer History Collection,* 77: 483.

71. Nora L. Lorrin interview with Frances Mary Rakes, April 12, 1938, El Reno, Oklahoma, in Foreman, *Indian Pioneer History Series,* 81: 476; Bureau of the Census, *Thirteenth Census of the United States, 1910: Population*: 3: 482.

72. Interview with Ned Warren, May 21, 1937, Oklahoma City, Oklahoma, in Foreman, *Indian Pioneer History Collection* 67: 27.

73. "My Experiences in the Old Indian Territory," Tom Cheney, October 27, 1937, in Foreman, *Indian Pioneer History Collection* 88: 273.

74. Albert McRill, *And Satan Came Also, An Inside Story of a City's Social and Political History* (Oklahoma City: Britton Publishing Company, 1955), 56, 74.

75. Jimmie Birdwell interview with George Plummer, July 19, 1937, Oklahoma City, in Foreman, *Indian Pioneer History Collection* 107: 374.

76. McRill, *And Satan Came Also*, 70, 28, 76.

77. Jimmie Lewis Franklin, "That Noble Experiment: A Note on Prohibition in Oklahoma," *Chronicles of Oklahoma* 43, no. 1 (Spring 1965): 25.

78. *Stillwater Gazette*, May 2, 1901.

79. *Beaver Journal*, June 28, 1907.

2. Oklahoma Goes Dry

1. "Oklahoma Report by League Superintendent Horatio T. Laughbaum," *Proceedings, Fifteenth National Convention of the Anti-Saloon League of America, November 10–13, 1913,* (Westerville, Ohio: American Issue Publishing Co., 1913), 317–20.

2. *Wisconsin Issue*, September 1907; Jack S. Blocker, *Retreat from Reform: The Prohibition Movement in the United States, 1890–1913* (Westport, Conn.: Greenwood Press, 1976), 158.

3. *Daily Oklahoman*, November 25, 1904; Larry E. Burgess, *The Lake Mohonk Conference of Friends of the Indian, Guide to the Annual Reports* (New York: Clearwater Publishing Company, Inc., 1975), 82. This conference of Friends of the Indian, many of whom were ministers, met annually from 1883 until 1916 in the Catskill Mountains of New York to discuss ways to ease the assimilation of American Indians into U.S. society.

4. LeGrand, "The Temperance Movement in Oklahoma," 25.

5. *Muskogee Democrat*, March 28, 1905.

6. Gaines M. Foster, *Moral Reconstruction: Christian Lobbyists and the Federal Legislation of Morality, 1865–1920* (Chapel Hill: University of North Carolina Press, 2002), 168–69, 175.

7. *Daily Oklahoman*, November, 17, 1907; *American Issue*, Oklahoma Edition, April 1915; *American Issue*, Oklahoma Edition, January 1916; *Enabling Act*, McRill file, Barde Collection, 3.

8. *Muskogee Democrat*, March 28, 1905.

9. *Daily Oklahoman*, November, 17, 1907; Paul Nesbitt, ed., "Governor Haskell Tells of Two Conventions," *Chronicles of Oklahoma* 14, no. 2 (June 1936): 215.

10. LeGrand, "The Temperance Movement in Oklahoma," 9–10.

11. *Muskogee Times-Democrat*, August 20, 1906.

12. *Daily Oklahoman*, November 17, 1907; Nesbitt, "Governor Haskell Tells of Two Conventions," 202.

13. Vertical Files, Oklahoma Territorial Museum, Guthrie, Okla..

14. *Muskogee Times-Democrat*, September 8, 1906.

15. *Muskogee Times-Democrat*, September 13, 1906.

16. *Beaver Journal*, June 28, 1907.

17. *Muskogee Times-Democrat*, September 8, 1906.

18. *Shawnee Herald*, July 1, 1906.

19. *El Reno News*, August 6, 1897. The counties that sent delegates were Canadian, Kingfisher, Kay, Blaine, Oklahoma, Garfield, Cleveland, Noble, and Logan. Jimmie Lewis Franklin, in *Born Sober*, asserts that the association formed in 1904, citing an article in *Daily Oklahoman*, April 4, 1907. It is possible the association reorganized itself in that year or that the *Oklahoman* article listed the year incorrectly. The association seems to have been quite small before 1904 as no mention of it was found in the newspapers other than the 1897 listing.

20. Franklin, *Born Sober*, 15, 18, 20.

21. Nesbitt, "Governor Haskell Tells of Two Conventions," 215.

22. E. M. Sweet, "C. N. Haskell and Oklahoma Prohibition," in Charles N. Haskell Collection, Manuscript Collections, Western History Collection, University of Oklahoma, Norman (hereafter cited as Haskell Collection).

23. *Proceedings of the Constitutional Convention of the Proposed State of Oklahoma, Held at Guthrie, Oklahoma, November 20, 1906 to November 16, 1907,* (Muskogee, Okla.: Muskogee Printing Co., n.d.), 59–200. This account mentions several more petitions relating to the liquor issue that failed to specify a stance, pro or con.

24. *Daily Oklahoman*, November, 17, 1907; Nesbitt, "Governor Haskell Tells of Two Conventions," 214.

25. *Checotah Enquirer*, August 9, 1907.

26. Congressional Testimony of Reverend E. C. Dinwiddie, May 20, 1926, Anti-Saloon League of America Series: Clipping File May 20–25, 1926, Box 7, Folder 61, Ohio State Historical Society, Columbus. Dinwiddie's testimony was part of a congressional hearing into the effectiveness of prohibition.

27. *Daily Oklahoman*, November 14, 1908.

28. Dinwiddie to Howard H. Russell, July 12, 1907, Anti-Saloon League of America Series, Samuel Edgar Nicholson Subseries: Correspondence 1907–1910, Box 1, Folder 1, Ohio State Historical Society, Columbus (hereafter cited as Anti-Saloon League of America Series, Nicholson Subseries).

29. *American Issue*, Oklahoma Edition, January 1916; *Daily Oklahoman*, November 17, 1907; *Muskogee Times-Democrat*, May 18, 1907; *American Issue*, Oklahoma Edition, May 1916.

30. *Daily Oklahoman*, November 17, 1908, Reverend J. J. Thomson contributed this article to the *Oklahoman*.

31. *Daily Oklahoman*, November 17, 1907.

32. *Muskogee Times-Democrat*, February 21, 1907.

33. *Muskogee Times-Democrat*, December 4, 1908; E. C. Dinwiddie to S. E. Nicholson, May 20, 1907, E. C. Dinwiddie to the Headquarters Committee of the Anti-Saloon League of America, July 5, 1907, Anti-Saloon League of America Series: Correspondence 1907–1910, Box 1, Folder 1.

34. E. S. Chapman to Miss Laura Church, March 8, 1911, Anti-Saloon League of America Series, Nicholson Subseries: Correspondence 1911, Box 1, Folder 2; K. Autin Kerr, *Organized for Prohibition: A New History of the Anti-Saloon League* (New Haven, Conn.: Yale University Press, 1985), 128–29; Foster, *Moral Reconstruction*, 182–83.

35. George D. Conger to Samuel E. Nicholson, December 3, 1910, Anti-Saloon League Series, Nicholson Subseries: Correspondence 1907–1910, Box 1, Folder 1.

36. Oklahoma Anti-Saloon League pamphlet, prohibition files, Barde Collection; U.S. Department of Commerce, Bureau of the Census, *Population of Oklahoma and Indian Territory* (Washington, D.C.: Government Printing Office, 1907), 11.

37. Standard deviation measures the dispersion of the numbers from the mean or average percentage. To determine this, one measures the distance from the mean (in this case 54.3 percent, the average vote on the liquor question), adds these figures together, squares that number, and then takes the root of that total. Doing so, I arrived at 8.4, a range within which most of the county vote totals fell. Nineteen fell beyond the range of standard deviation: eleven counties reporting unusually dry votes and eight reporting unusually wet votes.

38. Franklin, *Born Sober*, 21–22.

39. See in particular Charles Merz, *The Dry Decade* (Garden City, N.Y.: Doubleday, Doran & Company, Inc., 1930) and Andrew Sinclair, *Era of Excess: A Social History of the Prohibition Movement* (New York: Harper & Row, 1962).

40. LeGrand, "The Temperance Movement in Oklahoma," 13–15.

41. Norman H. Clark, *Deliver Us from Evil: An Interpretation of American Prohibition* (New York: W. W. Norton & Company, Inc., 1976), 45.

42. Bader, *Prohibition in Kansas*, 64.

3. Early Statehood

1. Franklin, *Born Sober*, 78.

2. Andrew Barr, *Drink: A Social History of America* (New York: Carroll & Graf Publishers, Inc., 1999), 177.

3. Kingsdale, "The 'Poor Man's Club,' " 472–89.

4. Franklin, *Born Sober*, 24–25.

5. Dew, "Moral Reform for the 'Magic City,' " 406–27.

6. *(Eufaula) Indian Journal*, February 7, 1908.

7. Gumprecht, "A Saloon on Every Corner," 146–73.

8. *Okarche Times*, November 15, 1907.

9. *Okarche Times*, December 20, 1907.

10. Henry Braun Papers, Vertical Files, Oklahoma Territorial Museum, Guthrie, Okla..

11. *A Diamond Jubilee: History of Tillman County, 1901–1976*, Vol. 1 (n.p.: Tillman County Historical Society, 1976), 345.

12. William Ray Tower, "A General History of the Town of Prague, Oklahoma, 1902–1948" (master's thesis, Oklahoma Agricultural and Mechanical College, 1948), 13; Gumprecht, "A Saloon on Every Corner," 165.

13. McRill, *And Satan Came Also*, 140–41.

14. *Tupelo Times*, November 281907; *Coalgate Courier*, November 21, 1907; *Muskogee Times Democrat*, December 31, 1907; *Muskogee Times Democrat*, June 5, 1908; McRill, *And Satan Came Also*, 119.

15. Fortson, *Pott Country and What Has Come of It*, 28.

16. *Muskogee Times-Democrat*, July 1, 1909; *Muskogee Times Democrat*, December 31, 1907.

17. *Muskogee Times-Democrat*, August 19, 1909.

18. *Coalgate Courier*, October 10, 1907.

19. Fred S. Caldwell, Counsel to the Governor, "Report on Prohibition Investigation and Prosecution Covering Period December 1, 1908 to December 31, 1910," Governor's Papers, Governor Charles N. Haskell, November 16, 1907, to January 9, 1911, Box 11, File 13, Oklahoma Department of Libraries, Archives, and Records, Oklahoma City (hereafter cited as Haskell Papers). Caldwell was earnest in his work. A former officer in the Oklahoma Anti-Saloon League, his appointment in 1908 as state enforcement attorney met with strong league approval.

20. B. B. Ross to Lee Cruce, January 14, 1911, Governor's Papers, Governor Lee Cruce: General Correspondence, 1911–1914, Box 10, File 4, Oklahoma Department of Libraries Archives and Records, Oklahoma City (hereafter cited as Cruce Papers).

21. *Daily Oklahoman*, December 31, 1908.

22. *Muskogee Times-Democrat*, December 4, 1907; *Muskogee Times-Democrat*, December 28, 1907.

23. *Muskogee Times-Democrat*, December 14, 1907.

24. *Muskogee Times-Democrat*, January 9, 1908; *Lexington Leader*, July 9, 1909.

25. Oklahoma, *Journal of the House of Representatives of the Regular Session of the First Legislature of Oklahoma*, (Guthrie, Okla.: Leader Printing and Manufacturing House, 1908), 36, 37.

26. Franklin, *Born Sober*, 26–27.

27. Oklahoma, *State of Oklahoma Session Laws of 1907–1908* (Guthrie, Okla.: Oklahoma Printing Co., 1908), 603, 599, 597.

28. Oklahoma, *State of Oklahoma Session Laws of 1907–1908*, 604, 605, 603, 608–609.

29. Oklahoma, *State of Oklahoma Session Laws of 1907–1908*, 606.

30. *Lexington Leader*, May 15, 1908.

31. *(Eufaula) Indian Journal*, August 21, 1908.

32. *Lexington Leader*, September 18, 1908.

33. Franklin, *Born Sober*, 28–32.

34. Franklin, *Born Sober*, 34, 33.

35. Franklin, *Born Sober*, 34–35.

36. *Lexington Leader*, July 24, 1908.

37. Franklin, *Born Sober*, 35.

38. *Muskogee Times-Democrat*, March 21, 1908.

39. *Muskogee Times-Democrat*, November 12, 1908; *Muskogee Times-Democrat*, December 24, 1908.

40. *Enid Weekly Eagle*, April 9, 1908.

41. W. F. Morton to Lee Cruce, June 1, 1911, Cruce Papers: General Correspondence, 1911–1914, Box 18, File 4.

42. *Harlow's Weekly*, January 22, 1919. The bill failed to become law.

43. *Muskogee Times-Democrat*, December 10, 1908.

44. *Muskogee Times-Democrat*, December 15, 1908.

45. *Muskogee Times-Democrat*, March 5, 1911; *Muskogee Times-Democrat*, August 12, 1909; *Muskogee Times-Democrat*, January 13, 1911.

46. *Muskogee Times-Democrat*, September 13, 1909; *Muskogee Times-Democrat*, November 9, 1909.

47. David R. Morgan, Robert E. England, and George G. Humphreys, *Oklahoma Politics and Policies: Governing the State* (Lincoln: University of Nebraska Press, 1991), xxiv, 7, 16, 105.

48. LeRoy H. Fischer, ed., *Oklahoma's Governors, 1907–1929: Turbulent Politics* (Oklahoma City: Oklahoma Historical Society, 1981), 7, 55, 58.

49. *United States Supreme Court Reports, Lawyers' Edition*, Vol. 55 (Rochester, N.Y.: The Lawyers' Co-Operative Publishing Company, 1911), 431–37.

50. *Daily Oklahoman*, April 15, 1909.

51. *Oklahoma City Times-Journal*, March 29, 1908.

52. *Daily Oklahoman*, April 15, 1909.

53. *Muskogee Times-Democrat*, January 14, 1909.

54. Fortson, *Pott Country and What Has Become of It*, 28.

55. Caldwell, "Report on Prohibition Investigation," Haskell Papers, Box 11, File 13.

56. Caldwell, "Report on Prohibition Invesgitation," Haskell Papers, Administrative File, Box 11, File 13.

57. *Muskogee Times-Democrat*, February 17, 1912; *Muskogee Times-Democrat*, April 18, 1912; *Muskogee Times-Democrat*, December 19, 1912.

58. Governor's Papers, Governor Robert L. Williams: Administrative File, 1914–1916, Box 1, File 4, Oklahoma Department of Libraries Archives and Records, Oklahoma City (hereafter cited as Williams Papers); *The State of Oklahoma Ex*

Rel. Board of County Commissioners of the County of Ottawa, State of Oklahoma (Plaintiff) vs *George O. Gibson (Defendant)*, Williams Papers: General Correspondence, 1916, Box 5, File 8.

59. *Harlow's Weekly*, July 18, 1917.

60. *Harlow's Weekly*, August 15, 1917.

61. *American Issue,* Oklahoma Edition, July 1910.

62. *American Issue,* August 1910; Oklahoma Methodist General Convention, *Minutes*, 1910, 267–68, quoted in Franklin, *Born Sober,* 47.

63. Oklahoma Baptist General Convention, *Minutes*, 1910, 69–70, quoted in Franklin, *Born Sober,* 47.

64. Franklin, *Born Sober,* 47–48

65. *American Issue,* Oklahoma Edition, November, 1910; *American Issue,* Oklahoma Edition, December, 1910; Pamphlet distributed by the Oklahoma Anti-Saloon League, Prohibition files, Barde Collection.

66. *American Issue,* Oklahoma Edition, December 1910; *Eufaula Republican,* 11 November 1910.

67. *American Issue,* Oklahoma Edition, July 1910; *American Issue,* Oklahoma Edition, November 1910; *American Issue,* Oklahoma Edition, December 1910; Pamphlet distributed by the Oklahoma Anti-Saloon League, Prohibition files, Barde Collection.

68. Phillip Mellinger, "Discrimination and Statehood in Oklahoma," *Chronicles of Oklahoma* 49, no. 3 (Autumn 1971): 340–77; Jimmie Lewis Franklin, *Journey toward Hope: A History of Blacks in Oklahoma* (Norman: University of Oklahoma Press, 1982); Garin Burbank, *When Farmers Voted Red: The Gospel of Socialism in the Oklahoma Countryside 1910–1914* (Westport, Conn.: Greenwood Press, 1976).

4. Paper Prohibition

1. *Baptist Informer,* May 23, 1910; *Muskogee Times-Democrat,* May 3, 1912; *U.S. Supreme Court Reports,* Lawyers' Edition, Vol. 56 (Rochester, N.Y.: The Lawyer's Co-Operative Publishing Company, 1911), 1248–61.

2. *Muskogee Times-Democrat,* June 10, 1912.

3. *Blackwell Times Record,* November 7, 1912; *Eufaula Republican,* November 15, 1912.

4. *Harlow's Weekly,* April 26, 1913; *Harlow's Weekly,* May 3, 1913.

5. *Harlow's Weekly,* December 5, 1914.

6. *Muskogee Times-Democrat,* June 27, 1913; *Muskogee Times-Democrat,* June 28, 1913.

7. *Muskogee Times-Democrat,* January 26, 1911; *Muskogee Times-Democrat,* May 24, 1912.

8. *Muskogee Times-Democrat,* November 5, 1908.

9. *Muskogee Times-Democrat,* January 7, 1911.

10. *Guymon Herald,* October 29, 1914.

11. *Muskogee Times-Democrat,* September 20, 1907; *Lehigh Leader* September 19, 1907; *Wilburton Gazette,* October 4, 1907; *Muskogee Times-Democrat,* February 6, 1908; *American Issue,* Oklahoma Edition, September 22, 1908; *American Issue,* Oklahoma Edition, May 1912; *Muskogee Times-Democrat,* November 25, 1915.

12. *Lehigh Leader,* October 10, 1907; *Wilburton Gazette,* October 11, 1907; *Lehigh Leader,* October 17, 1907.

13. McRill, *And Satan Came Also,* 119, 140–41; *Tupelo Times,* November 28, 1907; *Coalgate Courier,* November 21, 1907; *Muskogee Times-Democrat,* December 31, 1907; *Muskogee Times-Democrat,* June 5, 1908.

14. *American Issue,* Oklahoma Edition, October 1909; McRill, *And Satan Came Also,* 109, 110; *Muskogee Times-Democrat,* July 13, 1911; F. M. Stevens to Lee Cruce, August 15, 1911, Cruce Papers: General Correspondence, 1911–1914, Box 23, File 1.

15. *American Issue,* Oklahoma Edition, August 1915; McRill, *And Satan Came Also,* 155, 166–67, 191.

16. *Harlow's Weekly,* February 20, 1915; *Harlow's Weekly,* April 24, 1915.

17. McRill, *And Satan Came Also,* 175–78.

18. Charles L. Daugherty Collection, Manuscript Collection, Western History Collection, University of Oklahoma, Norman (hereafter cited as Daughtery Collection), Box 1, File 3.

19. *Muskogee Times-Democrat,* July 7, 1913; *American Issue,* Oklahoma Edition, September 1915.

20. *Harlow's Weekly,* July 25, 1917.

21. Caldwell, "Report on Prohibition Investigation," Haskell Papers, Box 11, File 13.

22. *Harlow's Weekly,* July 5, 1913.

23. Lilah D. Lindsey Collection, Series III, Box 2, Folder 19, McFarlin Library, University of Tulsa (hereafter cited as Lindsey Collection).

24. Foress B. Lillie Collection, Manuscript Collections, Western History Collections, University of Oklahoma, Norman.

25. Lee Cruce to Vic S. Decker, November 25, 1913, Cruce Papers: General eCorrespondence, Box 1, File 8; Lee Cruce to Pat Malloy, November 25, 1913, Cruce Papers: General Correspondence, Box 5, File 6; Lee Cruce to William Hall, November 29, 1913, Cruce Papers: General Correspondence, Box 5, File 1.

26. Frank M. Weaver to Lee Cruce, November 15, 1913, Cruce Papers: General Correspondence, Box 1, File 8; Westfall Drug to Lee Cruce, November 20, 1913, Cruce Papers: General Correspondence, Box 1, File 8; Roach and Veazey Drug Company to Lee Cruce, November 17, 1913, Cruce Papers: General Correspondence, Box 1, File 8.

27. *Muskogee Time-Democrat*, November 21, 1913; Various correspondence, November 20, 1913 through October 14, 1914, Cruce Papers: General Correspondence, Box 1, File 8; Box 5, Files 1, 3, 6, 7; Box 56, Files 5, 6.

28. Chief Clerk to Governor to Alexander Drug Co., December 18, 1917, Williams Papers: Administrative File, 1917–1919, Box 1, File 4; Chief Clerk to Governor to Alexander Drug Co. and Cardinal Drug Co., December 31, 1918, Williams Papers: Administrative File, 1917–1919, Box 1, File 4; Robert L. Williams to Attorney General's Office, November 18, 1918, Williams Papers: Administrative File, 1917–1919, Box 1, File 9.

29. *Rhodes v. Iowa*, 170 *United States Reports, Supreme Court*, 412 (1898), cited in James H. Timberlake, *Prohibition and the Progressive Movement, 1900–1920* (Cambridge, Mass.: Harvard University Press, 1963), 148.

30. Caldwell, "Report on Prohibition Investigation," Haskell Papers, Box 11, File 13; Timberlake, *Prohibition and the Progressive Movement*, 162; *Daily Oklahoman*, January 10, 1917, cited in Franklin, *Born Sober*, 65; *Harlow's Weekly*, March 15, 1913.

31. Governor Lee Cruce to Reverend G. Lee Phelps, March 8, 1913, Cruce Papers: General Correspondence, Box 48, File 5.

32. Timberlake, *Prohibition and the Progressive Movement*, 172.

33. Oklahoma, *State of Oklahoma Session Laws of 1917*, (Guthrie, Okla.: Co-Operative Publishing Co., 1917), 350.

34. Thomas Elton Brown, "Bible-belt Catholicism: A History of the Roman Catholic Church in Oklahoma, 1905–1945" (PhD diss., Oklahoma State University, 1974), 7, 8–9, 25; *Muskogee Times-Democrat*, September 10, 1906.

35. Klepner, *The Third Electoral System*, 181–85, 293–97, 315, 322

36. Franklin, *Born Sober*, 65–66; *Harlow's Weekly*, September 19, 1917.

37. Santa Fe Railroad Agent Baker to S. P. Freeling, August 24, 1917, Attorney General and Assistant A. G. Records, A. G. S. P. Freeling, Miscellaneous Correspondence, Box 1, File 4, Oklahoma Department of Libraries Archives and Records, Oklahoma City (hereafter cited as Attorney General Records); Robert L. Williams to S. P. Freeling, August 31, 1917, Attorney General and Assistant A. G. Records: Miscellaneous Correspondence, Box 1, File 4.

38. Thomas Elton Brown, "Oklahoma's 'Bone-Dry Law' and the Roman Catholic Church," *Chronicles of Oklahoma* 52, no. 3 (Fall 1974): 322.

39. *Harlow's Weekly*, October 17, 1917; Brown, "Oklahoma's 'Bone-Dry Law,' " 324–28; Franklin, *Born Sober*, 67, 69.

40. Timberlake, *Prohibition and the Progressive Movement*, 32; Clark, *Deliver Us from Evil*, 101.

41. *Okarche Times* May 18, 1917.

42. *Harlow's Weekly*, July 25, 1914.

43. Lee Cruce to Bishop Theodore Meerschaert, March 20, 1912, Cruce Papers: General Correspondence, Box 26, File 4; Lee Cruce to Reverend James Van Hulse, July 25, 1912, Cruce Papers: General Correspondence, Box 32, File 4.

44. *Muskogee Times-Democrat*, June 27, 1912; *Muskogee Times-Democrat*, August 14, 1912.

45. *American Issue*, Oklahoma Edition, April 1916; Bader, *Prohibition in Kansas*, 186.

46. Bader, *Prohibition in Kansas*, 186; *Harlow's Weekly*, September 19, 1917.

47. *Guymon Herald*, January 25, 1917; Robert L. Williams to S. P. Freeling, March 26, 1919; Williams Papers, Box 1, File 9; Robert L. Williams to S. P. Freeling, August 20, 1918, Williams Papers, Box 1, File 9.

48. Timberlake, *Prohibition and the Progressive Movement*, 174–76, 180; *Harlow's Weekly*, January 2, 1915. Proponents of the wartime act successfully argued that the ban should take effect in 1919, despite the previous November's cease-fire because the United States had not signed a peace treaty and U.S. forces remained in Europe, leaving the nation in a wartime condition.

49. *Harlow's Weekly*, October 10, 1917; *Harlow's Weekly*, December 26, 1917.

50. R. E. Wood to J. M. White, October 22, 1918, Attorney General and Assistant A. G. Records: Miscellaneous Correspondence, Box 1, File 17; Robert L. Williams to S. P. Freeling, November 18, 1918, Williams Papers: Administrative File, 1917–1919, Box 1, File 9.

51. *Harlow's Weekly*, December 8, 1921.

52. *Daily Oklahoman*, July 19, 1919; H. R. Christopher to Mrs. Clara F. Hartsog, September 5, 1919, James B. A. Robertson Papers: General Correspondence, 1919, Box 15, File 4, Oklahoma Department of Libraries Archives and Records (hereafter cited as Robertson Papers).

53. Paul Popewe to S. P. Freeling, August 16, 1918, Attorney General Civil Cases, Record Group 1-2, Box 19, File 940, Oklahoma Department of Libraries Archives and Records (hereafter cited as Attorney General Civil Cases).

54. J. J. Barnes, "Report on Ardmore, Healdton and Wirt," September 10, 1918, E. P. Hill to S. P. Freeling, October 21, 1918, Attorney General Civil Cases, Record Group 1-2, Box 19, File 940; J. J. Barnes, "Report on Ardmore, Healdton and Wirt," September 10, 1918, E. P. Hill to S. P. Freeling, October 26, 1918, Attorney General Civil Cases, Record Group 1-2, Box 19, File 940.

55. *Harlow's Weekly*, September 17, 1919, reprinted from the *Tulsa World*.

56. Timberlake, *Prohibition and the Progressive Movement*, 154, 180, 182–83; *Harlow's Weekly*, October 28, 1921; Bader, *Prohibition in Kansas*, 193.

5. Oklahoma Drys

1. *Stillwater Gazette*, January 31, 1901.

2. Oklahoma, *Journal of the House Proceedings of the Sixth Legislative Assembly*, 183–84.

3. *Indian Journal (Muskogee)*, August 2, 1901. This measure applied to the Big Pasture region in the southwest, which was opened to white settlement by sealed

bids in 1906; to the Osage Reservation (subsequently Osage county), which was opened to white settlement following allotment of American Indian lands there in 1906; and to the Ponca and Oto-Missouri lands and Kaw lands west of the Osage Reservation, which were allotted in 1904 and 1906, respectively.

4. *American Issue*, Oklahoma Edition, April 1915.

5. E. M. Sweet, "C. N. Haskell and Oklahoma Prohibition," Haskell Collection.

6. *Muskogee Times-Democrat*, November 14, 1907.

7. *American Issue*, Oklahoma Edition, September 1910; *American Issue*, Oklahoma Edition, November 1910; *American Issue*, November 1908; *American Issue*, Oklahoma Edition, September 1, 1908; *American Issue*, Oklahoma Edition, October 24, 1908; *American Issue*, Oklahoma Edition, May 1909; *American Issue*, Oklahoma Edition, June 1912; *American Issue*, Oklahoma Edition, October 1912; *American Issue*, Oklahoma Edition, December 1912; *American Issue*, Oklahoma Edition, February 1914; *American Issue*, Oklahoma Edition, December 1914; *American Issue*, Oklahoma Edition, May 1915; *American Issue*, Oklahoma Edition, August 1916. These citations are but a sample of such reports found in The *American Issue*, Oklahoma Edition.

8. Charles N. Haskell, "Seventh Special Message of the Governor to the Legislature, December 12, 1907," *Journal of the House of Representatives of the Regular Session of the First Legislature of Oklahoma* (Guthrie, Okla., 1908), 36–37; *American Issue*, Oklahoma Edition, March 1911.

9. William E. Johnson, *Ten Years of Prohibition in Oklahoma* (Westerville, Ohio: American Issue Publishing Company), 3.

10. *American Issue*, Oklahoma Edition, December 1909.

11. *American Issue*, Oklahoma Edition, June 1911.

12. *American Issue*, Oklahoma Edition, February 1915.

13. *Harlow's Weekly*, January 22, 1919.

14. Caldwell, "Report on Prohibition Investigation," Haskell Papers, Box 11, File 13; *American Issue*, Oklahoma Edition, July 1914.

15. H. T. Laughbaum to Lee Cruce, December 2, 1912, Cruce Papers: General Correspondence, Box 39, File 1; *American Issue*, Oklahoma Edition, April 1913; *American Issue*, Oklahoma Edition, January 1914.

16. Lee Cruce to William Bickle, December 9, 1912, Cruce Papers: General Correspondence, Box 37, File 4.

17. *Muskogee Times-Democrat*, December 15, 1913; *American Issue*, Oklahoma Edition, January 1914.

18. *American Issue*, Oklahoma Edition, September 1908.

19. *American Issue*, Oklahoma Edition, April 1909.

20. *American Issue*, Oklahoma Edition, April 1910.

21. "Address of Governor C. N. Haskell at the Southern States Anti-Saloon

League Annual Convention (Atlanta, Georgia, April 3, 1910)," Haskell Collection, Box H-26, File 5.

22. T. E. Sisson to Lee Cruce, December 9, 1912, Cruce Papers: General Correspondence, Box 36, File 1.

23. Reverend J. W. Kendall to Lee Cruce, June 23, 1911, Cruce Papers: General Correspondence, Box 17, File 7; Lee Cruce to Dr. B. W. Freer, June 23, 1911, Cruce Papers: General Correspondence, Box 17, File 2.

24. Lee Cruce to H. T. Laughbaum, July 12, 1911, Cruce Papers: General Correspondence, Box 18, File 1; Lee Cruce to J. C. Tucker, July 12, 1911, Cruce Papers: General Correspondence, Box 19, File 6.

25. Lee Cruce to J. T. McIntosh, November 21, 1911, Cruce Papers: General Correspondence, Box 35, File 3.

26. Charles West to Lee Cruce, March 16, 1911, Cruce Papers: General Correspondence, Box 11, File 3.

27. H. T. Laughbaum to Robert Williams, March 26, 1915, Williams Papers: General Correspondence, 1915, Box 3, File 4.

28. Chief Clerk of Governor Williams to H. T. Laughbaum, April 19, 1915, Williams Papers: General Correspondence, 1915, Box 8, File 5.

29. *Oklahoma Messenger (Stillwater)*, March 1921.

30. "Investigation of State Dispensary (transcript)," Haskell Papers: Administrative File, Box 11, File 7; Franklin, *Born Sober*, 35.

31. *Frederick Enterprise*, August 15, 1907; *Muskogee Times-Democrat*, August 12, 1907.

32. *Muskogee Times-Democrat*, October 4, 1913.

33. Reverend J. J. Thomson to Governor C. N. Haskell, October 15, 1908, Haskell Papers: Administrative File, Box 11, File 6.

34. "Address of C. N. Haskell, Governor of Oklahoma, Before the Oklahoma Prohibition Convention, April 15, 1908,"Haskell Collection, Box H-26, File 5.

35. "Address of Governor C. N. Haskell at the Southern States Anti-Saloon League," Haskell Collection, Box H-26, File 5.

36. *American Issue*, August, 1908.

37. *American Issue*, Oklahoma Edition, October 1909.

38. Lee Cruce to H. T. Laughbaum, July 12, 1913, Cruce Papers: General Correspondence, Box 52, File 6.

39. Caldwell, "Report on Prohibition Investigation," Haskell Papers, Box 11, File 13.

40. *Cherokee Messenger*, May 19, 1905.

41. *Muskogee Times-Democrat*, August 4, 1906; *Muskogee Times-Democrat*, June 5, 1907.

42. *Altus Times*, September 10, 1908; *Altus Times*, October 17, 1908.

43. *Muskogee Times-Democrat*, June 5, 1907; Cruce Papers: General Correspon-

dence, Box 8, File 1; Cruce Papers: General Correspondence, Box 9, File 4; Cruce Papers: General Correspondence, Box 14, File 6; Cruce Papers: General Correspondence, Box 16, File 5; Cruce Papers: General Correspondence, Box 17, File 4; McRill, *And Satan Came Also,* 120–21.

44. Haskell Papers, Box 11, File 13; Cruce Papers: General Correspondence, Box 48, File 6.

45. Charles West to Independent Law Enforcement Club, July 27, 1914, Cruce Papers: General Correspondence, Box 34, File 5.

46. *Muskogee Times-Democrat,* December 22, 1908; *Muskogee Times-Democrat,* December 28, 1908; *Muskogee Times-Democrat,* December 29 1908. *Boley Progress,* November 24, 1910.

47. Law and Order League of Miami petition, March 20, 1911, Cruce Papers: General Correspondence, Box 4, File 33b.

48. Lee Cruce to Reverend L. Q. Hargraves, November 28, 1911, Cruce Papers: General Correspondence, Box 34, File 5; Lee Cruce to Reverend L. Q. Hargraves, November 28, 1911, Cruce Papers: General Correspondence, Box 35, File 3.

49. Lee Cruce to H. K. Sheldon, January 5, 1912, Cruce Papers: General Correspondence, Box 36, File 1.

50. Caldwell, "Report on Prohibition Investigation," Haskell Papers, Box 11, File 13.

51. John Harold Scott to Lee Cruce, June 9, 1913, Cruce Papers: General Correspondence, Box 48, File 8.

52. *American Issue,* Oklahoma Edition, April 1909.

53. Charles N. Haskell, "First Message of the Governor to the Second State Legislature, 5 January, 1909," in Oklahoma, *Journal of the House of Representatives of the Regular Session of the Second State Legislature of Oklahoma* (n.p.: n.d.), 27–28.

54. *Enid Weekly Eagle,* August 13, 1908.

55. *Muskogee Times-Democrat,* January 20, 1909.

56. *American Issue,* Oklahoma Edition, July 1910; *Muskogee Times-Democrat,* July 22, 1910.

57. *American Issue,* Oklahoma Edition, July 1910.

58. H. T. Laughbaum to Lee Cruce, March 6, 1913, Cruce Papers: General Correspondence, Box 47, File 5; Lee Cruce to H. T. Laughbaum, March 10, 1913, Cruce Papers: General Correspondence, Box 47, File 5.

59. H. T. Laughbaum to Lee Cruce, June 2, 1914, Cruce Papers: General Correspondence, Box 59, File 3.

60. *Harlow's Weekly,* January 31, 1914.

6. Dry Oklahoma

1. Foster, *Moral Reconstruction,* 167.

2. LeGrand, "The Temperance Movement in Oklahoma," 29–30.

3. *Our Helper*, March 1904.

4. Lindsey, "History of Indian Territory Woman's Christian Temperance Union," February 9, 1918, Lindsey Collection, Series III, Box 2, Folder 17; LeGrand, "The Temperance Movement in Oklahoma," 29–30.

5. *Our Helper*, May 1903.

6. *Chickasha Daily Express*, June 4, 1901.

7. Tulsa county Women's Christian Union meeting minutes, December 27, 1905, WCTU ledger, Lindsey Collection, Series III, Box 3, File 1; Tulsa county Women's Christian Union meeting minutes, March 21, 1906; WCTU ledger, Lindsey Collection, Series III, Box 3, File 1; Tulsa county Women's Christian Union meeting minutes, December 11, 1906, WCTU ledger, Lindsey Collection, Series III, Box 3, File 1.

8. *Oklahoma Messenger*, August 1907.

9. See Betty DeBerg, *Ungodly Women: Gender and the First Wave of American Fundamentalism* (Minneapolis: Fortress Press, 1990).

10. Bureau of the Census, *Special Reports, Religious Bodies: 1906*, 252–54; Bureau of the Census, *Special Reports, Religious Bodies: 1916*, 210–21.

11. Undated (1910) resolution by Tulsa Women's Christian Temperance Union, Lindsey Collection, Series III, Box 2, Folder 20.

12. Abbie B. Hillerman, *History of the Woman's Christian Temperance Union of Indian Territory, Oklahoma Territory, State of Oklahoma* (Sapulpa, Okla.: Jennings Printing and Stationery Company, 1924), 43, 53, 73, 99.

13. Mrs. W. E. Roberts to Lee Cruce, July 19, 1911, Cruce Papers: General Correspondence, Box 19, File 2; Mrs. F. M. Ward to Lee Cruce, July 21, 1911, Cruce Papers: General Correspondence, Box 19, File 7.

14. Tulsa county Women's Christian Union meeting minutes, October 20, 1903, WCTU ledger, Lindsey Collection, Series III, Box 3, File 1; Tulsa county Women's Christian Union meeting minutes, May 5, 1905, WCTU ledger, Lindsey Collection, Series III, Box 3, File 1; Tulsa county Women's Christian Union meeting minutes, April 18, 1906, WCTU ledger, Lindsey Collection, Series III, Box 3, File 1; Tulsa county Women's Christian Union meeting minutes, April 26, 1906, WCTU ledger, Lindsey Collection, Series III, Box 3, File 1; Mrs. J. O. Misch, "Lilah D. Lindsey," *Chronicles of Oklahoma* 33, no. 2 (Summer 1955): 197; *Muskogee Times-Democrat*, August 12, 1910; Mrs. Abbie B. Hillerman to Lee Cruce, June 4, 1911, Cruce Papers: General Correspondence, Box 17, File 4.

15. E. M. Sweet, "C. N. Haskell and Oklahoma Prohibition," Haskell Collection, Box H-26, File 5.

16. *Oklahoma Weekly Times-Journal*, December 20, 1907; *Muskogee Times-Democrat*, December 23, 1907; *Shawnee Herald*, March 25, 1908.

17. Mabel R. Sutherland to Indian Territory Women's Christian Temperance Union members, undated, Lindsey Collection, Series III, Box 2, Folder 20.

18. Ruth Bordin, *Woman and Temperance: The Quest for Power and Liberty, 1873–*

1900 (Philadelphia: Temple University Press, 1981), xviii; Kerr, *Organized for Prohibition*, 89; Linda K. Kerber, "Separate Spheres, Female Worlds, Woman's Place: The Rhetoric of Women's History," *Journal of American History* 75, no. 1 (June 1988): 28.

19. Bordin, *Woman and Temperance*, 168, 173.

20. Misch, "Lilah D. Lindsey," 197.

21. Kerr, *Organized for Prohibition*, 118.

22. Kerr, *Organized for Prohibition*, 94, 95.

23. *American Issue*, Oklahoma Edition, April 1915.

24. Kerr, *Organized for Prohibition*, 81, 82.

25. *Daily Oklahoman*, November 14, 1908; *American Issue*, Oklahoma Edition, April 1915; Resolutions of the Oklahoma Anti-Saloon League Board of Trustees, April 9, 1909, Anti-Saloon League of America Series, Nicholson Subseries: Correspondence 1907–1910, Box 1, Folder 1; *Muskogee Times-Democrat*, July 28, 1908.

26. *Daily Oklahoman*, December 5, 1909; *American Issue*, Oklahoma Edition, December 1909. Oklahoma League President C. L. Stealey and attorney Laughbaum recruited subscriptions from area supporters to pay off the balance of the debt by the end of 1909.

27. *Daily Oklahoman*, August 7, 1908; *Daily Oklahoman*, December 5, 1909; *American Issue*, Oklahoma Edition, February 1909; *Illinois Issue*, May 5, 1911; *American Issue*, Oklahoma Edition, June 1912; "Horatio T. Laughbaum," Laughbaum manuscripts, Oklahoma Historical Society, Oklahoma City (hereafter cited as Laughbaum manuscripts).

28. *American Issue*, Oklahoma Edition, April 1915.

29. *American Issue*, Oklahoma Edition, January 1909; *American Issue*, Oklahoma Edition, December 1910; *American Issue*, Oklahoma Edition, November 1912; *American Issue*, Oklahoma Edition, December 1912; *American Issue*, Oklahoma Edition, May 1913; *American Issue*, Oklahoma Edition, May 1914; *American Issue*, Oklahoma Edition, November 1916.

30. *American Issue*, Oklahoma Edition, September 1908 through December 1916. Data was not found for 1911.

31. Bureau of the Census, *Special Reports, Religious Bodies: 1916*, 210–12.

32. *American Issue*, Oklahoma Edition, September 1908 through December 1916.

33. Bureau of the Census, *Special Reports, Religious Bodies: 1916*, 210–12; *Daily Oklahoman*, May 8, 1910; *Daily Oklahoman*, October 19, 1910.

34. Bureau of the Census, *Special Reports, Religious Bodies: 1916*, 210–12.

35. LeGrand, "The Temperance Movement in Oklahoma," 24, 26; *American Issue*, Oklahoma Edition, April 1915.

36. *Lawton Constitution*, May 11, 1905.

37. *(Vinita) Weekly Chieftain*, September 24, 1909; Robertson Papers: General Correspondence, 1920, Box 1, File 2.

38. Stephen J. England, *Oklahoma Christians: A History of Christian Churches and of the Start of the Christian Church (Disciples of Christ) in Oklahoma* (n.p.: Bethany Press, 1975), 119; *American Issue*, Oklahoma Edition, February 1909 to December 1916.

39. Mrs. G. T. Ralls, *Oklahoma Trails: A History of the Work of the Synod of Oklahoma of the Presbyterian Church in the United States* (Atoka, Okla.: Atoka Press, 1927), 26; *American Issue*, Oklahoma Edition, February 1909 to December 1916.

40. *Baptist Sunday School Evangel* (Muskogee), August 1907; Leon W. Wiley to Robert L. Williams, January 31, 1915, Williams Papers: General Correspondence, 1915, Box 5, File 6; J. M. Gaskin, *Baptist Milestones in Oklahoma* (Oklahoma City: Baptist General Convention of the State of Oklahoma, 1966), 195; Benny Carl Fox, "The Baptist General Convention of Oklahoma and Higher Education: The Formative Period, 1906–1915" (master's thesis, Oklahoma State University, Stillwater, 1965), 48; *American Issue*, Oklahoma Edition, February 1909 to December 1916.

41. Fox, "The Baptist General Convention of Oklahoma and Higher Education," 48; *American Issue*, Oklahoma Edition, February 1909 to December 1916.

42. *Daily Oklahoman*, May 8, 1906; *Daily Oklahoma State Capital*, July 9, 1905; *American Issue*, Oklahoma Edition, February 1909 to December 1916.

43. *Muskogee Times-Democrat*, April 3, 1911; *American Issue*, Oklahoma Edition, February 1909 to December 1916.

44. *Muskogee Times-Democrat*, October 8, 1913; *Harlow's Weekly*, April 25, 1914; *American Issue*, Oklahoma Edition, February 1909 to December 1916.

45. *Harlow's Weekly*, May 8, 1915; AntiHorse Thief Association Lodge 234 to James B. A. Robertson, Robertson Papers: General Correspondence, 1921, Box 5, File 3; *American Issue*, Oklahoma Edition, February 1909 to December 1916.

46. Williams Papers: State Council of Defense, Liberty Loans, Box 3, File 1; *Harlow's Weekly*, August 15, 1917; S. W. Hayes to Robert L. Williams, August 20, 1918, Williams Papers, State Council of Defense, Homeguard, Box 3, File 2.

47. Secretary to the Governor to Wentworth Stuart, July 22, 1919, Robertson Papers: General Correspondence, 1919, Box 1, File 4.

48. "Report of Commission Charged With Investigation of Matters With Reference to Coal Strike," Robertson Papers: General Correspondence, 1919, Box 11, File 10.

49. See Sellars, "Oil, Wheat, and Wobblies"; Kenny L. Brown, "Progressive in Oklahoma Politics, 1900–1913: A Reinterpretation" in "An Oklahoma I Had Never Seen Before," *Alternative Views of Oklahoma History* ed. Davis D. Joyce (Norman: University of Oklahoma Press, 1994); John Thompson, *Closing the Frontier: Radical Responses in Oklahoma, 1889–1923* (Norman: University of Oklahoma Press, 1986); and Burbank, *When Farmers Voted Red*.

50. *American Issue*, Oklahoma Edition, April 1913; *American Issue*, Oklahoma Edition, October 1914.

51. Secretary to the Governor to H. H. Holman, November 30, 1917, Wil-

liams Papers: State Council of Defense, Homeguard, Box 2, File 4; *Muskogee Times-Democrat*, December 15, 1913.

52. *(Eufaula) Indian Journal*, August 21, 1919.

53. *Blackwell Sunday Tribune*, July 18, 1926.

54. J. G. Street and D. H. Hammond to Robert L. Williams, October 28, 1914, Williams Papers: Appointments by County, Box 5, File 1.

55. Dr. A. Grant Evans to Lee Cruce, September 21, 1912, Cruce Papers: General Correspondence, Box 29, File 6.

56. Robert L. Williams to Dr. E. D. Cameron, March 30, 1915, Williams Papers: General Correspondence, 1915, Box 2, File 1; Robert L. Williams to Rev. J. W. Mosley, April 13, 1915, Williams Papers: General Correspondence, 1915, Box 8, File 5; Robert L. Williams to H. t. Laughbaum, April 13, 1915, Williams Papers: General Correspondence, 1915, Box 8, File 5.

57. *Muskogee Times-Democrat*, June 5, 1907; *Muskogee Times-Democrat*, January 9 1908; *Muskogee Times-Democrat*, December 22, 1908; *Muskogee Times-Democrat*, December 29, 1908.

58. Dr. S. T. Peet to Charles L. Daugherty, November 19, 1908, Daugherty Collection, Box 2, File 2.

59. W. A. Murphy to Charles L. Daugherty, December 7, 1912, Daugherty Collection, Box 1, File 11.

60. Timberlake, *Prohibition and the Progressive Movement*, 92–94, 99, 115.

61. Burbank, *When Farmers Voted Red*, 161.

7. Wet Oklahoma

1. Interview with B. McAlpin, January 3, 1938, Comanche, Oklahoma, in Foreman, *Indian Pioneer History Collection* 60: 307; interview with R. S. Lewis and W. J. Nicholson, July 5, 1937, Tulsa, Oklahoma, in Foreman, *Indian Pioneer History Collection* 61: 286; interview with Martha Campbell Lynn, July 22, 1937, Lone Wolf, Oklahoma, in Foreman, *Indian Pioneer History Collection* 61: 508; Grace Kelley interview with Arnold McMullen, March 11, 1938, Henryetta, Oklahoma, in Foreman, *Indian Pioneer History Collection* 78: 478.

2. Interview with Bill Hart, June 16, 1937, Okmulgee, Oklahoma, in Foreman, *Indian Pioneer History Collection* 63: 458; interview with Dixie H. Colbert, May 24, 1937, Sulphur, Oklahoma, in Foreman, *Indian Pioneer History Collection* 51: 304; interview with Mrs. Rachel Hudson, June 23, 1937, Bartlesville, Oklahoma, in Foreman, *Indian Pioneer History Collection* 30: 79; interview with W. A. Jolly, August 26, 1937, Ardmore, Oklahoma, in Foreman, *Indian Pioneer History Collection* 31: 331; interview with J. P. Miller, September 15, 1937, Pauls Valley, Oklahoma, in Foreman, *Indian Pioneer History Collection* 36: 291; interview with Al Thompson, July 29, 1937, Okmulgee, Oklahoma in Foreman, *Indian Pioneer History Collection* 46: 426;

interview with L. F. Baker, February 24, 1938, Henryetta, Oklahoma, in Foreman, *Indian Pioneer History Collection* 51: 88.

3. Theodore R. Hamilton interview with Wilson Gunter, April 21, 1938, McAlester, Oklahoma, in Foreman, *Indian Pioneer History Collection* 84: 511.

4. Interview with T. P. Wilson, McAlester, Oklahoma, in Foreman, *Indian Pioneer History Collection* 11: 501; interview with J. R. Burleson, July 13, 1937, Rush Springs, Oklahoma, in Foreman, *Indian Pioneer History Collection* 17: 394; interview with George Tanner, October 18, 1937, Poteau, Oklahoma, in Foreman, *Indian Pioneer History Collection* 46: 196.

5. Don Moon, Jr., interview with Clyde Stanley Hyde, February 3–5, 1938, Guthrie, Oklahoma, in Foreman, *Indian Pioneer History Collection* 85: 411; Don Moon, Jr., interview with Red L. Wenner, April 29, 1938, Guthrie, Oklahoma, in Foreman, *Indian Pioneer History Collection* 95: 509; interview with Moses Weinberger, August 5, 1937, Guthrie, Oklahoma, in Foreman, *Indian Pioneer History Collection* 67: 70.

6. Ophelia D. Vestel interview with W. H. Wilson, January 26, 1938, Lawton, Oklahoma, in Foreman, *Indian Pioneer History Collection* 94: 283; interview with Winifred M. Clark, September 20, 1936, Tecumseh, Oklahoma, in Foreman, *Indian Pioneer History Collection* 104: 325; *Shawnee Herald*, September 24, 1907.

7. Jasper H. Mead interview with B. M. Austin, November 9, 1937, Chickasha, Oklahoma, in Foreman, *Indian Pioneer History Collection* 99: 258; interview with Charles F. Stuart, May 19, 1937, Pawhuska, Oklahoma, in Foreman, *Indian Pioneer History Collection* 10: 192; Augusta H. Custer interview with Henry Slight, November 16, 1937, Geary, Oklahoma, in Foreman, *Indian Pioneer History Collection* 101: 466; Jimmie Birdwell interview with T. G. Netherton, September 9, 1937, Oklahoma City, Oklahoma, in Foreman, *Indian Pioneer History Collection* 102: 327; biography of Edmund Frantz in Foreman, *Indian Pioneer History Collection* 3: 580; Angie Debo, "The History of Marshall, Oklahoma" in Foreman, *Indian Pioneer History Collection* 2: 495; Gumprecht, "A Saloon on Every Corner," 146, 163.

8. Interview with Ed Coke, July 27, 1937, Kingfisher, Oklahoma, in Foreman *Indian Pioneer History Collection* 51: 295–96. Coke operated a territorial Kingfisher saloon before and provided a representative sketch of such establishments. Interview with T. J. Hicks, Purcell, Oklahoma, in Grant Foreman, *Indian Pioneer History Collection* 29: 85. Hicks, a black ranch hand who moved to Indian Territory in 1897, frequented Lexington's illegal Blue Front Saloon.

9. Interview with Ernest B. Morgan, August 9, 1937, Dewar, Oklahoma, in Foreman, *Indian Pioneer History Collection* 37: 204.

10. Interview with Tice Woods, April 14, 1938, Henryetta, Oklahoma, in Foreman, *Indian Pioneer History Collection* 75: 426.

11. Interview with Ed Coke, in Foreman, *Indian Pioneer History Collection* 51: 295–29.

12. Gomer Gower, "Experiences of Coal Miners in the Indian Territory, 1882–191," May 21, 1937 in Foreman, *Indian Pioneer History Collection* 105: 432.

13. Dew, "Moral Reform for the 'Magic City,' " 409–410; Grant Foreman, ed., *Indian Pioneer History Collection* 6: 437; interview with Shea Powell, April 22, 1937, Chickasha, Oklahoma, in Foreman, *Indian Pioneer History Collection* 70: 327; G. D. Boirum Collection, Manuscript Collections, Western History Collection, University of Oklahoma, Norman (hereafter cited as Boirum Collection).

14. Interview with George Tanner, October 18, 1937, Poteau, Oklahoma, in Foreman, *Indian Pioneer History Series* 46: 195; G. D. Boirum Collection.

15. *Muskogee Times-Democrat*, December 2, 1907; *Muskogee Times-Democrat*, August 25, 1910.

16. Kenny A. Franks, *The Rush Begins: A History of the Red Fork, Cleveland and Glenn Pool Oil Fields* (Oklahoma City: Western Heritage Books, Inc., 1984), 35; Ned DeWitt interview with an oil pipe-line worker, Works Progress Association Historic Sites and Federal Writers' Project, Manuscript Collection, Western History Collection, University of Oklahoma, Norman, Box 42, File 2 (hereafter cited as Works Progress Association Historical Sites); *Muskogee Times-Democrat*, August 7, 1911.

17. *Daily Oklahoman*, July 20, 1919.

18. Knox, "The Beginning of Perry Oklahoma," 22, 26; Interview with Harve Lovelday, September 17, 1937, Okemah, Oklahoma, in Foreman, *Indian Pioneer History Collection* 61: 428; Interview with Winifred M. Clark, September 20, 1936, Tecumseh, Oklahoma, in Foreman, *Indian Pioneer History Collection* 104: 325; Gumprecht, "A Saloon on Every Corner," 150.

19. Gumprecht, "A Saloon on Every Corner," 153–54; Saloon File, Barde Collection.

20. Linnaeus B. Ranch interview with L. E. Moyer, October 2, 1937, Gage, Oklahoma, in Foreman, *Indian Pioneer History Collection* 108: 481–85.

21. Durward Earl Newsom, *Drumright: The Glory Days of Boom Town* (Perkins, Okla.: Evans Publications, Inc., 1985), 50, 52–54.

22. Franks, *The Rush Begins*, 87, 94, 102, 104, 105.

23. Maude M. Fink interview with J. L. Avant, April 15, 1937, Clinton, Oklahoma, in Foreman, *Indian Pioneer History Collection* 99: 285; Fortson, *Pott County and What Has Come of It*, 79.

24. Anna R. Barry interview with Charles G. Watson, January 21, 1938, El Reno, Oklahoma, in Foreman, *Indian Pioneer History Collection* 95: 432.

25. Interview with Ike Nicholson, May 18, 1937, Bartlesville, Oklahoma, in Foreman, *Indian Pioneer History Collection* 38: 16–18; Alene D. McDowell interview with Mrs. Ruth Gilmore, April 26, 1938, Bartlesville, Oklahoma, in Foreman, *Indian Pioneer History Collection* 80: 140.

26. Interview with Mrs. Belle Gunn, June 9, 1937, El Reno, Oklahoma, in Foreman, *Indian Pioneer History Collection* 27: 82; Interview with David Newton Hatfield, April 23, 1937, in Foreman, *Indian Pioneer History Collection* 4: 470.

27. Newsom, *Drumright*, 50–54.

28. Interview with B. L. Bennett, July 9,1937, Durant, Oklahoma, in Foreman, *Indian Pioneer History Collection* 14: 353; Interview with Bush N. Bowman, June 12, 1937, Perry, Oklahoma, in Foreman, *Indian Pioneer History Collection* 16: 65–66; Interview with Jim Williams in Foreman, *Indian Pioneer History Collection* 46: 527.

29. *A Diamond Jubilee*, 1: 345; Interview with Moses Weinberger, August 5, 1937, Guthrie, Oklahoma, in Foreman, *Indian Pioneer History Collection* 67: 70.

30. *Okarche Times*, November 15, 1907; *Okarche Times*, December 20, 1907; *Okarche Times*, October 21, 1910; *Okarche Times*, May 18, 1917; Margaret Tulp, ed., *History of Canadian County Oklahoma* (El Reno, Okla.: Canadian County History Book Association, Inc., 1991), 144.

31. *Mangum Star*, August 8, 1907; *Daily Oklahoman* May 17, 1907; *Muskogee Times-Democrat*, June 21, 1907; *Checotah Enquirer*, August 9, 1907; *Lehigh Leader*, October 24, 1907.

32. *Daily Oklahoman*, May 15, 1915; *Enid Weekly Eagle*, July 16, 1908; Franklin, *Born Sober*, 27–35.

33. *American Issue*, Oklahoma Edition, September, May 1909; *(Vinita) Weekly Chieftain*, May 13, 1910.

34. Charles L. Daugherty to Moman Pruiett, July 9, 1909, Daugherty Collection, Box 2, File 2.

35. *American Issue*, Oklahoma Edition, May 1910; Franklin, *Born Sober*, 48.

36. *El Reno News*, August 6, 1897; *Shawnee Herald*, June 25, 1907.

37. *Daily Oklahoman*, May 1, 1907; Prohibition files, Barde Collection.

38. Bureau of the Census, *Thirteenth Census of the United States, 1910*, 3: 466, 467, 471, 473, 475, 477; Richard Rohrs, *The Germans in Oklahoma: The German-American Experience in Oklahoma* (Stillwater: Oklahoma State University, 1981), 1, 18–19.

39. *American Issue*, Oklahoma Edition, May 1909; Rohrs, *The Germans in Oklahoma*, 28.

40. *Daily Oklahoman*, April 18 and 20, 1918; *Harlow's Weekly*, November 14, 1917.

41. Haskell Papers: Correspondence, Box 1, File 6; *American Issue*, Oklahoma Edition, December 1910.

42. Prohibition files, Barde Collection; *American Issue*, Oklahoma Edition, September 1913, October 1913, April 1914.

43. *Purcell Register*, January 10, 1907; *Oklahoma City Times*, February 19, 1909; *Daily Oklahoman*, January 27, 1907; Prohibition files, Barde Collection; *Daily Oklahoman*, May 15, 1915.

8. The Oklahoma Liquor Question as a Class Issue

1. Federal Writers' Project of Oklahoma, Works Projects Administration, *Labor History of Oklahoma* (Oklahoma City: A. M. Van Horn, 1939), 22.

2. Interview with George Tanner, October 18, 1937, Poteau, Oklahoma, in Foreman, *Indian Pioneer History Collection* 46: 192–93, 195.

3. Gomer Gower interview with H. Lee Jackson, April 23, 1938, Poteau, Oklahoma, in Foreman, *Indian Pioneer History Collection* 86: 15; Interview with Roderick Dhu Perry, April 1, 1938, Collinsville, Oklahoma, in Foreman, *Indian Pioneer History Collection* 70: 187; Ruby Wolfenberger interview with Mack Wafer, March 23, 1938, Sentinel, Oklahoma, in Foreman, *Indian Pioneer History Collection* 95: 201.

4. *Harlow's Weekly*, September 7, 1912.

5. Ibid., March 1, 1913; November 7, 1914; April 3, 1915.

6. *Boley Progress* May 11, 1905; *Muskogee Times-Democrat* August 26, 1908; Earnest P. Bicknell to Lee Cruce, March 21, 1912, Cruce Papers: General Correspondence, Box 24, File 2.

7. United Mine Workers petition of Governor Lee Cruce for appropriation for a school of mines at Wilburton, March 1912, Cruce Paper:, General Correspondence, Box 27, File 5; Felix M. Gray, "History of Nowata County" (master's thesis, Oklahoma Agricultural and Mechanical College, 1937), 31; *Muskogee Times-Democrat*, November 22, 1912; *Muskogee Times-Democrat*, December 3, 1912; *Harlow's Weekly*, September 14, 1912.

8. *Muskogee Times-Democrat*, February 8, 1907; May 2, 1907.

9. Steven Lee Sewell, "Industrial Unionism and the Oklahoma Coal Industry, 1870–1935" (PhD diss., Oklahoma State University, 1992), 57–58.

10. *Muskogee Times Democrat*, April 5, 1906; *Coalgate Courier*, October 10, 1907; *Wilburton Gazette*, July 5, 1907.

11. Bureau of the Census, *Thirteenth Census of the United States, 1910*, 3: 482; Fred S. Caldwell, "List of Persons who Paid the Special U.S. tax for Liquor Dealers Compiled by Fred S. Caldwell up to 12-2-1908," Haskell Papers: Administrative File, Box 2, File 14. Paying this tax left one susceptible to state prosecution but provided immunity from federal officials until the 1912 ruling that former Indian Territory lands remained under the earlier federal liquor ban.

12. Mrs. Rose Gavin Brunson to Lee Cruce, February 12, 1913, Cruce Papers: General Correspondence, Box 55, File 4.

13. *Wilburton Gazette*, September 23, 1910; *Wilburton News*, September 7, 1910; *Wilburton Gazette*, September 30, 1910.

14. *American Issue*, Oklahoma Edition, September 221908; *Lehigh Leader*, October 20, 1910.

15. Bureau of the Census, *Thirteenth Census of the United States, 1910*, 3: 476; Bureau of the Census, *Fourteenth Census of the United States, 1920*, 3: 822.

16. E. H. Post to Lee Cruce, July 30, 1911, Lee Cruce Papers: General Correspondence, Box 18, File 7; Robert L. Williams to Reverend C. S. Stubblefield, January 20, 1916, Williams Papers: General Correspondence, 1916, Box 6, File 8; S. C. Fullerton to Robert L. Williams, January 20, 1916, Williams Papers: General Correspondence, 1916, Box 5, File 27.

17. *The State of Ok Ex Rel. Board of County Commissioners of the County of Ottawa, State of Oklahoma (Plaintiff) v. George O. Gibson (Dependent)*, Williams Papers: General Correspondence, 1916, Box 5, File 8.

18. Lt. J. H. Carey to Commanding Officer, November 5, 1919, Robertson Papers: General Correspondence, 1919, Box 11, File 5.

19. *Muskogee Times-Democrat*, November 2, 1906; *Harlow's Weekly*, August 23, 1913; November 20, 1918.

20. *Muskogee Times-Democrat*, February 6, 1907; March 3, 1907; *Harlow's Weekly*, June 12, 1915.

21. *Muskogee Times-Democrat*, November 15, 1906; *Daily Leader-Guthrie*, August 16, 1909.

22. "The Work's Safer Now'days," Ned DeWitt interview with an electrician at Seminole, Oklahoma, in Works Progress Association Historic Sites Box 43, File 9.

23. "Hot Oil," Ned DeWitt interview with an ex-convict from the oil fields, in Works Progress Association Historic Sites, Box 43, File 1.

24. Ned DeWitt interview with a foreman, in Works Progress Association Historic Sites, Box 42, File 28.

25. "Refinery Worker," Ned DeWitt interview with a refinery worker in Cyril, Oklahoma, in Works Progress Association Historic Sites, Box 43, File 21.

26. Ned DeWitt interview with an oil driller, in Works Progress Association Historic Sites, Box 42, File 26.

27. Dan Clifton to Robert Williams, July 14, 1915, Williams Papers: General Correspondence, 1915, Box 11, File 1.

28. Pauline P. Jackson, "Life and Society in Sapulpa," *Chronicles of Oklahoma* 43, no. 3 (Autumn 1965): 303; *American Issue*, Oklahoma Edition, March 1912.

29. Charles E. Helphrey to Lee Cruce, March 6, 1913, Cruce Papers: General Correspondence, Box 47, File 1; *Harlow's Weekly*, May 22, 1915.

30. Sapulpa residents' petition to Robert L. Williams, April 20, 1915, Williams Papers: General Correspondence, 1915, Box 8, File 7.

31. Lee Cruce to Mrs. E. M. Larmer, July 28, 1913, Cruce Papers: General Correspondence, Box 52, File 6; Robert L. Williams to Reverend Robert Van Meigs, October 29, 1915, Williams Papers: General Correspondence, 1915, Box 17, File 5; Gray, "History of Nowata County," 31, 36; J. W. Biffle to Lee Cruce, June 5, 1914, Cruce Papers: General Correspondence, Box 57, File 1.

32. *Guymon Herald*, March 29, 1917; Robert L. Williams to S. Prince Freeling, November 20, 1918, Williams Papers: Administrative File, 1917–1919, Box 1, File 9.

33. C. C. Suman to James B. A. Robertson, March 21, 1919, Robertson Papers: General Correspondence, 1919, Box 12, File 1; Ben C. Heald to James B. A. Robertson, March 25, 1919, Robertson Papers: General Correspondence, 1919, Box 15, File 4; Reverend W. A. Roach to James B. A. Robertson, June 14, 1919, Robertson Papers: General Correspondence, 1919, Box 27, File 5; William Noble to

James B. A. Robertson, July 3, 1919, Robertson Papers: General Correspondence, 1919, Box 27, File 5.

34. J. G. Martin and others to James B. A. Robertson, November 23, 1921, Robertson Papers: General Correspondence 1921, Box 6, File 3.

35. "I Take A Small Profit," Ned DeWitt interview with Cappy, in Works Progress Association Historic Sites, Box 43, File 18; Ned DeWitt interview with a rough neck, in Works Progress Association Historic Sites, Box 42, File 21.

36. *Muskogee Times-Democrat*, May 5, 1909; Reverend W. E. Harris to Lee Cruce, November 27, 1913, Cruce Papers: General Correspondence, 1911–1914, Box 5, File 1.

37. *Working* Man (Lawton), October 6, 1910. The editor reprinted this anti-prohibition editorial twice before the election.

38. Burbank, *When Farmers Voted Red*, xiv, 33.

39. *Indiahoma Union Signal*, August 23, 1906; October 25, 1906; December 13, 1906.

40. *Indiahoma Union Signal*, August 28, 1907; September 5, 1907; September 12, 1907.

41. *Lexington Leader*, September 3, 1909; W. T. Holland interview with Mary Gillette Engle, March 14, 1938, in Foreman, *Indian Pioneer History Collection* 91: 144; *Boley Progress*, July 27, 1905.

42. *Lexington Leader*, July 24, 1908; *Muskogee Times-Democrat*, January 31, 1910.

43. Alfred Baker to Lee Cruce, February 27, 1911, Cruce Papers: General Correspondence, Box 7, File 2.

44. *Muskogee Times-Democrat*, July 29, 1912.

45. *Muskogee Times-Democrat*, October 14, 1908; *Lexington Leader*, June 19, 1908.

46. *Muskogee Times-Democrat*, February 29, 1912.

47. Ibid., March 8, 1909; February 9, 1910.

48. Ibid., December 21, 1912.

49. Michael Kaplan, "New York City Tavern Violence and the Creation of a Working-Class Male Identity," *Journal of the Early Republic* 15 (Winter 1995): 592, 595, 614, 601.

50. Thompson, *Closing the Frontier*, 44.

51. Ned DeWitt Interview with a farm (oil field) boss, in Works Progress Administration Historic Sites, Box 42, File 20.

52. *Boley Progress*, May 11, 1905; *Muskogee Times-Democrat*, August 26, 1908; Cruce Papers: General Correspondence, Box 24, File 2.

53. Kingsdale, "The 'Poor Man's Club,' " 476, 479; Kathy Peiss, *Cheap Amusements: Working Women and Leisure in Turn-of-the-Century New York* (Philadelphia: Temple University Press, 1986), 17; Roy Rosenzweig, *Eight Hours for What We Will: Workers and Leisure in an Industrial City, 1870–1920* (Cambridge: Cambridge University Press, 1983), 36, 51.

54. *Oklahoma Messenger (Stillwater)*, August 1907; *Oklahoma Messenger (Stillwater)*, October 1909.

55. J. K. Green to Lee Cruce, July 22, 1911, Cruce Papers: General Correspondence, Box 17, File 3; *American Issue*, Oklahoma Edition, November 1911.

56. *Oklahoma Staats* Zeitung (Enid), March 28, 1919.

Conclusion

1. *(Eufaula) Indian Journal*, December 30, 1920; *Daily Oklahoman*, April 26, 1922, page 1; J. C. Martin to Attorney General S. P. Freeling, June 27, 1921, Robertson Papers: General Correspondence 1921, Box 6, File 3.

2. *Daily Oklahoman*, April 20, 1923; Sam W. Tuck to Ed Dabney, December 12, 1923, Attorney General and Assistant Attorney General Papers: Ed Dabney Personal Correspondence, Box 1, File 14; Ed Dabney to J. D. Montgomery, March 2, 1924, Attorney General and Assistant Attorney General Papers: Misc. Correspondence by Subject, Legislature 1923–1924.

3. Subscription Department Report of the Audit of June 30, 1921, Anti-Saloon League of America Series: Audits, The Ohio State Historical Society, Box 3, Folder 6 (hereafter cited as Anti-Saloon League of America Series: Audits); Anti-Saloon League of America Series: Audits, Box 2, Folder 4.

4. Hearings on Prohibition Modification Proposals before United States Senate Judiciary Committee, April 26, 1926, Anti-Saloon League of America Series: Clippings File, The Ohio State Historical Society, April 26 through May 1, 1926, Box 4, Folder 4. (hereafter cited as Anti-Saloon League of America Series: Clippings File).

5. *New York Times*, July 10, 1932, Anti-Saloon League of America Series: History, The Ohio State Historical Society, Box 5, Folder 48 (hereafter cited as Anti-Saloon League of America Series: History).

6. Summary of Prohibition Enforcement During the Fiscal Year Ended June 30, 1925, Anti-Saloon League of America Series: Clippings File, May 3–7, 1926, Box 4, Folder 5; *New York Times*, October 21, 1929, Anti-Saloon League of America Series: Enforcement, The Ohio State Historical Society, March throughDecember 1929, Box 4, Folder 32 (hereafter cited as Anti-Saloon League of America Series: Enforcement); *New York Times* January 28, 1930, Anti-Saloon League of America Series: Enforcement, Box 5, Folder 33.

7. Charles C. Alexander, *The Ku Klux Klan in the Southwest* (Frankfurt: University of Kentucky Press, 1965), 21, 43, 55; *Stonewall Weekly News*, September 22, 1921.

8. *Weekly Herald (Muskogee)*, November 15, 1921; *Fairview Republican*, January 27, 1922; *Oklahoma Herald*, September 5, 1922; *Oklahoma Herald*, September 19, 1922; *Harlow's Weekly*, November 24, 1921. From its first issue, the *Weekly Herald*

supported the Klan. Its name changed to the *Oklahoma Herald* early in 1922 and, subsequently the editor acknowledged that it was associated with the hooded order.

9. *Oklahoma Herald*, February 21, 1922; *Oklahoma Leader*, December 19, 1921; *Weekly Herald (Muskogee)*, December 13, 1921; *Weekly Herald (Muskogee)*, January 3, 1922; *Daily News (Pryor)*, August 22, 1922; *Oklahoma Herald* May 16, 1922; Tipton Klan letter of July 4, 1922, John C. Walton Collection, Western History Collection, University of Oklahoma, Norman. Box 17, File 16 (hereafter cited as Walton Collection); *Weekly Herald*, January 10, 1922; *Oklahoma Herald*, October 17, 1922; *Oklahoma Herald*, May 8, 1923.

10. James B. A. Robertson to W. L. Johnson, September 25, 1922, Robertson Papers: General Correspondence 1922, Box 3, File 11; N. Clay Jewett article in the *Imperial Nighthawk*, November 7, 1923, Carter Blue Clark Collection, Western History Collection, University of Oklahoma, Norman Box 1, File 1 (hereafter cited as Clark Collection).

11. *Oklahoma Herald*, October 3,1922; *Oklahoma Herald*, October 31,1922; 9 *Oklahoma Herald*, October 9, 1923; Howard A. Tucker, *A History of Governor Walton's War on the Ku Klux Klan, The Invisible Empire* (Oklahoma City: Southwest Publishing Co., 1923), 47; James Lowell Showalter, "Payne County and the Hooded Klan, 1921–1924" (PhD diss., Oklahoma State University, 2000), 74–75; Alexander, *The Ku Klux Klan*, 109, 134; *Harlow's Weekly*, December 1, 1923.

12. *American Issue*, Oklahoma Edition, 1912–19131913; Alexander, *The Ku Klux Klan*, 60.

13. Franklin, *Born Sober*, 107, 109.

14. Ibid., 111, 114.

15. Ibid., 119–20, 124, 129, 133.

16. John C. Burnham, *Bad Habits: Drinking, Smoking, Taking Drugs, Gambling, Sexual Misbehavior, and Swearing in American History* (New York: New York University Press, 1993), 1, 11–12.

17. Timberlake, *Prohibition and the Progressive Movement*, 1–3; Richard Hofstadter, *The Age of Reform: From Bryan to F.D.R.* (New York: Vintage Books, 1855), 211–12.

18. Burbank, *When Farmers Voted Red*, 161.

19. *The Prohibition Agitator*, June 13, 1906.

20. *Muskogee Times-Democrat*, May 20, 1907.

21. A. M. McDonald to Lee Cruce, July 10, 1911, Lee Cruce Papers: General Correspondence, 1911–1914, Box 18, File 3.

22. *Muskogee Times-Democrat*, December 11, 1908.

23. Burton, *Indian Territory and the United States*, xiv.

24. *Boley Progress*, January 4, 1912.

25. Brown, "Bible-belt Catholicism," 7, 32–33, 74, 28–29.

Bibliography

Archival Sources

Anti-Saloon League of America Series, The Ohio State Historical Society.

Attorney General and Assistant A. G. Papers, Oklahoma Department of Libraries Archives and Records, Oklahoma City.

Attorney General Civil Cases, Oklahoma Department of Libraries Archives and Records, Oklahoma City.

Boirum, G. D. Collection. Manuscript Collections, Western History Collection, University of Oklahoma, Norman.

Carter Blue Clark Collection. Western History Collection. University of Oklahoma, Norman.

Daugherty, Charles L. Collection. Manuscript Collections, Western History Collection, University of Oklahoma, Norman.

Enabling Act, McRill file, Frederick S. Barde Collection, Oklahoma Historical Society, Oklahoma City.

Ferguson, Thomas Benton Collection, Manuscript Collections, Western History Collection, University of Oklahoma, Norman.

Governor's Papers: Governor Charles N. Haskell (November 16, 1907 to January 9, 1911), Oklahoma Department of Libraries Archives and Records, Oklahoma City.

Governor's Papers: Governor Lee Cruce (January 9, 1911 to January 13, 1915), Oklahoma Department of Libraries Archives and Records, Oklahoma City.

Governor's Papers: Governor Robert L. Williams (January 11, 1915 to January 13, 1919), Oklahoma Department of Libraries Archives and Records, Oklahoma City.

Governor's Papers: Governor James B. A. Robertson (January 13, 1919 to January 8, 1923), Oklahoma Department of Libraries Archives and Records, Oklahoma City.

Haskell, Charles N. Collection, Manuscript Collections, Western History Collection, University of Oklahoma, Norman.

Laughbaum Manuscripts, Oklahoma Historical Society, Oklahoma City.

Lillie, Forress B. Collection, Manuscript Collections, Western History Collection, University of Oklahoma, Norman.

Lindsey, Lilah D. Collection, McFarlin Library, Tulsa University.

Prohibition Files, Frederick S. Barde Collection, Oklahoma Historical Society, Oklahoma City.

Purdum, Helen Collection, Manuscript Collections, Western History Collection, University of Oklahoma, Norman.

Saloon File, Frederick S. Barde Collection, Oklahoma Historical Society, Oklahoma City.

Tilghman, William Matthew Papers, Manuscript Collections, Western History Collection, University of Oklahoma, Norman.

Vertical Files. Oklahoma Territorial Museum, Guthrie, Oklahoma.

Walton, John C. Collection. Western History Collection, University of Oklahoma, Norman.

Woodrow, Thomas W. Papers, Manuscript Collections, Western History Collection, University of Oklahoma, Norman.

Works Progress Association Historical Sites and Federal Writers' Project, Manuscript Collections, Western History Collection, University of Oklahoma, Norman.

Government Documents

U.S. Department of Commerce, Bureau of the Census. *Fourteenth Census of the United States, 1920: Population,* 3. Washington, D.C.: Government Printing Office, 1923.

U.S. Department of Commerce, Bureau of the Census. *Population of Oklahoma and Indian Territory.* Washington, D.C.: Government Printing Office, 1907.

U.S. Department of Commerce, Bureau of the Census. *Special Reports: Religious Bodies, 1906. Part I: Summary and General Tables.* Washington, D.C.: Government Printing Office, 1910.

U.S. Department of Commerce, Bureau of the Census. *Special Reports: Religious Bodies, 1916. Part I: Summary and General Tables.* Washington, D.C.: Government Printing Office, 1919.

U.S. Department of Commerce, Bureau of the Census. *Thirteenth Census of the United States, 1910: Population,* 3. Washington, D.C.: Government Printing Office, 1913.

U.S. Department of Interior. *Letter from the Secretary of the Interior to the President of the Senate Transmitting Correspondence with the President Relating to the Coal, Oil, and Timber Lands in Indian Territory*. Washington, D.C.: Government Printing Office, 1907.

U.S. Department of Interior. William M. Jenkins. *Report of the Governor of Oklahoma to the Secretary of the Interior, 1901*. Washington, D.C.: Government Printing Office, n.d.

U.S. Department of Labor. *Twelfth Annual Report of the Commissioner of Labor: Economic Aspects of the Liquor Problem, 1897*. Washington, D.C.: Government Printing Office, 1898.

U.S. Supreme Court Reports, Lawyers' Edition, Vol. 55. Rochester, N.Y.: The Lawyers' Co-Operative Publishing Company, 1911.

Periodicals

Altus Times, 1908

Alva Review, 1902

American Issue, July 1908–November 1908

American Issue, Oklahoma Edition, September 1908–December 1916

Baptist Informer, 1910

Baptist Sunday School Evangel (Muskogee), 1907

Beaver Journal, 1907

Blackwell Morning Tribune, 1926–1932

Blackwell Times Record, 1912–1919

Boley Progress, 1905–1926

Checotah Enquirer, 1907–1910

Cherokee Phoenix and Indian Advocate (Tahlequah), 1833

Cherokee Republican, 1910

Cherokee Messenger, 1905

Chickasha Daily Express, 1900–1901

Coalgate Courier, 1907–1910

Constructive Socialist (Alva), 1907

Daily Leader (Guthrie), 1909

Daily News (Pryor), 1922

Daily Oklahoman (Oklahoma City), 1900–1925

Daily Oklahoma State Capital, 1905

El Reno News, 1897–1901

Enid Weekly Eagle, 1908–1909

(Eufaula) Indian Journal, 1901–1920

Eufaula Republican, 1907–1910

Fairview Republican, 1922

Frederick Enterprise, 1907

Guymon Herald, 1914–1917
Harlow's Weekly: A Journal of Comments and Current Events, 1912–1921
Illinois Issue, 1911
Indiahoma Union Signal, 1906–1907
Indian Journal (Muskogee), 1908
Kingfisher Free Press, 1891–1903
Lawton Constitution, 1905
Lehigh Leader, 1907–1910
Lexington Leader, 1908–1909
Mangum Star, 1907
McIntosh County Democrat, 1910
Muskogee Democrat, 1900–1906
Muskogee Times-Democrat, 1906–1920
Okarche Times, 1907–1920
Oklahoma City Times-Journal, 1903–1908
Oklahoma City Times, 1908–1909
Oklahoma Herald, 1922–1923
Oklahoma Leader, 1921
Oklahoma Messenger (Stillwater), 1921
Oklahoma Neuigkeiten *(Perry)*, 1912–1923
Oklahoma Staats Zeitung *(Enid)*, 1914–1920
Our Helper, 1903–1904
Pauls Valley Enterprise and Valley News, 1906
Prohibition Agitator, 1906
Purcell Register, 1907
Shawnee Herald, 1906–1907
Sooners in the War, 1919
Stillwater Advance, 1901–1907
Stillwater Gazette, 1900–1910
Stonewall Weekly News, 1921
Tupelo Times, 1907
(Vinita) Weekly Chieftain, 1910
Weekly Herald (Muskogee), 1921–1922
Wilburton Gazette, 1907–1910
Wilburton News, 1907–1910
Wisconsin Issue, 1906
Working Man (Lawton), 1910

Published Primary Sources

Brooks, Charles L., ed. *Minutes of the Sixty-Seventh Session of the East Oklahoma Conference of the Methodist Episcopal Church, South: For the Conference Year, 1911–12.*

———. *Minutes of the Sixty-Ninth Session of the East Oklahoma Conference of the Methodist Episcopal Church, South: For the Conference Year, 1913–14.*

Cherrington, Ernest H., ed. *The Anti-Saloon League Year Book, 1909–1920, 1922–1924: An Encyclopedia of Facts and Figures Dealing with the Liquor Traffic and the Temperance Reform.* Chicago: The Anti-Saloon League of America, n.d.

Dunkle, W. F., ed. *Official Minutes and Annual Report of the Oklahoma Conference of the Methodist Episcopal Church, South: For the Conference Year, 1905–6.*

———. *Official Minutes and Annual Report of the Sixty-Second Session of the Oklahoma Conference of the Methodist Episcopal Church, South: For the Conference Year, 1906–7.*

Foreman, Grant, ed. *Indian Pioneer History Collection.* Works Progress Administration Project S-149, 1937–1938.

Laughbaum, Horatio T. "Oklahoma." *Proceedings, Fifteenth National Convention of the Anti-Saloon League of America, November 10–13, 1913.* Westerville, Ohio: The American Issue Publishing Company, 1914.

Conference of the Methodist Episcopal Church, South: For the Conference Year, 1914–15.

Minutes of the Seventieth Session of the East Oklahoma Conference Methodist Episcopal Church, South: For the Conference Year, 1914–15.

Minutes of the Seventy-First Session of the East Oklahoma Conference Methodist Episcopal Church, South: For the Conference Year, 1915–16.

Minutes of the Seventy-Fourth Session of the East Oklahoma Conference Methodist Episcopal Church, South: For the Conference Year, 1918–19.

Minutes of the Seventy-Sixth Session of the East Oklahoma Conference Methodist Episcopal Church, South: For the Conference Year, 1920–21.

Norman Transcript.

Oklahoma. *Journal of the House of Representatives of the Regular Session of the First Legislature of Oklahoma.* Guthrie, Okla.: Leader Printing and Manufacturing House, 1908.

Oklahoma. *Journal of the House of Representatives of the Regular Session of the Fourth Legislature of Oklahoma.* Oklahoma City: Harlow-Ratliff Printing Company, 1913.

Oklahoma. *Journal of the House of Representatives of the Regular Session of the Second State Legislature of Oklahoma.* n.p.: n.p., n.d.

Oklahoma. *Journal of the House of Representatives of the Regular Session of the Sixth Legislature of Oklahoma.* n.p.: n.p., n.d.

Oklahoma. *Journal of the House Proceedings of the Sixth Legislative Assembly of the Territory of Oklahoma, Beginning January 8, 1901, Ending March 8, 1901.* n.p.: n.p., n.d.

Oklahoma. *Journal Proceedings of the House of Representatives of the Third Legislature — Regular Session State of Oklahoma.* Oklahoma City: Warden Printing Company, 1911.

Oklahoma. *Oklahoma Reports, Volume X: Cases Determined in the Supreme Court of the*

Territory of Oklahoma at January 1901 and Previous Terms and not Published in Former Volumes. Guthrie, Okla.: State Capital Printing Company, 1901.

Oklahoma. *Oklahoma Reports, Volume XI: Cases Determined in the Supreme Court of the Territory of Oklahoma at the June 1901 Term, January 1902 and June 1902 Terms.* Guthrie, Okla.: State Capital Printing Company, 1902.

Oklahoma. *State of Oklahoma Session Laws of 1907–1908.* Guthrie: Oklahoma Printing Company, 1908.

Oklahoma. *State of Oklahoma Session Laws of 1909.* Oklahoma City: Oklahoma Engraving and Printing Company, 1909.

Oklahoma. *State of Oklahoma Session Laws of 1910.* Guthrie, Okla.: The State Capital Company, 1910.

Oklahoma. *State of Oklahoma Session Laws of 1910–1911.* Guthrie, Okla.: The Leader Printing Company, 1911.

Oklahoma. *State of Oklahoma Session Laws of 1913.* Guthrie, Okla.: Co-operative Publishing Company, 1913.

Oklahoma. *State of Oklahoma Session Laws of 1915.* Oklahoma City: State Printing and Publishing Company, 1915.

Oklahoma. *State of Oklahoma Session Laws of 1916.* Guthrie, Okla.: Co-operative Publishing Company, 1916.

Oklahoma. *State of Oklahoma Session Laws of 1917.* Guthrie, Okla.: Co-operative Publishing Company, 1917.

Oklahoma. *State of Oklahoma Session Laws of 1919.* Oklahoma City: Harlow Publishing Company, 1919.

Oklahoma. *Territory of Oklahoma Session Laws of 1903.* Guthrie, Okla.: State Capital Publishing Company, 1903.

Oklahoma. *Wilson's Revised and Annotated Statutes of Oklahoma, 1903, Vol. I.* Guthrie, Okla.: State Capital Publishing Company, 1903.

Proceedings of the Constitutional Convention of the Proposed State of Oklahoma, Held at Guthrie, Oklahoma, November 20, 1906 to November 17, 1907. Muskogee, Okla.: Muskogee Printing Co., n.d.

Proceedings, Fifteenth National Convention of the Anti-Saloon League of America, November 10–13, 1913. Westerville, Ohio: American Issue Publishing Company, 1913.

Proceedings, The Twentieth National Convention of the Anti-Saloon League of America, December 6–8, 1921. Washington, D.C.: S. E. Nicholson, 1921.

Roberts, J. C., and C. H. Woods. *Report of the Attorney General of the Territory of Oklahoma.* Guthrie, Okla.: State Capital Publishing Company, 1902.

Sweet, E. M., Jr., ed. *Official Minutes and Annual Report of the Sixty-Third Session of the Oklahoma Conference of the Methodist Episcopal Church, South: For the Conference Year, 1907–8.*

———. *Minutes and Annual Report of the Sixty-Fourth Session of the Oklahoma Conference of the Methodist Episcopal Church, South: For the Conference Year, 1908–9.*

————. *Minutes of the Sixty-Fifth Session of the Oklahoma Conference of the Methodist Episcopal Church, South: For the Conference Year, 1909–10.*

————. *Minutes of the Sixty-Sixth Session of the East Oklahoma Conference of the Methodist Episcopal Church, South: For the Conference Year, 1910–11.*

Books and Articles

Alexander, Charles C. *The Ku Klux Klan in the Southwest.* Frankfurt: University of Kentucky Press, 1965.

Allen, Iva Williams. "Early Days in Meers." *Chronicles of Oklahoma* 32, no. 3 (Autumn 1954): 278–89.

Anderson, Ken. "Frank Frantz: Governor of Oklahoma Territory, 1906–1907." *Chronicles of Oklahoma* 53, no. 1 (Spring 1975): 128–44.

Asbury, Herbert. *The Great Illusion: An Informal History of Prohibition.* Garden City, N.Y.: Doubleday & Company, 1950.

Babcock, Sidney H., and John Y. Bryce. *History of Methodism in Oklahoma: Story of the Indian Mission Annual Conference of the Methodist Episcopal Church, South.* N.p.: Sydney Henry Babcock, 1937.

Bachhofer, Aaron II. "Strange Bedfellows: Progressivism, Radicalism, and the Oklahoma Constitution in Historical Perspective." *Chronicles of Oklahoma* 77, no. 3 (Fall 1999): 244–71.

Bader, Robert Smith. *Prohibition in Kansas: A History.* Lawrence: University of Kansas Press, 1986.

Baker, Paula. "The Domestication of Politics: Women and American Political Society, 1780–1920." *American Historical Review* 89, no. 3 (June 1984): 620–47.

————. *The Moral Frameworks of Public Life: Gender, Politics, and the State in Rural New York, 1870–1930.* New York: Oxford University Press, 1991.

Barr, Andrew. *Drink: A Social History of America.* New York: Carroll & Graf, 1999.

Bederman, Gail. *Manliness and Civilization: A Cultural History of Gender and Race in the United States, 1880–1917.* Chicago: University of Chicago Press, 1995.

Bendroth, Margaret. "Rum, Romanism, and Evangelism: Protestants and Catholics in Late-Nineteenth-Century Boston." *Church History* 68, no. 3 (September 1999): 627–47.

Bendroth, Margaret Lamberts. *Fundamentalism and Gender, 1875 to the Present.* New Haven, Conn.: Yale University Press, 1993.

————. "Fundamentalism and the Family: Gender, Culture, and the American Pro-Family Movement." *Journal of Women's History* 10, no. 4 (Winter 1999): 35–54.

Bernard, Richard. *The Poles in Oklahoma.* Norman: University of Oklahoma Press, 1980.

Bicha, Karel D. *The Czechs in Oklahoma.* Norman: University of Oklahoma Press, 1980.

Blakey, Ellen Sue, Robbie Boman, Jim Downing, Ina Hall, John Hamill, and Peggi Ridgeway. *The Tulsa Spirit.* Tulsa, Okla.: Heritage Press, Inc., 1979.

Bland, Sister Joan. *Hibernian Crusade: The Story of the Catholic Total Abstinence Union of America.* Washington, D.C.: Catholic University of America Press, 1951.

Blessing, Patrick. *The British and Irish in Oklahoma.* Norman: University of Oklahoma Press, 1980.

Blochowiak, Mary Ann. " 'Woman with a Hatchet': Carry Nation Comes to Oklahoma Territory." *Chronicles of Oklahoma* 59, no. 2 (Summer 1981): 132–51.

Blocker, Jack S. *Retreat from Reform, The Prohibition Movement in the United States 1890–1913.* Westport, Conn.: Greenwood Press, 1976.

——. *American Temperance Movements: Cycles of Reform.* Boston: Twayne, 1989.

Boles, David C. "The Prairie Oil & Gas Company, 1901–1911." *Chronicles of Oklahoma* 46, no. 2 (Summer 1968): 189–200.

Bordin, Ruth. *Woman and Temperance: The Quest for Power and Liberty, 1873–1900.* Philadelphia: Temple University Press, 1981.

Botkin, Sam L. *The Episcopal Church in Oklahoma.* Oklahoma City: American-Bond Printing Company, 1958.

Brill, H. E. *Story of the Methodist Episcopal Church in Oklahoma.* Oklahoma City: Oklahoma City University Press, 1939.

Brown, Kenny L. *The Italians in Oklahoma.* Norman: University of Oklahoma Press, 1980.

——. "Progressivism in Oklahoma Politics, 1900–1913: A Reintepretation," in "An Oklahoma I Had Never Seen Before" *Alternative Views of Oklahoma History,* ed. Davis D. Joyce. Norman: University of Oklahoma Press, 1994.

——. "William C. Grimes: Acting Governor of Oklahoma Territory, 1901." *Chronicles of Oklahoma* 53, no. 1 (Spring 1975): 93–108.

Brown, Thomas Elton. "Oklahoma's Bone Dry Law and the Roman Catholic Church." *Chronicles of Oklahoma* 52, no. 3 (Fall 1974): 316–30.

Brunk, Gregory. "Freshman vs. Incumbents: Congressional Voting Patterns on Prohibition Legislation during the Progressive Era." *Journal of American Studies* 24, no. 2 (August 1990): 235–42.

Bryant, Keith L., Jr. "Labor in Politics: The Oklahoma State Federation of Labor during the Age of Reform." *Labor History* 11, no. 3 (Summer 1970): 249–76.

Burbank, Garin. "The Political and Social Attitudes of Some Early Oklahoma Democrats." *Chronicles of Oklahoma* 52, no. 4 (Winter 1974–1975): 439–55.

——. *When Farmers Voted Red: The Gospel of Socialism in the Oklahoma Countryside, 1910–1914.* Westport, Conn.: Greenwood Press, 1976.

Burgess, Larry E. *The Lake Mohonk Conference of Friends of the Indian, Guide to the Annual Reports.* New York: Clearwater, 1975.

Burnham, John C. "New Perspectives on the Prohibition 'Experiment' of the 1920's," *Journal of Social History* 2 (1968): 51–68.

———. *Bad Habits: Drinking, Smoking, Taking Drugs, Gambling, Sexual Misbehavior, and Swearing in American History*. New York: New York University Press, 1993.

Burrill, Robert M. "The Osage Pasture Map." *Chronicles of Oklahoma* 53, no. 2 (Summer 1975): 204–11.

Burton, Jeffrey. *Indian Territory and the United States, 1866–1906: Courts, Government, and the Movement for Oklahoma Statehood*. Norman: University of Oklahoma Press, 1995.

Butterfield, Reverend Andrew E. *Comanche, Kiawa and Apache Missions: Forty-two Years Ago and Now*. Childress, Tex.: n.p., 1934.

Carney, George O. "Oklahoma's Territorial Delegates and Progressivism, 1901–1907." *Chronicles of Oklahoma* 52, no. 1 (Spring 1974): 38–51.

Casey, Orben J. "Governor Lee Cruce, White Supremacy and Capital Punishment, 1911–1915." *Chronicles of Oklahoma* 52, no. 4 (Winter 1974–1975): 456–75.

———. "Governor Lee Cruce and Law Enforcement, 1911–1915." *Chronicles of Oklahoma* 54, no 4 (Winter 1976–1977): 435–60.

Cassal, Reverend Hilary. "Missionary Tour in the Chickasaw Nation and Western Indian Territory." *Chronicles of Oklahoma* 34, no. 4 (Winter 1956–1957): 397–416.

Clark, Blue. "Delegates to the Constitutional Convention." *Chronicles of Oklahoma* 48, no. 4 (Winter 1970–71): 400–15D.

Clark, Norman H. *Deliver Us from Evil: An Interpretation of American Prohibition*. New York: W. W. Norton, 1976.

Clark, Stanley. "Immigrants in the Choctaw Coal Industry." *Chronicles of Oklahoma* 33, no. 4 (Winter 1955–1956): 440–55.

Clegg, Leland, and William B. Oden. *Oklahoma Methodism in the Twentieth Century*. Oklahoma City: Oklahoma Conference, The Methodist Church, 1968.

Clemens, Elisabeth S. "Organizational Repertoires and Institutional Change: Women's Groups and the Transformation of American Politics, 1890-1920." *American Journal of Sociology* 98, no. 4 (January 1993): 755–98.

Coleman, McAlester. *Nation* 117 (5 September 1923): 239–40.

Colvin, D. Leigh. *Prohibition in the United States: A History of the Prohibition Party and the Prohibition Movement*. New York: George H. Doran Company, 1926.

Corwin, Hugh D. "Protestant Missionary Work among the Comanches and Kiowas." *Chronicles of Oklahoma* 46, no. 1 (Spring 1968): 41–57.

Creel, Von Russell. "Socialists in the House: The Oklahoma Experience, Part I." *Chronicles of Oklahoma* 70, no. 3 (Summer 1992): 144–83.

Curtis, Ralph E., Jr. "Relations between the Quapaw National Council and the Roman Catholic Church, 1876–1927." *Chronicles of Oklahoma* 55, no. 2 (Summer 1977): 211–21.

DeBerg, Betty. *Ungodly Women: Gender and the First Wave of American Fundamentalism*. Minneapolis: Fortress Press, 1990.

Debo, Angie. *And Still the Waters Run: The Betrayal of the Five Civilized Tribes.* Princeton, N.J.: Princeton University Press, 1940.

Denzin, Norman K. "Notes on the Criminogenic Hypothesis: A Case Study of the American Liquor Industry." *American Sociological Review* 42, no. 6 (December 1977): 905–20.

Dew, Jay R. "Moral Reform for the 'Magic City': Temperance in Guthrie, Oklahoma, 1889–1907." *Chronicles of Oklahoma* 77, no. 4 (Winter, 1999–2000): 406–27.

A Diamond Jubilee: History of Tillman County, 1901–1976, Vol. 1. N.p.: Tillman County Historical Society, 1976.

Edgley, Charles, and Dennis Brissett. *A Nation of Medlers.* Boulder, Colo.: Westview Press, 1999.

Encyclopedia of Southern Baptists, Vol. 2. Nashville: Broadman Press, 1958.

England, Stephen J. *Oklahoma Christians: A History of Christian Churches and of the Start of the Christian Church (Disciples of Christ) in Oklahoma.* N.p.: Bethany Press, 1975.

Evans, Ralph, and Helen Evans. *The Cross to the Crown: A History of the Southern Baptist Churches of Enon Baptist Association in Southern Oklahoma.* Ardmore, Okla.: Enon Baptist Association, n.d.

Federal Writers' Project of Oklahoma, Works Projects Administration. *Labor History of Oklahoma.* Oklahoma City: A. M. Van Horn, 1939.

Finney, Frank F. "The Osage Indians and the Liquor Problem before Statehood." *Chronicles of Oklahoma* 34, no. 4 (Winter, 1956–1957): 456–64.

Fischer, LeRoy H. "Oklahoma Territory, 1890–1907." *Chronicles of Oklahoma* 53, no. 1 (Spring 1975): 3–8.

———, ed. *Oklahoma Governors, 1907–1929: Turbulent Politics.* Oklahoma City: Oklahoma Historical Society, 1981.

Foreman, Grant. "A Century of Prohibition." *Chronicles of Oklahoma* 12, no. 2 (June 1934): 133–41.

Forbes, Gerald. "History of the Osage Blanket Lease." *Chronicles of Oklahoma* 19, no. 1 (March 1941): 70–81.

Fortson, John. *Pott County and What Has Come of It: A History of Pottawatomie County.* N.p.: Pottawatomie County Historical Society, 1936.

Foster, Gaines M. *Moral Reconstruction: Christian Lobbyists and the Federal Legislation of Morality, 1865–1920.* (Chapel Hill: University of North Carolina Press, 2002).

Fowler, James H. "Tar and Feather Patriotism: The Suppression of Dissent in Oklahoma During World War One." *Chronicles of Oklahoma* 56, no. 4 (Winter 1978–1979): 409–30.

———. "Creating an Atmosphere of Suppression, 1914–1917." *Chronicles of Oklahoma* 59, no. 2 (Summer 1981): 202–23.

Fowler, Oscar P. *The Haskell Regime: The Intimate Life of Charles Nathaniel Haskell.* Oklahoma City: Boles Printing Company, Inc., 1933.

Franklin, Jimmie Lewis. *Born Sober: Prohibition in Oklahoma, 1907–1959*. Norman: University of Oklahoma Press, 1971.

———. *Journey toward Hope: A History of Blacks in Oklahoma*. Norman: University of Oklahoma Press, 1982.

———. "A Note on Prohibition in Oklahoma." *Chronicles of Oklahoma* 43, no. 1 (Spring 1965): 19–34.

———. "That Noble Experiment: A Note on Prohibition in Oklahoma," *Chronicles of Oklahoma* 43, no. 1 (Spring 1965): 19–34.

Franks, Kenny A. *The Oklahoma Petroleum Industry*. Norman: University of Oklahoma Press, 1980.

———. *Rag Town: A History of the Greater Healdton-Hewitt Oil Field*. Oklahoma City: Western Heritage Books, 1986.

———. *The Rush Begins: A History of the Red Fork, Cleveland and Glenn Pool Oil Fields*. Oklahoma City: Western Heritage Books, 1984.

French, Laurence A., and Jim Hornbuckle. "Alcoholism among Native Americans: An Analysis." *Social Work* 25 (July 1980): 275–80.

Gaskin, J. M. *Baptist Milestones in Oklahoma*. Oklahoma City: Baptist General Convention of the State of Oklahoma, 1966.

Gibson, Arrel. *The Chickasaws*. Norman: University of Oklahoma Press, 1971.

Gilfoyle, Timothy J. "The Moral Origins of Political Surveillance: The Preventative Society in New York City, 1867–1918." *American Quarterly* 38, no. 4 (Autumn 1986): 637–52.

Gill, Jerry L. "Thomas Benton Ferguson: Governor of Oklahoma Territory, 1901–1906." *Chronicles of Oklahoma* 53, no. 1 (Spring 1975): 109–27.

Gilmore, Glenda Elizabeth. *Gender and Jim Crow: Women and the Politics of White Supremacy in North Caroline, 1896–1920*. Chapel Hill: University of North Carolina Press, 1996.

Goldberg, Michael Lewis. *An Army of Women: Gender and Politics in Gilded Age Kansas*. Baltimore: Johns Hopkins University Press, 1997.

Gordon, Elizabeth Putnam. *Women Torch-Bearers: The Story of the Woman's Christian Temperance Union*, 2nd ed. Evanston, Ill.: National Woman's Christian Temperance Union Publishing House, 1924.

Gorn, Elliott J. " 'Good-Bye Boys, I Die a True American': Homicide, Nativism, and Working-Class Culture in Antebellum New York City." *Journal of American History* 74, no. 2 (September 1987): 388–410.

"The Grandfather Clause in Oklahoma." *Outlook* 95 (August 20, 1910): 853–54.

Green, Elna C. *Southern Strategies: Southern Women and the Woman Suffrage Question*. Chapel Hill: University of North Carolina Press, 1997.

Gregory, Robert. *Oil in Oklahoma*. Muskogee, Okla.: Leake Industries, 1976.

Gumprecht, Blake. "A Saloon on Every Corner: Whiskey Towns of Oklahoma Territory, 1889–1907." *Chronicles of Oklahoma* 74 no. 2 (Summer 1996): 146–73.

Gusfield, Joseph. *Contested Meanings: The Construction of Alcohol Problems*. Madison: The University of Wisconsin Press, 1996.

———. "Social Structure and Moral Reform: A Study of the Woman's Christian Temperance Union." *American Journal of Sociology* 61, no. 3 (November 1955): 221–32.

———. *Symbolic Crusade: Status Politics and the American Temperance Movement*, 2nd. ed. Urbana: University of Illinois Press, 1986.

Haddock, Louise, and Dr. J. M. Gaskin. *Baptist Heroes in Oklahoma (Grandfather Tells Tommy and Lee Ann the History of the Oklahoma Baptists)*. Oklahoma City: Baptist General Convention of Oklahoma, 1976.

Hale, Douglas. *The Germans from Russia in Oklahoma*. Norman: University of Oklahoma Press, 1980.

Harlow, Victor E. *Oklahoma: Its Origins and Development*. Oklahoma City: Harlow Publishing Corporation, 1935.

Harper, Richard H. "The Missionary Work of the Reformed (Dutch) Church in America, In Oklahoma, Part III: Work among the People." *Chronicles of Oklahoma* 19, no. 3 (June 1941): 170–79.

Harris, Carl V. "Reforms in Government Control of Negroes in Birmingham, Alabama, 1890–1920." *Journal of Southern History* 38, no. 4 (November 1972): 567–600.

Haskell, H. J. "Martial Law in Oklahoma." *Outlook* 135 (September 26, 1923): 183.

Hays, Samuel P. *The Response to Industrialism, 1885–1914*. Chicago: University of Chicago Press, 1957.

Hazell, Thomas Arthur. "George Washington Steele: Governor of Oklahoma Territory, 1890–1891." *Chronicles of Oklahoma* 53, no. 1 (Spring 1975): 9–22.

Heidenreich, C. Adrian. "Alcohol and Drug Use and Abuse among Indian-Americans: A Review of Issues and Sources." *Journal of Drug Issues* 6, no. 3 (Summer 1976): 256–72.

Henslick, Harry E. "Abraham Jefferson Seay: Governor of Oklahoma Territory, 1892–1893." *Chronicles of Oklahoma* 53, no. 1 (Spring 1975): 28–45.

Hill, Mozell C. "Basic Racial Attitudes toward Whites in the Oklahoma All-Negro Community." *American Journal of Sociology* 49, no. 6 (May 1944): 519–23.

Hillerman, Abbie B. *History of the Woman's Christian Temperance Union of the Indian Territory, Oklahoma Territory, and the State of Oklahoma*. Sapulpa, Okla.: Jennings Printing and Stationary Company, 1925.

Hilton, O. A. "The Oklahoma Council of Defense and the First World War." *Chronicles of Oklahoma* 20, no. 2 (March 1942): 18–42.

A History of the Parish of St. John the Baptist Catholic Church Edmond, Oklahoma, 1889–1989. Edmond, Okla.: St. John the Baptist Catholic Church, 1989.

Hofstadter, Richard. *The Age of Reform: From Bryan to F.D.R.* New York: Vintage Books, 1955.

Hohner, Robert A. "Bishop Cannon's Apprenticeship in Temperance Politics, 1901–1918." *Journal of Southern History* 34, no. 1 (February 1968): 33–49.

Jackson, Pauline P. "Life and Society in Sapulpa." *Chronicles of Oklahoma* 43, no. 3 (Autumn 1965): 297–318.

James, Louise Boyd. "The Woman Suffrage Issue in the Oklahoma Constitutional Convention." *Chronicles of Oklahoma* 56, no. 4 (Winter 1978–1979): 379–92.

Jeltz, Wyatt F. "The Relations of Negroes and Choctaw and Chickasaw Indians." *Journal of Negro History* 33, no. 1 (January 1948): 24–37.

Jensen, Richard J. *The Winning of the Midwest: Social and Political Conflict, 1888–1896.* Chicago: University of Chicago Press, 1971.

Johnson, Paul E. *A Shopkeeper's Millennium: Society and Revivals in Rochester, New York, 1815–1837.* New York: Hill and Wang, 1978.

Johnson, William E. *Ten Years of Prohibition in Oklahoma.* Westerville, Ohio: American Issue Publishing Company, n.d.

Johnson, W. H. "The Saloon in Indian Territory." *North American Review* 146 (March 1888): 340–41.

Kalisch, Philip A. "Ordeal of the Oklahoma Coal Miners: Coal Mine Disasters in the Sooner State, 1886–1945." *Chronicles of Oklahoma* 48, no. 3 (Autumn 1970): 331–40.

Kaplan, Michael. "New York City Tavern Violence and the Creation of a Working-Class Male Identity." *Journal of the Early Republic* 15 (Winter 1995): 591–617.

Kazin, Michael. *The Populist Persuasion: An American History.* New York: Basic Books, 1995.

Kerber, Linda K. "Separate Spheres, Female Worlds, Woman's Place: The Rhetoric of Women's History." *Journal of American History* 75, no. 1 (June 1988): 9–39.

Kerr, K. Austin. *Organized for Prohibition, A New History of the Anti-Saloon League.* New Haven, Conn.: Yale University Press, 1985.

Kimmel, Michael. *Manhood in America: A Cultural History.* New York: The Free Press, 1996.

Kingsdale, Jon M. "The 'Poor Man's Club': Social Functions of the Urban Working-Class Saloon." *American Quarterly* 25, no. 4 (October 1973): 471–89.

Kjaer, Jens Christian. "The Lutheran Mission at Oaks, Oklahoma." *Chronicles of Oklahoma* 28, no. 1 (Spring 1950): 42–51.

Kleppner, Paul. *The Cross of Culture: A Social Analysis of Midwestern Politics, 1850–1900.* New York: Free Press, 1970.

———. *The Third Electoral System, 1853–1892: Parties, Voters, and Political Cultures.* Chapel Hill: University of North Carolina Press, 1979.

Kroecker, Marvin E. *Comanches and Mennonites on the Oklahoma Plains: A. J. and Magdelena Becker and the Post Oak Mission.* Fresno, Calif.: Centers for Mennonite Brethren Studies, 1997.

Krout, John Allen. *The Origins of Prohibition.* New York: Alfred A. Knopf, 1925.

Kyvig, David E. "Women against Prohibition." *American Quarterly* 28, no. 4 (Autumn 1976): 465–82.

Lee, Alfred McClung. "Techniques of Social Reform: An Analysis of the New Prohibition Drive." *American Sociological Review* 9, no. 1 (February 1944): 65–77.

Lyon, Vincent T. "The Repeal of Prohibition: The End of Oklahoma's Noble Experiment." *Chronicles of Oklahoma* 76, no. 4 (Winter, 1998–1999): 416–35.

Maxwell, Amos D. "The Sequoyah Convention." *Chronicles of Oklahoma* 28, no. 2 (Summer 1950): 161–92.

———. "The Sequoyah Convention, Part II." *Chronicles of Oklahoma* 28, no. 3 (Autumn 1950): 299–340.

McDonagh, Eileen L. "Woman Suffrage in the Progressive Era: Patterns of Opposition and Support in Referenda Voting, 1910–1918." *American Political Science Review* 79, no. 2 (June 1985): 415–35.

McKenzie, Frederick Arthur. *"Pussyfoot" Johnson, Crusader-Reformer-A Man Among Men*. New York: Fleming H. Revell Company, 1920.

McMasters, Clyde Valancourt. *Witnessing throughout the Twentieth Century: First Presbyterian Church Sapulpa, Oklahoma Celebrates One Hundred Years*. Franklin, Tenn.: Providence House, 1995.

McReynolds, Edwin C. *Oklahoma: A History of the Sooner State*. Norman: University of Oklahoma Press, 1954.

McRill, Albert. *And Satan Came Also: An Inside Story of a City's Social and Political History*. Oklahoma City: Britton Publishing Company, 1955.

McRill, Leslie. "An Early Crusader for Law and Order in Oklahoma: Thompson Benton Ferguson." *Chronicles of Oklahoma* 36, no. 1 (Spring 1958): 79–87.

Mellinger, Phillip. "Discrimination and Statehood in Oklahoma." *Chronicles of Oklahoma* 49, no. 3 (Autumn 1971): 340–78.

———. "Agrarian Socialism and the Negro in Oklahoma, 1900–1918." *Labor History* 11, no. 3 (Summer 1970): 277–84.

Merz, Charles. *The Dry Decade*. Garden City, N.Y.: Doubleday, Doran & Company, Inc., 1930.

Miles, Ray. *"King of the Wildcatters": The Life and Times of Tom Slick, 1883–1930*. College Station: Texas A&M University Press, 1996.

Milligan, Dorothy, ed. *The Indian Way, Cherokees*. Quanah, Tex: Nortex Press, 1977.

———. *The Indian Way, Chickasaws*. Quanah, Tex.: Nortex Press, 1976.

———. *The Indian Way, Choctaws*. Quanah, Tex.: Nortex Press, n.d.

Misch, Mrs. J. O. "Lilah D. Lindsey." *Chronicles of Oklahoma* 33, no. 2 (Summer 1955): 195–200.

Monahan, David, ed. *One Family: One Century, A Photographic History of the Catholic Church in Oklahoma 1875–1975*. Oklahoma City: Archdiocese of Oklahoma City, 1977.

Morgan, David R., Robert E. England, and George G. Humphreys. *Oklahoma Politics and Policies: Governing the State*. Lincoln: University of Nebraska Press, 1991.

Morgan, James F. "William Cary Renfrow: Governor of Oklahoma Territory, 1893–1897." *Chronicles of Oklahoma* 53, no. 1 (Spring 1975): 46–65.

Morris, John W., Charles R. Goins, and Edwin C. McReynolds, eds. *Historical Atlas of Oklahoma*, 3rd ed. Norman: University of Oklahoma Press, 1986.

Murdock, Catherine Gilbert. *Domesticating Drink: Women, Men, and Alcohol in America, 1870–1940*. Baltimore: Johns Hopkins University Press, 1998.

Morton, Michael. "No Time to Quibble: The Jones Conspiracy Trial of 1917." *Chronicles of Oklahoma* 59, no. 2 (Summer 1981): 224–36.

Murphy, Mary. "Bootlegging Mothers and Drinking Daughters: Gender and Prohibition in Butte, Montana." *American Quarterly* 46, no. 2 (June 1994): 174–94.

"The Negro in Oklahoma." *Outlook* 95 (18 June 1910): 328.

Nesbitt, Paul, ed. "Governor Haskell Tells of Two Conventions." *Chronicles of Oklahoma*, 14, no. 2 (June 1936): 190–217.

Neuringer, Sheldon. "Governor Walton's War on the Ku Klux Klan: An Episode in Oklahoma History." *Chronicles of Oklahoma* 45, no. 2 (Summer 1967): 153–79.

Newsom, Durward Earl. *Drumright: The Glory Days of a Boom Town*. Perkins, Okla.: Evans Publications, 1985.

Odegard, Peter. *Pressure Politics: The Story of the Anti-Saloon League*. New York: Columbia University Press, 1928.

Ownby, Ted. *Subduing Satan: Religion, Recreation, and Manhood in the Rural South, 1865–1920*. Chapel Hill: University of North Carolina Press, 1990.

Patterson, Michael S. "The Fall of a Bishop: James Cannon, Jr., versus Carter Glass, 1909–1934." *Journal of Southern History* 39 no. 4 (November 1973): 491–518.

Peake, Kenneth J., and Patricia A. Peake. *Kansas Temperance: Much Ado about Booze, 1870–1920*. Manhattan, Kans.: Sunflower University Press, 2000.

Pegram, Thomas R. *Battling Demon Rum: The Struggle for a Dry America, 1880–1933*. Chicago: Ivan R. Dee, 1998.

———. "Temperance Politics and Regional Political Culture: The Anti-Saloon League in Maryland and the South, 1907–1915." *Journal of Southern History* 63, no. 1 (February 1997): 57–90.

Peiss, Kathy. *Cheap Amusements: Working Women and Leisure in Turn-of-the-Century New York*. Philadelphia: Temple University Press, 1986.

Petrin, Ronald A. *French Canadians in Massachusetts Politics, 1815–1915: Ethnicity and Political Pragmatism*. Philadelphia: The Balch Institute Press, 1990.

Porter, Delmer W. "William Miller Jenkins: Governor of Oklahoma Territory, 1901." *Chronicles of Oklahoma* 53, no. 1 (Spring 1975): 83–92.

Powers, Madelon. *Faces along the Bar: Lore and Order in the Workingman's Saloon, 1870–1920*. Chicago: University of Chicago Press, 1998.

Ralls, Mrs. G. T. *Oklahoma Trails: A History of the Work of the Synod of Oklahoma of the Presbyterian Church in the United States*. Atoka, Okla.: Atoka Press, 1927.

Reese, Linda Williams. *Women of Oklahoma, 1890–1920*. Norman: University of Oklahoma Press, 1997.

Richards, Eugene S. "Trends of Negro Life in Oklahoma as Reflected by Census Reports." *Journal of Negro History* 33, no. 1 (January 1948): 38–52.

Rorabaugh, W. J. *The Alcoholic Republic: An American Tradition*. New York: Oxford University Press, 1979.

Rohrer, James R. "The Origins of the Temperance Movement: a Reinterpretation." *Journal of American Studies* 24, no. 2 (August 1990): 228–35.

Rohrs, Richard C. *Crossroads Oklahoma: The German-American Experience in Oklahoma*. Stillwater: Oklahoma State University, 1981.

———. *The Germans in Oklahoma*. Norman: University of Oklahoma Press, 1980.

Rosenzweig, Roy. *Eight Hours for What We Will: Workers and Leisure in an Industrial City, 1970–1920*. Cambridge: Cambridge University Press, 1983.

Rotundo, E. Anthony. *American Manhood: Transformations in Masculinity from the Revolution to the Modern Era*. New York: Basic Books, 1993.

Salinger, Sharon V. *Taverns and Drinking in Early America*. Baltimore: Johns Hopkins University Press, 2002.

Sinclair, Andrew. *Era of Excess: A Social History of the Prohibition Movement*. New York: Harper and Row, 1962.

Smith, Michael M. *The Mexicans in Oklahoma*. Norman: University of Oklahoma Press, 1980.

Stearns, Peter N. *Be a Man! Males in Modern Society*. New York: Holmes and Meier, 1979.

Stewart, Justin. *Wayne Wheeler Dry Boss, An Uncensored Biography of Wayne B. Wheeler*. New York: Fleming H. Revell Company, 1928.

Strickland, Rennard. *The Indians in Oklahoma*. Norman: University of Oklahoma Press, 1980.

Thompson, John. *Closing the Frontier: Radical Responses in Oklahoma, 1889–1923*. Norman: University of Oklahoma Press, 1986.

Timberlake, James H. *Prohibition and the Progressive Movement 1900–1920*. Cambridge, Mass.: Harvard University Press, 1963.

Tobias, Henry J. *The Jews in Oklahoma*. Norman: University of Oklahoma Press, 1980.

Tolman, Keith. "The Sacramental Wine Case of 1917–18." *Chronicles of Oklahoma* 62, no. 3 (Autumn 1984): 312–24.

Tropman, John E. *Conflict in Culture: Permissions versus Controls and Alcohol Use in American Society*. Lanham, Md.: University Press of America, 1986.

Tucker, Howard A. *A History of Governor Walton's War on the Ku Klux Klan, the Invisible Empire*. Oklahoma City: Southwest Publishing Co., 1923.

Tulp, Margaret, ed. *History of Canadian County, Oklahoma*. El Reno, Okla.: Canadian County History Book Association, 1991.

Tyrell, Ian. *Women's World, Women's Empire: The Woman's Christian Temperance Union in International Perspective, 1880–1930*. Chapel Hill: University of North Carolina Press, 1991.

Unrau, William E. *White Man's Wicked Water: The Alcohol Trade and Prohibition in Indian Country, 1802–1892*. Lawrence: University Press of Kansas, 1996.

Wickett, Murray R. *Contested Territory: Whites, Native Americans, and African Americans in Oklahoma, 1865–1907*. Baton Rouge: Louisiana State University Press, 2000.

Wiebe, Robert H. *The Search for Order, 1877–1920*. New York: Hill and Wang, 1967.

Williams, Nudie E. "Cassius McDonald Barnes: Governor of Oklahoma Territory, 1897–1901." *Chronicles of Oklahoma* 53, no. 1 (Spring 1975): 66–82.

———. "They Fought for Votes: The White Politician and the Black Editor." *Chronicles of Oklahoma* 64, no. 1 (Spring 1986): 18–35.

Willibrand, W. A. "German in Okarche, 1892–1902." *Chronicles of Oklahoma* 28, no 3 (Autumn 1950): 284–91.

Woody, Carroll H., and Samuel A. Stouffer. "Local Option and Public Opinion." *American Journal of Sociology* 36, no. 2 (September 1930): 175–205.

Wright, James R., Jr. "The Assiduous Wedge: Woman Suffrage and the Oklahoma Constitutional Convention." *Chronicles of Oklahoma* 51, no. 4 (Winter 1973–1974): 421–43.

Yakey, Jack R. "Robert Martin: Acting Governor of Oklahoma Territory, 1891–1892." *Chronicles of Oklahoma* 53, no. 1 (Spring 1975): 23–27.

Theses and Dissertations

Brown, Thomas Elton. "Bible-belt Catholicism: A History of the Roman Catholic Curch in Oklahoma, 1905–1945." PhD diss., Oklahoma State University, 1974.

Bush, Charles C. "The Green Corn Rebellion." Master's thesis, University of Oklahoma, 1932.

Fox, Benny Carl. "The Baptist General Convention of Oklahoma and Higher Education: The Formative Period, 1906–1915." Master's thesis, Oklahoma State University, 1965.

Gray, Felix M. "History of Nowata County." Master's thesis, Oklahoma Agricultural and Mechanical College, 1937.

Hinds, Elwood Michael, Jr. "A History of Congregationalism in Oklahoma from 1817 to 1943." Master's thesis, Oklahoma Agricultural and Mechanical College, 1942.

Knox, Ethel Katherine. "The Beginning of Perry Oklahoma." Master's thesis, Oklahoma Agricultural and Mechanical College, 1937.

LeGrand, Walter. "The Temperance Movement in Oklahoma." Master's thesis, Oklahoma Agricultural and Mechanical College, 1948.

Meredith, Howard L. "A History of the Socialist Party in Oklahoma." PhD diss., University of Oklahoma, 1969.

Pickens, Donald Kenneth. "The Principles and Program of Oklahoma Socialism, 1900–1918." Master's thesis, University of Oklahoma, 1957.

Sellars, Nigel Anthony. "Oil, Wheat, and Wobblies: The Industrial Workers of the World in Oklahoma, 1905–1930." PhD diss., University of Oklahoma, 1998.

Sewell, Steven Lee. "Industrial Unionism and the Oklahoma Coal Industry, 1870–1935." PhD diss., Oklahoma State University, 1992.

Showalter, James Lowell. "Payne County and the Hooded Klan, 1921–1924." PhD diss., Oklahoma State University, 2000.

Smith, Willard Preston. "The Agricultural Development of Kiowa County." Master's thesis, Oklahoma Agricultural and Mechanical College, 1939.

Tolson, Arthur Lincoln. "The Negro in Oklahoma Territory, 1889–1907: A Study in Racial Discrimination." PhD diss., University of Oklahoma, 1966.

Tower, William Ray. "A General History of the Town of Prague, Oklahoma, 1902–1948." Master's thesis, Oklahoma Agricultural and Mechanical College, 1948.

Wanken, Helen M. " 'Woman's Sphere' and Indian Reform: The Women's National Indian Association, 1879–1901." PhD diss., Marquette University, 1981.

Index

231